Best Ever Apartment Syndication Book

Joe Fairless and Theo Hicks

All Rights Reserved

Text Copyright © 2018 Joe Fairless

DEDICATION

I dedicate this book to YOU.

YOU are seeking a higher level. But YOU are doing more than just seeking. YOU are acting on your desires by buying this book.

So what's next?

Reading it, naturally. But why is it that some people buy a book but never read it? I'm guilty of that. I have a dozen or so books on my bookshelf that I bought but didn't read.

Why is that? Well, I guess it's because when I bought the book it was relevant to me at the time but when I got the book, or got to the book, it no longer was as relevant, so I did other things with my time.

So, that brings us back to this book.

Why am I dedicating this book to YOU? Because I created this book for YOU. Just for YOU. This book is exactly what YOU need to do an apartment syndication. This book has all the info in it that I have used to build a multimillion-dollar real estate empire. This book is what YOU have been waiting for. There is nothing else out there that gives YOU the step-by-step guide to doing an apartment syndication.

Enjoy YOUR book.

It will be a game changer for YOU, YOUR family, YOUR friends and those around YOU.

A special thank-you to Frank Roessler, who provided valuable insights included in this book, as well as Jonathan Russo, who offered his feedback on the chapter focused on underwriting.

TESTIMONIALS

"By following the processes outlined in this book, my real estate portfolio went from $2 million to over $7 million in one year."

-**Danny Randazzo,** *Randazzo Capital*

"After applying the principles Joe talks about in this book, we've been able build a 700-unit (and growing) portfolio."

-**Andrew Campbell,** *Wildhorn Capital*

"Joe's apartment syndication system has been instrumental in my success and has exponentially accelerated my timeline. It has helped me eliminate limiting beliefs and has given me the confidence to pursue transactions much larger than I envisioned. In the 18 months since I've learned the principles outlined in this book, I've partnered on 437 units and our newly-formed company has been the lead sponsor on 261 units (with another 587 units under contract). Most excitingly, I've recently been able to leave my day job as a tax attorney and become a full-time multifamily real estate investor."

-**Kent Piotrkowski**

"I've known about Joe's apartment syndication principles for approximately a year and have achieved more than I expected to accomplish in that time. They have helped me reach my goals faster and with more confidence than I anticipated."

-**Mark Circa,** *Hardscrabble Investments*

"Summer of 2017, I was walking out of a failed business attempt looking where to go from there. After listening to 'Best Real Estate Investing Advice Ever Show,' I contacted Joe Fairless for apartment syndication advice. After I explained my history and lack of real estate background, he provided me with the principles outlined in this book. Joe is a one-of-a-kind guy. His principles have taught me more than I ever imagined. I have been able to close 106 units within 12 months. If you're looking for real estate knowledge, I would give this book an A+. Thank you, Joe."

-Stephen Wood, *Iron Wood Capital*

"10 months ago, my son and I learned about the principles outlined in this book and nothing has been the same since. We followed every step of Joe's instructions and advice, which helped us close on our first deal, a 261-unit apartment community in Houston. If you told me 10 months ago that we would own 261 units valued at $15M and that I would have personally raised $1.75M I would have said you were nuts! Joe's process is very comprehensive and engendered a lot of confidence that we could do the same thing as the people we were listening to on Joe's podcast. So much so that we already have another property in escrow, a 587-unit property in Houston."

-**Todd Beardsley**, *Menlo Atherton Capital Partners*

"If buying large apartments feels daunting, Joe has developed a practical, proven strategy to provide a clear roadmap for success. I've successfully employed these strategies and watched numerous others do the same to raise millions to acquire apartments."

-**John Casmon**, *Casmon Capital Group*

"Joe's simple yet powerful principles helped me uncover my ability to build deep investor relations and successfully raise millions for apartment community investing. My journey from CTO to Commercial Real Estate would have been tough without the systems outlined in this book."

                        -**Iqbal Mutabanna,** *IHM Business Group*

"Through the application of the strategies outlined in this book, I've been able to transition from a passive investor into the general partnership of 2 large apartment communities valued at over $50M. And all of this in well under 1 years' time. The actionable knowledge that I've gained and this ROI speaks for itself – thank you Joe!"

                                                     -**Melinda Warren**

"Learning and applying Joe's apartment syndication principles has 10X'd our company Viking Capital. Starting with a 6 million dollar deal as our 1st project we now have just purchased a 268-unit $35 million deal. Joe's apartment syndication system simply works. He is humble but ambitious, conservative in his analysis but delivers explosive growth, all the while being charitable with his time and resources. I am proud to call him a friend and mentor. This book will level up your real estate career. Joe is an unstoppable tour de force!"

                            -**Vikram Raya,** *Viking Capital*

WHAT YOU WILL LEARN – AN OVERVIEW

This book does not just tell you **what** to do. It tells you **how** to do it. It includes step-by-step processes for **what** to do, as well as systems, examples from my investment experience and guided exercises for you to complete to learn **how** to go from having no experience, no money and no deals to completing your first apartment syndication.

Moreover, I wanted to add MASSIVE value to your business in the earliest pages of this book.

I'm dedicating this chapter to give you an overview of **what** you need to know to complete your first apartment syndication, which I will accomplish by addressing the 11 bullet points from the back cover of this book. Then, read the entire book to learn the **how**.

1. Becoming an expert on the apartment syndication terminology (Chapters 1–4)
When starting any new endeavor, the first step is always education. For you, that's comprehending the fundamental apartment syndication knowledge required in order to qualify to become an apartment syndicator and to effectively communicate with your team members and passive investors.

The two main requirements needed before becoming an apartment syndicator are education and experience.

To cover the educational requirement, I'll cover the important terminology, which includes defining what an apartment syndication and a qualified investor is, along with a list of over 80 apartment syndication related terms and definitions (which can be found at the back of the book for your convenience). Additionally, you will learn about the two most important factors in apartment syndications – the cash-on-cash return and the internal rate of return – and how those two factors will be the measurement of a deal's success.

To cover the experience requirement, you will rank your prior real estate and business experience and determine what you need to do (if anything) before moving forward in the apartment syndication process.

2. Setting a specific, quantifiable goal and creating a long-term, motivating vision (Chapter 5–6)

Once you have the educational and experience requirements covered, the next step is to set compelling goals. This starts by answering the money question. That is, how do you make money as an apartment syndicator?

After you learn about the six most common ways an apartment syndicator makes money, you can set your first 12-month goal. Rather than just setting a goal for how much money you want to make, you will complete a guided exercise to calculate how much money you need to raise in order to hit your financial goal in 12 months.

In addition to your 12-month goal, you will create an affirmation statement that is a psychologically compelling long-term vision that includes a list of things that both inspire and disgust you to keep you motivated and on-track.

Lastly, you will learn about the five-step Ultimate Success Formula (which I got from a Tony Robbins' seminar) that all past and present entrepreneurs who have attained massive success in their given field have followed.

3. Building a powerful brand that attracts passive investors (Chapters 7–12)

A powerful brand is the foundation of any successful business, and the same applies to apartment syndications. The centerpiece of your brand will be a thought leadership platform, which is an interview-based, online network where you consistently offer valuable content to a your loyal following free of charge.

As a novice apartment syndicator, you will face a credibility problem, and your thought leadership platform is a major part of the solution. Through your thought leadership platform, you will position yourself as an expert in the apartment syndication field. Additionally, you will build upon your initial apartment syndication education by having conversations with active real estate entrepreneurs, probing them for the best advice they have to offer. Lastly, you will get your name and voice in front of real estate professionals while you sleep, which will help you source apartment deals and private capital, as well as network with potential team members. Overall, the benefits of a powerful thought leadership platform are countless.

Before launching your thought leadership platform, you will perform an exercise to define your target audience. That is, who do you want to attract with your thought leadership platform? (The answer is passive investors!). Then, you will follow my proven system I used to create the world's longest running daily real estate podcast in order to create a powerful thought leadership platform, which includes selecting a platform that aligns with your unique talents, the three keys to success and the five-step process to develop an educational and entertaining platform.

Additionally, you will learn how to create the three complementary components of your brand: the company name, logo and business cards, website and company presentation.

4. Evaluating and selecting the real estate market that will be the launching point for your apartment empire (Chapters 13–16)

To conclude the first part of the book (The Experience), you will select and evaluate a target market. That is the primary geographic location in which you will focus your search for potential investments. There are more than 19,000 cities located in the United States, and it is impossible (and a waste of your most valuable resource – your time) to target every single one.

One objection others may have about you is that you are starting after the 2008 crash. I hear you. I've heard that from a handful of people as well. However, I spent an inordinate amount of time studying the reasons why investors lost it all during the crash, as well as interviewing over 1,000 investors who experienced failures and successes during the crash. As a result of these investigations and learnings, I determined that there are three laws that were the difference between those who were successful and those who failed during the crash.

They are *The Three Immutable Laws of Real Estate Investing*:

1. Buy for cash flow (not appreciation)
2. Secure long-term debt
3. Have adequate cash reserves

If you follow these three laws, your business will not only survive, but thrive during the next crash. And, don't worry, we'll get into these more in depth later.

With those three laws in mind, in order to select a target market, you will first perform an exercise to narrow down the 19,000 cities to seven potential target markets based on where you live, where you have lived and the top real estate markets in the country.

Then, you will take those seven markets through my six-step market evaluation process. You will record demographic and economic data across seven factors and interpret the data by determining market insights. Based on the data and market insights, you will rank the seven potential markets, selecting the top one or two markets for further investigation. Lastly, you will create a database of at least 200 properties and a summary report for the one or two target markets. At this point, you will have qualified one or two target markets AND created a database of properties whose owners you can reach out to and generate potential leads.

5. Surrounding yourself with an all-star real estate team (Chapters 17–19)
Now that you have the education to become an apartment syndicator and selected one or two target markets, the next step is to create your all-star real estate team. Your core real estate team will consist of a real estate broker, accountant, property management company, mortgage broker, real estate attorney, securities attorney and a mentor/consultant.

The decision to or not to hire a mentor/consultant depends on your expectations and why you want to hire one in the first place. A good mentor is an active, successful apartment syndicator, provides you with system for how you can replicate their success, an ally that you can call upon in times of need and has good connections in the syndication industry. A good mentor will not be your knight in shining armor that magically solves all of your problems, nor should they offer a "done-for-you" program. Additionally, before hiring a mentor (if you end up doing so), you should have defined a specific outcome you want to achieve. Know exactly what you want to get out of the relationship, whether it's a proven system, an experienced ally or excellent connections.

To find the other members of your core real estate team, leverage your mentor's relationships and the relationships you created through your thought leadership platform. Once you find one solid team member, you can ask them for referrals to fill the remaining positions. However, regardless of where or how you found someone, always interview them yourself, keeping in mind that they are interviewing you as well.

Each member of your team will have their own motivations, so it is your job to prove to them that by becoming a part of your team, they will achieve their goals too. For each team member, I outline the questions you need to be prepared to answer during the interview, as well as how to approach winning them over by proactively fulfilling their needs.

6. Tapping into your existing network to find passive investors (Chapters 20–24)

The other part of your core real estate team are your passive investors. This might be one of the reasons why you purchased this book – to learn how to find private capital.

The first step towards finding private capital is learning why someone would invest with you. Surprisingly, the answer isn't to make money. Instead, it is because they trust you. Trust is created in three important ways – through time, displaying your expertise and creating personal connections – which I will show you how to do.

The best way to find passive investors with which you already have a trusting relationship is through your existing network. To create a network, or to expand it, I provide five solutions: 1) build a thought leadership platform, 2) join and participate on BiggerPockets, 3) attend or create a meetup group, 4) volunteer and 5) build personal connections. For this last approach, you will perform an exercise to create a list of passive investors and obtain their verbal investment commitments, an exercise I used to raise $1,160,500 for my very first apartment deal.

Besides trust, another challenge you will face is your lack of apartment syndication experience. Why would someone invest with you if you've never completed a syndication deal before? To overcome this challenge, you will learn about the system I use for approaching initial conversations with prospective passive investors before finding a deal. This includes creating alignment of interests to offset your lack of apartment syndication experience, as well as learning how to address the top objections and questions you will get from passive investors about you, your team and your business plan.

7. Selecting the ideal business plan to maximize returns to passive investors (Chapter 25)
Before finding a deal, you will need to know what to look for. Similar to the selecting a target market, you cannot pursue every single investment opportunity. There are simply too many. Instead, you must set the initial investment criteria of your business plan in order to screen incoming deals. This includes answering the following questions: What is your investment strategy (i.e. value-add, distressed or turnkey)? Where will you invest (i.e. your one or two target markets)? What date of construction range will you target? And what is the maximum number of units you are capable of purchasing given certain price per unit assumptions?

8. Creating a lead-generation machine that pumps out qualified off-market apartment deals (Chapter 26–28)
Once you have the money lined up and created the team who will help you execute the business plan, the next step is to find your first deal.

First, you will learn the difference between on-market and off-market apartment deals, and the reasons why off-market deals are better for both you and the seller (yes, I said seller too!). Essentially, on-market deals are listed by a real estate broker while for off-market deals, you're dealing directly with the owner.

Then, you will learn about the top 10 ways to generate off-market deals in your market, which include the exact process for how to do so for each method. I will also provide you with a deal-finding tracker in order to track the process of your various lead generation strategies.

When you are implementing one or more of these ten strategies, you may discover that you are unable to generate qualified leads due to the competitive nature of the market. As an added bonus, I will provide you with the secret to finding qualified off-market deals in a hot market – when you find one deal, find a complementary property in the immediate area and reach out to the owner, asking to purchase their asset too (I've done this – it works!).

For another bonus: there are two types of markets: a market with lots of deals but no money or a market with no deals but lots of money. If you discover that your target market is the former, leverage your thought leadership platform to attract out-of-market capital. If you discover that your target market is the latter, use my secret from finding deals in a hot market or use the abundance of in-market capital to invest in a qualified out-of-state market.

9. Learning the science behind evaluating, qualifying and submitting offers on apartment deals (Chapter 29–32)

As you receive on-market leads from your real estate broker and off-market leads from your marketing machine, you will need to determine if the lead warrants an offer. This process is called underwriting.

In order to underwrite a deal properly, you will need to acquire the rent roll, the trailing 12-month profit and loss statement (T-12) and, if it is an on-market deal, the offering memorandum. The rent roll is a summary of the current rental information. The T-12 contains detailed information on the income and expenses over the last 12-months. And the offering memorandum is a sales package created by the listing real estate broker that highlights the important information of the apartment offering.

You will use these three pieces of information to underwrite the deal. Using your own financial model or the simplified model I offer for free, you will underwrite the deal using my company's six-step process: 1) reading through the offering memorandum (if it is an on-market deal), 2) inputting the rent roll and T-12, 3) setting assumptions for how you will operating the property, 4) calculating an offer price, 5) performing your own rental comparable analysis and 6) visiting the asset in-person to perform additional due diligence.

Once you've completed the entire six-step underwriting process, you've arrived at the point where you need to determine if you will submit an offer. If the results of the underwriting process meet or exceed your and your investors' return goals, you will submit a letter of intent, which is a non-binding letter that represents your intent to purchase the property. If your letter of intent is ultimately accept, you will sign a purchase and sale agreement officially putting the property under contract to purchase.

10. Preparing and presenting an apartment offering to your passive investors and securing financial commitments (Chapter 33–42)

Congrats, the property is under contract and you'll now enter the due diligence phase. During this phase, you will obtain and review 10 reports about the property in order to confirm the assumptions you made during the underwriting process and decide if you need to update your offer price and terms or cancel the contract. If you decide to move forward, you will secure financing from a lender. You will learn about the two main types of financing and what you need to do in order to qualify for your first loan, which involves bringing on a loan guarantor who meets the liquidity, net worth and experience requirements set forth by the lender.

At the same time, you will present the new apartment offering to and secure commitments from your passive investors. First, you will use the results of your underwriting and due diligence to create an investment summary document, which outlines the main highlights of the investment and the market, as well as the return projections to your passive investors. Then, using the investment summary as a guide, you will present the new investment offering to your passive investors, using the nine-step process I've used to present deals to thousands of passive investors. Finally, you will officially secure commitments from your passive investors by preparing and having them sign five investor forms.

11. Impressing your investors by effectively implementing the business plan and exceeding their expectations (Chapter 43–46)
After the deal has passed the due diligence process and you've secured commitments from passive investors, you'll close on the deal!

Upon closing, you will notify your investors using the email template I've provided and you will begin your duties as the asset manager.

Your 10 responsibilities as the asset manager are:

1. Implement the business plan
2. Conduct weekly performance reviews with your property manager

BEST EVER APARTMENT SYNDICATION BOOK

3. Send the correct distributions to your passive investors
4. Provide monthly recap emails to your investors
5. Manage the renovations
6. Maintain economic occupancy
7. Plan trips to the property
8. Frequently analyze the competition
9. Frequently analyze the market
10. Resolve issues as they arise.

In regards to maintaining economic occupancy, I provide the 19 best practices for doing so – although, your property management company should implement these best practices on their own.

The last step of the syndication process, and when you and your investors make the BIG money, is to sell the property. In order to maximize the sales price, which in turn will maximize the returns, follow my eight-step process for selling your apartment community.

So there you go, that's what to do. Now, let's get into how to do it!

FOREWORD

As a Master Coach, I've dedicated over 15,000 hours to working with entrepreneurs and real estate investors all over the globe, helping them achieve success and build incredible wealth. I'm passionate about helping others realize their potential in real estate while creating an extraordinary quality of life at the same time. Every so often, I am amazed when a client that I coach achieves a phenomenal level of success in a short amount of time.

That certainly was the case with Joe Fairless, who went from owning four single-family homes to acquiring more than **4,000 units, totaling over $400,000,000 in real estate under management** while creating the world's longest-running daily real estate podcast, the **Best Real Estate Investing Advice Ever Show**. I'm proud to have had a front-row seat for Joe's life these past few years as I was able to witness all of the things that it took for him to achieve success along the way.

In this book, Joe shares the simple, straightforward truth behind building wealth and creating extraordinary results in multifamily real estate. By following Joe's step-by-step process, not only will you discover how to make it big in real estate but you'll also gain time to pursue other passions and have more freedom in your life. That's exactly what Joe has done for himself and he's now ready to share his successful process with the world.

Having interviewed some of the most successful real estate investors of all time, Joe knows the real-life strategies and investing secrets that are proven to work time and time again.

Whether it's finding incredible on-market or off-market deals, learning how to speak to and influence real estate brokers and passive investors or discovering hidden profits by adding massive value to properties, Joe shares what every real estate investor needs to know to be successful in today's market.

He has shared and tested these strategies and techniques with hundreds of clients that he has mentored and now he's sharing them with you. It doesn't matter what level you're at as they will work just as well for new multifamily investors as they will for seasoned multifamily real estate investors.

People always ask me, "Trevor, what's the secret to Joe's success?" My answer is that you first have to master your psychology and then execute your plan with a proven strategy. To put it into simple terms, you must always begin with your mindset, and then you must model best practices in real estate investing if you want to get from where you are to where you truly want to be. And of course, to be successful at anything takes consistency, commitment and focus each and every step of the way.

That's what this book is offering you: the strategies and insights that will give you the competitive edge for creating success in multifamily real estate investing. **Joe's process is proven, practical and has been applied by hundreds of his students who have had amazing results time after time in their own multifamily investments.**

In summary, if you want to be successful in real estate, then you owe it to yourself to start right now by reading this book cover to cover. It will change your life and give you a definitive roadmap for creating wealth and passive income through smart real estate investing faster than you ever thought possible.

Sincerely,
Trevor McGregor (aka Joe's Coach)

TABLE OF CONTENTS

Dedication	iii
Testimonials	v
What You Will Learn – An Overview	ix
Foreword	xxi
Introduction	1

Part I: The Experience

Chapter 1: An Apartment Syndication Is What Again?	11
Chapter 2: Getting to the "Spooky" OPM – Other People's Money	13
Chapter 3: Can't Wait! How Do I Get Started?	23
Chapter 4: Your Focus is CoC Return and IRR	25
Chapter 5: The Money Question	31
Chapter 6: So, What's Your Goal?	36
Chapter 7: It's All about the Brand, Baby!	51
Chapter 8: You Have to Aim Before You Can Shoot!	58
Chapter 9: Building Your Personal Best-Ever Brand	62
Chapter 10: The Road to Selective Fame	76
Chapter 11: Entertain While Educating	83
Chapter 12: Manufacturing a Mastermind	91

Chapter 13: Time for Target Practice!   99

Chapter 14: Narrowing It Down to the Top Seven Markets   101

Chapter 15: Get Ready to Hit the Target   110

Chapter 16: Describe the Target   129

Part 2: The Money

Chapter 17: Your Core Apartment Syndication Team   141

Chapter 18: To Be Mentored or Not to Be Mentored...   142

Chapter 19: How to Build Your All-Star Team   147

Chapter 20: Why Would Someone Invest with You?   169

Chapter 21: How to Find Passive Investors   173

Chapter 22: The Courting Process   180

Chapter 23: Hey, I Object!   186

Chapter 24: Laying the Ground Rules   203

Part 3: The Deal

Chapter 25: A Deal Won't Qualify Itself   211

Chapter 26: Your First Time Is Always the Most Challenging   223

Chapter 27: How to Find Your First Apartment Deal   227

Chapter 28: Deal-Finding Tracker   244

Chapter 29: Time to Nerd Out on Math   253

Chapter 30: Gather Your Intel   255

Chapter 31: The Underwriting Process   264

Chapter 32: What Do You Have to Offer?   307

Part 4: The Execution

Chapter 33: So You're Saying There's a Chance?	317
Chapter 34: The Due Diligence Report Cards	319
Chapter 35: Your Final Exam	324
Chapter 36: Yay or Nay?	331
Chapter 37: You Can Take It to the Bank	332
Chapter 38: Time to Commit	343
Chapter 39: Painting the Full Picture	346
Chapter 40: It's My Honor to Introduce You to...	356
Chapter 41: You Have the Right to One Phone Call	359
Chapter 42: The Five Investor Forms Your Investors Will Sign	375
Chapter 43: You've Reached the (First) Finish line	381
Chapter 44: Anticipating the Finish	383
Chapter 45: The Road Ahead	389
Chapter 46: Finish Strong to Collect Your Jackpot	400
Conclusion	405
Glossary of Terms	407
About the Authors	427

PART 1: THE EXPERIENCE

KNOWLEDGE — Chapters 1-4
1. What is apartment syndication?
2. How to Get Started
3. What to focus on

GOALS — Chapters 5-6
1. How do you make money?
2. Set 12-month goal and long-term vision
3. Ultimate Success Formula

BRAND BUILDING — Chapters 7-12
1. Why you need a brand
2. Select a target audience
3. How to build a brand

MARKET EVALUATION — Chapters 13-16
1. 3 Immutable Laws of Real Estate
2. Evaluate 7 markets
3. Pick 1-2 Target Markets

PART 2: THE MONEY

BUILD TEAM — Chapters 17-19
1. Find core real estate team members
2. Hire a mentor or consultant

FIND CAPITAL — Chapters 20-24
1. Why will they invest?
2. Build passive investor database
3. Create partnership structure

PART 3: THE DEAL

FIND DEALS — Chapters 25-28
1. Set investment criteria
2. On-market vs. off-market deals
3. How to find your first deal

UNDERWRITING — Chapters 29-31
1. Information needed to underwrite a deal
2. The 6-step underwriting process

SUBMIT OFFER — Chapter 32
1. How to submit an offer on a deal
2. Best-and-final offer
3. Purchase sales agreement

PART 4: THE EXECUTION

DUE DILIGENCE — Chapters 33-37
1. 10 due diligence reports
2. Secure financing from lender

SECURE CAPITAL — Chapters 38-42
1. Create investment summary
2. New investment offering call
3. Secure investor commitments

CLOSE — Chapters 43-44
1. Closing process
2. Notify passive investors

EXECUTE BUSINESS PLAN — Chapters 45-46
1. 10 asset management duties
2. How to sell the apartment

INTRODUCTION

You want to do what I do?

GREAT!

You need experience, money, deal flow and the ability to execute a business plan.

Damn, wait, I didn't mean to kill the mood so soon. Let me try that again.

What I should have said is that you need to be capable of putting together an experienced team, resourceful enough to find money, smart enough to learn about and implement a proven system that generates deals, and diligent enough to bring all of that together to create and execute a business plan.

Ah, much better, right? Because you are capable of doing just that!

You ARE capable of doing that because others before you, me included, have done it. That means you can, too. You know what will help you get there? Reading this book... because when I started out in real estate investing there wasn't a book like the one you are about to read that walked you through the process of apartment syndication, which is what I do!

This book gives you an advantage in apartment syndication that nobody has ever had before. Further, it gives you the potential to create generational wealth. To go from making what you earn now to becoming a multi-millionaire and beyond.

But first, to realize your massive potential, you need the right mindset and strategies.

Let me back up...

I remember when I moved from Lubbock, Texas, to East Flatbush, Brooklyn, in June of 2005 after graduating from Texas Tech University. Besides the culture shock from going from cows and cotton to sky scrapers and hidden sunlight, I was hit hard in the face with a rude financial awakening. My annual salary was $30,000, which netted me about $1,500 a month. My rent was $750 a month, so I had a whopping $750 a month remaining to buy food and a subway card, make monthly payments to knock down $18,000 in student loans, pay utility bills, and get a beer every now and then with friends. Putting it mildly, things were tight.

Hey, but maybe they weren't as tight as the situation you find yourself in right now. I get it. But assets don't just mean income and savings. There are assets you have right now!

Let's do a quick exercise together to prove that point.

In my asset pool I get to count a few good ones. For example, I am fortunate because I have a mom who is caring, loving, supportive, and emotionally connected with others. My dad is kind; he taught me about character and tries to look at the positive side of things, regardless of what life throws at him. This became clear when I got in trouble a couple (or more than a couple) of times in high school. On one of those occasions my dad had me stand in front of a mirror with an inscription on it about what it meant to be a man of character. I had to read it aloud. Talk about a lasting impression.

I also am fortunate to have had a step-dad who loved me unconditionally as if I were his natural son. This man showed me what hard work looks like and the importance of staying loyal to the people in your circle. Without him I would not be where I am today. Period.

I am the youngest of four kids. My siblings are 8, 10, and 12 years older than me. I was a mistake, ahem, I mean a pleasant surprise. I mean, a blessing... yes, that's it! I was a blessing.

My oldest brother, Nick, taught me the importance of truly caring for others. When you're in a room with him and you don't know anyone, he will introduce himself. He will make sure you are comfortable and he will ask intelligent, thoughtful questions. It comes naturally to him because he truly cares about your comfort and learning more about you than telling folks he meets all about him.

My sister, Amber, taught me how to be tenacious and street smart. I'm sure she won't like how I phrased it as "street smart," but I mean it as a sincere compliment. Perhaps I could call it emotional intelligence, but that's not as fun. Amber can read people better than anyone I know. She has a gift of meeting someone and instantly knowing if the person is hiding something or being genuine.

My other brother, Steve, taught me how to be a man of my word. He's a West Point graduate, so that makes sense, right? He also included me in things even though I am 8 years younger than he is. I remember playing football with his friends and him, going on road trips and spending time in a stinky high school weight room as a 9-year-old.

Why am I telling you this?

Because I want you to understand that regardless of your situation currently or your life circumstance, regardless of what happened to you as a child, nothing in life has meaning until you choose to give it meaning. You have the power to choose what you learn or don't learn from any given life experience. When we start thinking that life is happening for us and not to us, our life experiences become empowering. We learn things along the way and apply them to our life, which enhances our time on earth, optimizes the value we create, and, consequently, can make us a whole bunch of money!

Believe me, I could choose to list negative things that each of these people did in my life just as they could about me. But why focus on the negative? That gets us nowhere in life or in business. Instead, let's focus on those empowering things that have happened in our lives or in our relationships with others because that's what will propel us forward.

So write down who has been and/or is in your life. These people are called assets.

Next to each name write down some empowering things they have taught you.

Name: _____

Empowering lessons they taught you: _____
_____
_____

Name: _____

Empowering lessons they taught you: _____
_____
_____

Name: _____

Empowering lessons they taught you: _____
_____
_____

Here are the skills I learned from others I grew up with:

- Be loving
- Be emotionally connected with others
- Be kind
- Be a person of character

- Work hard
- Stay loyal to those in your circle (assuming the circle is continually assessed)
- Truly care for others
- Ask thoughtful questions
- Be tenacious
- Be street smart (i.e., emotionally intelligent)
- Be a person of your word
- Involve others in your journey so they can benefit and it becomes more rewarding for you, too

Think these skills are directly applicable to building a multi-million-dollar real estate empire?

You bet!

The funny thing is that my list of empowering people in my life is just my immediate family. If I listed everyone from whom I have learned something I'd be arrested for chopping down all the trees on earth to print this book! Since I've never been to jail and would prefer not to go, I'll just leave it at family members. My point is that you can list out others whom you have learned something from and then see how that helps you in your business.

Think of them as assets in your life.

Having a hard time thinking of people who have taught you empowering life lessons? I suggest you look in the mirror, my friend, because the problem isn't the world; it's you. And it isn't that YOU are the problem. Nope. It's that your INTERPRETATION of events is the problem.

It's best to choose to interpret things that happen for you in life in a way that empowers you to do bigger and better things. Think of each life experience as a door that keeps opening to another and another.

That said, while I didn't start off rich, I leveraged my life experiences to take me to a higher and higher level. I still do. That's what you'll do if you want to be successful in apartment syndication because everyone, EVERYONE, has some challenge they must overcome to do apartment syndication or take their apartment syndication game to the next level.

Those challenges fall into four categories. Any of these sound familiar?

1. Lack of experience
   a. "I've never done a large apartment deal before."
   b. "I don't know how to build the right team."
   c. "I want to buy larger deals but I'm not sure how to run the numbers."
2. Lack of money
   a. "I don't have the money to buy a large deal."
   b. "Nobody I know has money."
   c. "I'm an introvert. I'm not good at sales. I can't raise money."
   d. "I'm scared to use other people's money. What if I lose it?"
   e. "The market isn't good for investing in apartment deals. Nobody would invest."
3. Lack of deals
   a. "I have money but I can't find any deals."
   b. "The market is too hot. There are too many people looking for deals."
4. Lack of execution
   a. "I am good at planning, but I always have trouble implementing my plans."
   b. "I am indecisive when it comes to making a financial commitment."

Repeat after me:

> "I am not alone in initially feeling this way, but others have solved these challenges, so I will, too."

Doesn't that feel good? Say it again. It just might put a smile on your face as it does mine.

You do not have a unique challenge. The challenge you have with apartment syndication falls into one of those categories and it has been solved before.

This book will solve your challenges while educating you through the process of how to buy apartments with investors. By the end of the book you will:

1. Know how to leverage other people and platforms to gain the experience.
2. Build a money-raising machine that attracts investors to you.
3. Create a deal-tracking system that brings in quality leads for you to buy.
4. Learn the exact steps required to close on a deal and successfully execute a business plan.

That's why this book is structured in four sections: experience, money, deals, and execution.

Once you have mastered those four areas you'll be ready and raring to go.

So... let's go. Let's do this thing...

PART 1: THE EXPERIENCE

PART 1: THE EXPERIENCE

YOU ARE HERE

KNOWLEDGE — Chapters 1-4
1. What is apartment syndication?
2. How to Get Started
3. What to focus on

GOALS — Chapters 5-6
1. How do you make money?
2. Set 12-month goal and long-term vision
3. Ultimate Success Formula

BRAND BUILDING — Chapters 7-12
1. Why you need a brand
2. Select a target audience
3. How to build a brand

MARKET EVALUATION — Chapters 13-16
1. 3 Immutable Laws of Real Estate
2. Evaluate 7 markets
3. Pick 1-2 Target Markets

PART 2: THE MONEY

BUILD TEAM — Chapters 17-19
1. Find core real estate team members
2. Hire a mentor or consultant

FIND CAPITAL — Chapters 20-24
1. Why will they invest?
2. Build passive investor database
3. Create partnership structure

PART 3: THE DEAL

FIND DEALS — Chapters 25-28
1. Set investment criteria
2. On-market vs. off-market deals
3. How to find your first deal

UNDERWRITING — Chapters 29-31
1. Information needed to underwrite a deal
2. The 6-step underwriting process

SUBMIT OFFER — Chapter 32
1. How to submit an offer on a deal
2. Best-and-final offer
3. Purchase sales agreement

PART 4: THE EXECUTION

DUE DILIGENCE — Chapters 33-37
1. 10 due diligence reports
2. Secure financing from lender

SECURE CAPITAL — Chapters 38-42
1. Create investment summary
2. New investment offering call
3. Secure investor commitments

CLOSE — Chapters 43-44
1. Closing process
2. Notify passive investors

EXECUTE BUSINESS PLAN — Chapters 45-46
1. 10 asset management duties
2. How to sell the apartment

CHAPTER 1

AN APARTMENT SYNDICATION IS WHAT AGAIN?

Before we get into the tactics of how to do apartment syndications – rather, how you make money syndicating apartments, how to find apartment deals, how to raise capital from passive investors, and more – first let's take a giant step back. Let's address the fundamentals.

WHAT IS AN APARTMENT SYNDICATION?

First and foremost, what the heck is apartment syndication?

Simply put, an apartment syndication is the pooling of money from numerous investors that will be used to buy an apartment building(s) and execute the project's business plan.

You, the syndicator – also commonly referred to as a sponsor or general partner – are tasked with raising money from qualified investors and then using that money to buy apartment buildings. Typically an apartment syndication structure is best used when buying large apartment buildings or even complexes.

WHAT IS A "QUALIFIED INVESTOR"?

So, what's a "qualified investor"? Generally, there are two types of qualified investors:

1. Accredited investors
2. Sophisticated investors

An accredited investor is a person with an annual income of $200,000 (or $300,000 for joint income) that he/she has earned and can prove for the last two years or an individual with a net worth that exceeds $1 million. This definition can change, so for the most up-to-date accredited investor qualifications, visit the SEC.gov website.

A sophisticated investor does not meet the accredited investor requirements, but he/she has the knowledge and experience in financing and business matters, and therefore is capable of evaluating the merits and risks of the prospective investments.

After closing on your apartment deal, you (the syndicator) are responsible for ongoing property management, which includes ensuring the completion of the capital improvements, overseeing the property management company, communicating regular updates to the limited partners (i.e., the passive investors who made the deal possible), and, ultimately, overseeing the business plan.

When I first got going with large apartments (i.e., the "asset"), I didn't realize there was a business plan for each deal. I just thought I'd buy it, then the property cash would flow and then I would get to sit back while the checks rolled in. Um, not so much. All I can say is that I was just a young grasshopper back then. The reason I decided to write this book is to help you avoid my mistakes. I don't want you to take the hard road and make the same mistakes I – and others – did. So, keep reading!

CHAPTER 2

GETTING TO THE "SPOOKY" OPM – OTHER PEOPLE'S MONEY

Before we go further, do me a favor and answer the six quick questions below with a simple Yes or No. I call this my sanity checklist!

1. Do you have a fear of using other people's money?
2. Do you have any reservations about partnering with investors?
3. Do you think your relationship with your friends will be forever changed if you partner with them on a deal?
4. After successfully completing 10 or more syndications, do you think you'll be 10X more concerned with gaining and maintaining trust with your passive investors?
5. Do you think after you've done 10+ successful syndicated deals your ongoing awareness of the importance of being trusted with investors' capital will only be magnified 10X?
6. Is Third Eye Blind the best band ever?

If you answered "No" to all of the questions, you might be a sociopath. Seek help from a trained psychological professional. If you answered "Yes" to any or all of the questions, congrats, you're sane.

I believe you should have an initial fear of using other people's money. If you've never raised private capital before, there's a lot to learn. There are the right words to say and ways to lay down your deals so investors are eager to participate.

You should have a reservation about partnering with investors because it's a big responsibility. You are entering into a legal and binding contract.

Your relationship with your family and friends will forever be changed when they invest with you. Even when the deal does very well, it still adds a different dimension to your relationships, which will be way more business focused. Be prepared for this change and know it's coming if you decide to involve family and friends. (These are often referred to as "pillow investors." I'll let you figure out why.)

And, after doing 10+ syndicated deals, I can tell you the one big thing that changes in terms of concern for investors is that it gets magnified. This makes all the sense in the world, because the longer you have a business partnership with the investors, the closer you get emotionally and the more you care for them. It's not called a relationship for nothing!

As for my last question, obviously Third Eye Blind is the best band ever. No explanation needed for this one. ;)

Assuming you are aware that partnering with investors comes with MASSIVE responsibility on your part and that your ongoing concern will only grow for investors as you do more deals (because they are helping you achieve your goals so your dreams can come true), let us now proceed.

If you don't understand these things, go back and answer the first five questions again. The right answer is YES for each. If you answered NO to all of these questions, please accept my apologies for calling you a sociopath. I'm here to help you become the best apartment syndicator you can be! Let my questions be your guide.

HOW TO OVERCOME THE FEAR OF USING OPM?

Aside from being one of the most common questions I get from coaching clients and fellow real estate investors who are entertaining the idea of apartment syndication, it was the main question that kept me stuck. I wanted to transition from being a single-family property investor to being a syndicator, but the thought of using other people's money (OPM) to scale my business scared me.

The steps involved in overcoming one's fear of using OPM vary from situation to situation. For me, it was out of necessity. I couldn't see how I could scale the single-family-residence investing model to the tune of $10,000 per month in profits, which was my original investing goal. While it is certainly possible to build a real estate investing business around single-family homes, that strategy wasn't congruent with my patience level and financial situation at the time. I needed things to happen faster. That meant I needed to invest in more doors at one time. I needed to invest in multifamily properties and, better yet, apartment buildings!

I came to this obvious conclusion when creating a spreadsheet so I could accurately calculate how many single-family homes I would need to buy to generate $10,000 per month in passive profits. Setting my goal, over the next three years I purchased four single-family homes in Texas. I was on track to achieve my goal! However, I faced a dilemma – how was I going to continue to save up for all the future down payments I would need?

Faced with that reality, I knew my spreadsheet plan wasn't an accurate reflection of where I was and where I wanted to be... unless I lived to be 400 years old. (Fingers crossed!)

Plus, I spent way more time than I expected on managing my little portfolio of single-family homes, even though I hired a full-time property manager. I was still inundated with paperwork and submitting checks to lenders and insurance brokers.

The many tasks required to close deals were too time consuming. That wouldn't have been a problem, except for the fact that each home was only generating $100 to $250 per month, and then the cost incurred from one move-out or one maintenance issue would wipe out the profits for an entire year.

It was frustrating. I was rolling along, earning about $1,000 a month across my four homes, but then I had a move-out at one of the properties. Factoring in all make-ready expenses, it cost me approximately $5,000 before we could lease the unit again. Then it struck me like a heavy apple on my noggin. If that happened on two homes I would basically break even. Three move-outs during a 12-month period would sink me. The math just didn't add up to this setup being a short- and medium-term venture in profitability. My stomach hurt.

I knew there had to be a better, and more time-efficient way to scale my real estate business. So I did a bit of research and signed up for a *Rich Dad, Poor Dad* seminar to learn about other investment niches.

Having four properties under my belt, I walked into that seminar with my chest puffed up, feeling like Stephan Jenkins after singing "Motorcycle Drive By" to a sold-out crowd. I could feel my ego quickly deflate with the opening line of the seminar, "You will not get rich on single-family homes. It's going to have to be apartments or mobile home trailer parks."

UGH...

I wasn't familiar with trailer parks, but I had lived in an apartment in 5th and 6th grade after my parents divorced. Plus, at the time of the seminar I was living in an apartment in NYC. So, I have an understanding of apartment living. With this newfound knowledge, I got my hands on every apartment investing book I could find.

Then I realized that I faced a similar dilemma to the one I faced with buying single-family properties. What about the down payments? How was I going to afford the down payment for an apartment building when it would be greater than the sum total of the down payments for my four single family homes?

This realization did not hold me back. I found a solution through my research: apartment syndications!

Two Requirements Before Becoming an Apartment Syndicator

There are two other requirements you must meet before pursuing a career as an apartment syndicator. The first is education, which is the purpose of this book. Finish reading it and you can check that requirement off your list.

The second requirement is experience. You might think I mean apartment syndication experience or even real estate experience. NOPE! You need a track record in business, which can be real estate or some other business endeavor. If it's a successful entrepreneurial endeavor, all the better.

Why?

Well, if you don't have a track record in business, why would someone trust you with their money? How can you expect an investor to back your deal(s)?

Here's an exercise that will help you. Right now, this very moment, honestly assess both your real estate and business experience. Here are a few questions to help you get started:

- **Real Estate Experience**
  - What are your real estate accomplishments?
  - Do you currently or have you previously owned profitable properties?
  - Do you have a track record of successfully investing your own money and making money?
  - Do you have any experience with or education on commercial real estate?

- **Business Experience**
    - What are your business accomplishments?
    - Have you ever started a business? Was it profitable?
    - If you are or were a W2 employee, have you received promotions or awards?
    - Would your business colleagues and/or employers describe you as someone who exceeds expectations?

If you have success in business, you can easily translate that into buying apartment buildings and complexes with investors. However, if you lack real estate knowledge and experience, it is vital that you surround yourself with the right team and advisors who have done successful deals in real estate.

If you already have real estate experience, it will be a more seamless transition! However, it might be a challenge for you to find passive investors. If your experience is solely focused on real estate, you will likely have fewer relationships with individuals outside the real estate world.

In my humble opinion, it's better to have investors who aren't focused on real estate for their full-time occupations. The reason is that non-full-time real estate investors tend to want to passively invest, whereas full-time real estate professionals tend to want a more active role in the deal.

My company's deals are only for passive investors. Non-real estate professionals may have some interest in real estate, but they don't have time to invest themselves and they don't really care to learn how. That's why they want to invest with you – because they are busy making money elsewhere. They just want that money to grow without effort on their part!

That said, there are always exceptions. In fact, some of my largest investors are full-time real estate investors who did very well in the past but now want to take a more passive role. Age and life experience can be a root cause. Maybe they are just tired of doing the work.

If you are lacking in both areas of business and real estate success, you don't really have the foundation to become an apartment syndicator YET. But you can get there! Start to work on establishing success in real estate using your own money or by building up a solid reputation in the business world.

What do I mean by lacking? On an experience scale of 1 to 10, with 10 being someone who has taken an apartment deal full cycle and a 1 being someone who hasn't done a single real estate deal and isn't involved in the real estate industry in any form (i.e., they aren't or haven't worked with a broker, agent, or property management company). They haven't started or owned their own business. They aren't an entrepreneur and don't understand that mindset. If they have a W2 job, they haven't received any promotions or awards, either because they are very new to the company or because they are working for a company that doesn't have a lot of career growth potential. (Or maybe they like hiding out in a middle management role where they don't have to make any real decisions.) However, they are excited about real estate and the prospect of completing their first deal. They read about real estate transactions and strategies. They dream of doing deals and walking away from the 9-to-5.

Near the opposite end of the spectrum, a 7 or 8 is someone who has previous experience with investing in apartments. Maybe they haven't completed a large apartment syndication, but they've personally invested in smaller multifamily properties and they've made a profit. They've gotten a taste for having a few units under one roof (or in the same small area). They get the formula of "more doors = more profit"! Or they are or were once an apartment broker, property manager, or lender. Since they are or were involved in the apartment investing industry, they have the relationships and most of the education required to syndicate a deal. All they need to do is find a deal and get out there to raise private money!

A 4 or 5 would be someone in the situation I was in prior to syndicating my first deal. I had a strong track record in both business and non-commercial real estate. As I already mentioned, I acquired four single-family homes. That means I was familiar with the real estate transaction process, I was comfortable with handling a portfolio worth hundreds of thousands of dollars, and that gave me a foundation of knowledge on which to build. Plus, I taught a class on single-family property investing, so I was already perceived as a thought leader in the real estate industry.

From a business perspective, I was the youngest Vice President of a large advertising firm in New York City. In that role, I worked with Fortune 500 companies, helping them create and implement successful advertising campaigns. Through this experience, I honed my written and verbal communication skills. In particular, I learned the importance of addressing questions and concerns in a timely manner and to proactively address potential follow-up questions to minimize the amount of back-and-forth communications. (Time is the most precious resource we have!)

Let me tell you, you'd be surprised by just how much your investor will appreciate this style of communication. Because of the relationships I formed from my business experience, I could easily create a list of potential passive investors. In fact, the two investors who invested the largest sum of money into my first deal were people I met during my advertising career. As you see, I had some real estate credibility and access to investors' money on a small scale. However, I still needed to educate myself on apartment investing and syndications, surround myself with an expert team, and find a deal.

Using the questions previously listed about your background, assess where you fall on the real estate and business experience scale.

You don't need to answer "yes" to every question. But before you're ready to start your syndication journey, do yourself a big favor. Get a very strong real estate background and a very strong business background and gain a moderate level of success in both categories. I would say a "passing grade" is being at least a 4 on the experience scale.

Even if you have past success in business and in another real estate niche, you still don't have the right amount of experience investing in apartment buildings. This is one of the biggest challenges you will face starting out. The solution is having alignment of interest with your investors, which you will accomplish in part by surrounding yourself with an experienced team (which will be discussed in Chapter 23).

Don't Be Selfish

If you ace (or at least pass) the experience exam, but you think you will be bad at or are fearful of raising capital from others, it's likely that you have a limiting belief about what is possible for yourself. Let's do this:

Imagine the city you live in has the plague. And there is one person who knows the antidote to the plague. All that person has to do is gather the townspeople and tell them what the antidote is so they can then apply it. The problem? The person who knows the antidote has stage fright and doesn't like speaking in front of crowds. How inconvenient. What would YOU say to that person if you were living in that city? You'd say "get your booty on stage and give us the information," correct?

The same thing applies here my friend. YOU have the potential to greatly influence many people's lives in a positive way. And if you don't realize that potential then you're being a little selfish because you're not giving to others and helping them reach their financial goals. Which, by the way, will help you reach yours too (and then some).

Let me elaborate.

A core belief that enables me to direct my focus away from my needs and toward helping other human beings and helping them attain their needs and goals is that *people are inherently good.*

If people are inherently good, that means if they had more free time they would be naturally drawn to do "good" things that would benefit other people. One of the best ways to increase the amount of free time someone has is to help them achieve their financial goals. Once that happens all that time spent on accumulating wealth can now be spent on doing things they really want to do. And since people are inherently good, those things will logically be done to benefit other people. If I am able to help people achieve their financial goals, they will benefit... and everyone will benefit, including me.

My business and my investors have benefited greatly from focusing on helping others achieve their financial goals. You may wonder what this has to do with raising and using OPM, but being fearful of using OPM is actually an act of selfishness that keeps you from helping other people.

This fear will be one of the biggest barriers to your success that you will encounter. You must embrace the idea of using OPM. Of course it will require a mindset shift, but you can do it. I promise.

Overall, before starting your apartment syndication journey, you must have the correct mindset and have a proven track record in real estate and/or business. This isn't something you can acquire overnight, But there's really good news. If you are lacking in these areas, there's no better time to start on a new path than right now!

CHAPTER 3

Can't Wait! How Do I Get Started?

Now that you've cultivated the proper mindset and forged success in real estate and/or business, how do you get started in apartment syndication?

THE APARTMENT SYNDICATION CRASH COURSE
Before building a team, reaching out to investors or looking for deals, you need to set yourself up for success. You need to get educated!

Since you are reading this book, you are already on the right track. In fact, you're ready for the next to-do in our lesson plan!

When I bring on a new client who wants to become a syndicator, one of the first exercises I ask them to perform is memorize important apartment syndication terminology. The primary purpose of this exercise is to introduce them to terms and concepts they must understand in order to comprehend the steps later on in the syndication process.

Second, and even more important, the goal is for them to become competent enough to effectively communicate with investors, brokers, and property managers without sounding like a newbie who doesn't know what they're talking about.

The first important concept to understand is value-add investing. My clients and I are all value-add apartment investors.

Therefore, this book will focus on the apartment syndication process for value-add investors. (I will outline the advantages of value-add investing compared with turnkey and distressed investing in Chapter 25)

NOTE: Value-add investors purchase apartments and increase the value of the asset by increasing the income and/or decreasing the expenses. There are countless ways of adding value to an apartment building. Generally, the syndicator will increase the rental rates by performing interior and/or exterior renovations and decrease the expenses by improving the operations.

If your goal is to be a terrific apartment syndicator, there are definitions of important apartment syndication terms you must memorize and be able to accurately use during a conversation. **At this point, I recommend going to the Glossary at the end of the book to review the terms and definitions, along with the accompanying examples of each term.** All examples are from an actual apartment syndication my company completed, which is a 216-unit we purchased for $12,200,000.

When I started out, I created a notecard for each apartment syndication term I needed to memorize. On one side I would list the term. On the other side I would list the definition and formula. I would carry these flashcards with me wherever I went, reviewing them whenever I had a spare moment. I read them on the L-train to and from work every day. I also used them as bookmarks in the apartment investing books I was reading.

I recommend using a similar approach. Create notecards and recite the definitions and practice using the formulas until they become second nature. Most, if not all, of these terms will come up in every conversation with investors, brokers, and lenders when discussing a deal. In short, you have to be able to talk the talk before you can walk the walk!

CHAPTER 4

YOUR FOCUS IS COC RETURN AND IRR

As an apartment syndicator (and more specifically, a value-add syndicator), the terms "cash-on-cash (CoC) return" and "internal rate of return" (IRR) will be your main focus when underwriting a deal. I'll be telling you more about this in Chapter 31, so keep reading.

For now, the short story is that we use CoC and IRR to screen deals, because they are both the basis for determining the asset's value (remember that value is equal to income divided by capitalization rate). The higher the apartment value, the higher the CoC and IRR; the lower the apartment value, the lower the CoC and IRR.

When I am analyzing a deal, the apartment must have an IRR of at least 14% with a 5-year exit to the limited partners (i.e., passive investors) and have the ability to pay my investors at least 8% CoC return annualized over the hold period.

NOTE: The 8% CoC return doesn't include profits from sale.

When factoring in the profits from sale, **the annualized CoC return should be around 20%.** Investors get pretty excited about this level of return!

However, unless you find an extremely distressed apartment building owner/operator, you will likely never find a property that will achieve these two requirements at closing without any additional action on your part. To maximize both CoC return and IRR, the ideal and recommended business approach is the value-add model.

You need to understand something about me. I am a firm believer in the value-add business model and personally follow that model in my business. My company buys apartment buildings and improves the interior and exterior with the purpose of increasing the net operating income (NOI). Also called "forced appreciation," this increases the value of the property. You are forcing the value of the property up by making improvements.

When appreciation is forced, something we did made the income of the property increase and/or the expenses decrease, resulting in an increase in value. When the value is increased, both the CoC return and IRR increase, which means we can pay our investors their preferred returns and split the remaining profits!

When it comes to real estate investing, forced appreciation is the key to generating wealth. This is especially true when investing in large multifamily properties. You aren't going to get rich on single-digit CoC (unless you buy in a market that appreciates like crazy. Then you do a cash-out refinance or 1031 exchange into something larger). You get rich when you force appreciation and add hundreds of thousands or millions of dollars in equity with the gains realized at sale or at refinance.

For example, we purchased a 250-unit apartment building in a market with a cap rate of 7.8%. Here is a table showing the property value increases based on the increase in unit rental rates from what we did to add value (notice what happens when you just add $25 to the rent per unit – meaning that you don't always have to do a lot to force appreciation):

Increase in Rent (per unit)	Increase in Gross Rent	Increase in Property Value
$25	$75,000	$961,538
$50	$150,000	$1,923,077
$75	$225,000	$2,884,615
$100	$300,000	$3,846,154
$125	$375,000	$4,807,692
$150	$450,000	$5,769,231

On that particular deal, we were able to increase the rents by over $100! That was nearly $4,000,000 in equity, which allowed us to refinance and return equity to our investors. For example, we bought the 250-unit property for $14,100,000, put in about $2,000,000 in renovations and, due to the increase in income from increasing the rents, it appraised for $21,600,000 16 months later! That's $5,500,000 in "free" equity.

Obviously, increasing the unit rent will require a capital investment upfront, and the higher the rental increase, the higher initial investment. But as you can see, an increase of just $25 per unit results in over $1 million in equity created.

Forced appreciation is the main wealth producer and way to optimize CoC return and IRR. If you plan to get wealthy doing deals in real estate, this model can certainly get you there!

PART 1: THE EXPERIENCE

KNOWLEDGE — Chapters 1-4
1. What is apartment syndication?
2. How to Get Started
3. What to focus on

YOU ARE HERE

GOALS — Chapters 5-6
1. How do you make money?
2. Set 12-month goal and long-term vision
3. Ultimate Success Formula

BRAND BUILDING — Chapters 7-12
1. Why you need a brand
2. Select a target audience
3. How to build a brand

MARKET EVALUATION — Chapters 13-16
1. 3 Immutable Laws of Real Estate
2. Evaluate 7 markets
3. Pick 1-2 Target Markets

PART 2: THE MONEY

BUILD TEAM — Chapters 17-19
1. Find core real estate team members
2. Hire a mentor or consultant

FIND CAPITAL — Chapters 20-24
1. Why will they invest?
2. Build passive investor database
3. Create partnership structure

PART 3: THE DEAL

FIND DEALS — Chapters 25-28
1. Set investment criteria
2. On-market vs. off-market deals
3. How to find your first deal

UNDERWRITING — Chapters 29-31
1. Information needed to underwrite a deal
2. The 6-step underwriting process

SUBMIT OFFER — Chapter 32
1. How to submit an offer on a deal
2. Best-and-final offer
3. Purchase sales agreement

PART 4: THE EXECUTION

DUE DILIGENCE — Chapters 33-37
1. 10 due diligence reports
2. Secure financing from lender

SECURE CAPITAL — Chapters 38-42
1. Create investment summary
2. New investment offering call
3. Secure investor commitments

CLOSE — Chapters 43-44
1. Closing process
2. Notify passive investors

EXECUTE BUSINESS PLAN — Chapters 45-46
1. 10 asset management duties
2. How to sell the apartment

CHAPTER 5

THE MONEY QUESTION

A question I hear a lot from people who want to get into apartment syndication is about the syndication compensation structure. That's what I'll explain in this chapter.

Once you understand how syndicators are paid, you'll have the information required to (1) decide whether you want to pursue the syndication model, (2) establish your quantifiable goals, and (3) structure deals with investors. That last one is after you know what you're doing, of course!

What do you want to earn as a syndicator? $60,000? $120,000? $1 million? Many, many millions? These are attainable goals. But first you have to understand the fee structures... how you make your money in a deal.

First, you will receive a fee for putting together an apartment syndication. That's called the "acquisition fee," which is a percentage of the purchase price (1% to 5% of the purchase price is the industry standard). If your goal is to make $60,000 at closing, you need to purchase (acquire) a $3,000,000 asset, assuming a 2% acquisition fee.

Most of these types of deals require 35% of the purchase price to close, and that's **AFTER** factoring in the down payment, closing costs, renovation improvements, and your fees.

So, to make a $60,000 acquisition fee on the $3,000,000 asset, you'll need to raise $1,050,000 in private capital. To make a $120,000 acquisition fee, you'll raise $2.1 million. And so on. But you're not done there. On top of the acquisition fee, there are various other fees you can charge to make even more money over the course of the project AND upon selling.

How Do You Make Money?

Here are six of the most common fees you can charge as a syndicator:

1. Profit Split

Depending on how the partnership is structured, the syndicator can earn a portion of the total profits.

For example, a partnership can be structured so that the overall profits from the project (ongoing cash flow plus sales proceeds) are split 50/50 between the general partner (syndicator) and limited partner (passive investors).

If you have one limited partner who invested $1,000,000 into a property with a total project profit of $3,000,000, the limited partners and general partners would receive $1,500,000 each.

2. Acquisition Fee

The acquisition fee is an upfront fee paid by the new buying partnership entity for finding, analyzing, evaluating, financing, and closing the deal.

The acquisition fee ranges from 1% to 5% of the purchase price, depending on the size and scope of the project. On very large deals with a lot of potential for profit, I've seen a fee as high as 5% of the purchase price. On a $20 million deal, the acquisition fee would be between $100,000 on the low end and $1,000,000 on the high end.

3. Asset Management Fee

The asset management fee is an ongoing annual fee paid from the property operation for property oversight. Generally the asset management fee is 2% of collected income. Other syndicators charge a per-unit asset management fee (for example, $250 per unit per year). However, since you're collecting a flat fee regardless of whether you've hit your return projections, a per-unit asset management fee doesn't show alignment of interests.

4. Property Management Fee

The property management fee is an ongoing fee for managing the day-to-day operations of the property (collecting rent, paying bills, running the property, doing the accounting) that is paid from the operations of the property on a monthly basis. This fee ranges from 2% to 8% of the total monthly collected revenues of the property, depending on the size of the deal (the larger the deal, the lower the management fee). If the gross rent is $165,000 a month, the property management fee would be between $4,950 and $9,900 a month.

This fee is not common for people starting out in syndication, because it's usually best to use a third-party property management company. However, as you grow your portfolio, you might find that it makes more sense to take the property management in-house, in which case you would build out a property management team and receive the fee.

5. Refinancing Fee

The refinancing fee is paid for the work required to refinance a property. At time of closing the new loan, a fee of 0.5% to 2% of the total loan amount is paid to the syndicator if a certain hurdle is reached. For example, you might have a return hurdle on a refinance of 50%. So, when you refinance, if you return 50% or more to the limited partners, you get your agreed-upon fee.

6. Guaranty Fee

The guaranty fee is typically a one-time fee paid to a loan guarantor at closing. The loan guarantor guarantees the loan. The general partner (i.e. your company) may bring on an individual with a high net-worth/balance sheet to sign on the loan to get the best terms possible. Or, the general partner may sign on the loan themselves, collecting the fee or deciding to forgo it.

At close, a fee of as low as 0.5% to 2% and as high as 3.5 to 5% of the principal balance of the mortgage is paid to the loan guarantor. The riskier the financing or more complicated the deal, the higher the guaranty fee. For example, a nonrecourse loan will have a lower fee than a recourse loan.

If the general partner doesn't have a good relationship with the loan guarantor, that individual will charge a higher fee as well. In some instances, the general partner will offer the loan guarantor a percentage of the general partnership (5% to 30%) in addition to or instead of the one-time upfront fee.

In Chapter 37, I go into more details on the loan guarantor.

This is the list of the six most common syndicator fees. However, and I cannot emphasize this enough, DO NOT take fees unless it shows an alignment of interests and you are adding value to the respective aspect of the process.

DO NOT overload the partnership with excessive fees.

As an example of a typical fee structure my company follows, here is what we charged on that 250-unit deal we purchased for $14,100,000:

- **Asset management fee:** 2% of collected monthly income, provided that preferred return was paid to the limited partners.
- **Acquisition fee:** 2% of the gross transaction amount paid at closing.
- **Refinancing fee:** 2% of the original principal amount paid at closing of the new loan.
- **Guaranty fee:** 0.83% of the outstanding principal balance paid at closing.

- **Profit split:** 30% the total profits.

In that example, the return projections were as follows:

- **Asset management fee:** Year one projected collected income was $2,447,334; 2% of that is $48,946.68 annually, or $4,078.89 per month.
- **Acquisition fee:** 2% of the $14,100,000 purchase price is $282,000.
- **Refinancing fee:** Since we were able to add $5,500,000 in equity in less than a year, at refinance we would return more than 50% of the limited partners' equity. Therefore, 2% of the original principal amount is $234,000.
- **Guaranty fee:** The initial loan amount was $11.7 million; 0.83% of that is $97,110.
- **Profit split:** The total profits are split 70/30 between the LP and GP. However, the LP receives an ongoing preferred return of 8% before the GP receives a distribution. We also had an IRR hurdle; once the LP IRR reaches 20%, the profit split is 50/50. With this structure, the payments to the GP equate to approximately $108,000 annually, or $9,000 per month. At sale, we projected a $6,668,727. With a 70/30 split and a 50/50 split once a 20% LP IRR is hit, the payment to the GP at sale equates to $2,217,152.

Overall, after five years, the general partners will earn a total of $3,614,996.

Think that could help you with your financial goals? Well, then, keep reading and let's do this thing!

CHAPTER 6

SO, WHAT'S YOUR GOAL?

Now that you understand how syndicators get paid, you can establish a financial goal. While studying the apartment syndication terms and formulas, it's time to start thinking about:

1. Your 12-month goal, and
2. Your long-term vision.

WHAT'S YOUR 12-MONTH GOAL?

When establishing goals, you always want them to be BOTH specific and quantifiable. For example, my long-term goal is to control $1 billion in assets by my 40th birthday. It's a quantifiable value ($1 billion) that I set out to achieve by a specific date (my 40th birthday).

For the 12-month goal, we already have the specific part down – 12 months from now. We just need to select a dollar value. Maybe, this is the dollar value you need in order to replace the income you earn from your full-time job or to afford your ideal lifestyle... or something else entirely. That part is up to you. Answer the following:

My 12-month goal is $_____.

Now let's get even more specific. You need to determine what you have to do to achieve that stated goal. Some people will determine how many deals they need to complete to achieve their goal. However, I don't like that approach.

Going back to what I said earlier, that approach is not specific enough and it doesn't account for losing money on a deal. For example, if your goal is to complete five deals, but you lose $1,000,000 on each deal, you've technically achieved your goal. And your reward is that you get to file for bankruptcy and live under a bridge. (I know... not funny.)

Instead, you need to determine **how much money you need to raise to achieve your goal**. This can be calculated in different ways depending on how you structure the deal with investors (which we will discuss in Chapter 24). Right now, to keep things simple and conservative, I recommend calculating the amount of money you need to raise using the acquisition fee. The acquisition fee is only one component of how you make money in apartment syndications. You will also make a small ongoing cash flow while you execute the business plan. Then, you will get your big payday at sale. However, since you will not receive that payday for 5 or more years (depending on how long you plan on holding onto your deal) and you won't know how much ongoing cash flow you will receive until you begin underwriting deals, the acquisition fee is the best factor to use when setting your short-term goals. As you approach the end of the business plan on your deals, you can update your 12-month goals to include the projected profits for sale.

Let's say your goal is to create an annual income of $100,000 in the next 12 months, and you structure your deals so that your compensation is a 2% acquisition fee. To make $100,000 from the acquisition fee, you must then syndicate $5,000,000 worth of deals ($100,000 / 2% acquisition fee). The typical equity raise for an apartment deal is 35% of the all-in price. Obviously, this varies based on the type of loan you get, your business plan, and general partner fees, but let's just go with this structure initially.

Calculating this deal, 35% of $5,000,000 is $1,750,000. In this case, your specific goal is to have at least $1,750,000 in verbal commitments from investors. Additionally, on top of your $100,000 acquisition fee, you will make money ongoing from the other fees charged (asset management fee, profit split), as well as a big payday once you sell the asset!

Now that you know how much money you need to raise to achieve your 12-month goal, begin the process of reprogramming your mind to include the new goal by creating an affirmation statement, which you will write 15 times each morning for the next 30 days.

For example, following the "acquisition fee only" payment structure, your affirmation would read, "On___/___/_____, I have raised $1,750,000 in equity from passive investors, and I used that equity to syndicate $5,000,000 worth of successfully performing apartment communities earning me a total of $100,000 in acquisition fees."

Fill in the blanks to create your own affirmation statement. Commit to writing it out 15 times each morning for the next 30 days:

On ___/___/_____, I have raised $_____ in equity from passive investors, and I used that equity to syndicate $_____ worth of successfully performing apartment communities earning me a total of $_____ in acquisition fees.

WHAT'S YOUR LONG-TERM VISION?

Don't stop at setting a 12-month goal. You'll want to create a compelling long-term vision with the purpose of keeping you motivated and on track. (That's what I do and it works!)

To aid in the creation of a long-term vision, I use a powerful written exercise I like to call "Gotta Get Yo Mind Right Before You Get Yo Money Right."

In the spaces below, complete the following statements:

1. **What gets me excited about real estate is...**

_____

_____

_____

2. **Once I achieve my goal, I will benefit by...**

_____

_____

_____

3. **If I don't achieve my goal, I will be disgusted with myself because I will not get to (or I will unfortunately have to)...**

_____

_____

_____

4. **What negative consequences have I already experienced as a result of not achieving my goal?**

_____

_____

_____

For an even more powerful affirmation statement, you can add in your responses to the above questions, making a paragraph-long affirmation statement that you recite in the mirror each morning, before you go to bed, or whenever you need a motivational boost.

    I chose these four questions for very specific psychological reasons.

    The first question is to elicit your passions for real estate. That's your "why" behind your interest in real estate. If you aren't passionate, or don't know what aspects of real estate get you really passionate, you will likely fold when the going gets tough. Worst case, you won't get started at all.

The second question is to help you create an ideal toward which you will want to be pulled. The third and fourth questions are to help you create a worst-case scenario to avoid.

Some people are motivated by striving for success and meaning; others are motivated by avoiding failure. These four questions speak to both types of individuals.

When you get to a step in the syndication process that feels overwhelming, you will come back to these four questions (and your answers), reviewing your inspirations for becoming a syndicator and the things that disgust you in regard to not achieving your syndication goals.

Make your responses as specific as possible.

An example of a poor inspiring response is "Once I achieve my goal, I will benefit by having more money, having more freedom of time, and being able to travel." An example of a great, inspiring response is "Once I achieve my goal, I will benefit by having more money to **buy Texas Rangers season tickets for my immediate and extended family**, having more freedom of time **to go on a jog at 2pm on a Wednesday,** and being able to travel **with the love of my life to Paris, France, and take a picture in front of the Eiffel Tower."**

See and *feel* the difference between those two visions?

Regarding what disgusts you, a poor statement would be "By not achieving my goal, I will be disgusted, because I will not get to have more money and more freedom."

Instead, be specific. For example, I was disgusted by the idea of having to go back to my advertising job. Everyone I worked with knew the reason I left was to pursue an apartment syndication career. The thought of having to walk back into that same office defeated... a failure and an embarrassment... made me literally sick to my stomach.

Finally, I ask the third and fourth questions because one of my fundamental beliefs, which I took from Tony Robbins and which is highlighted on my vision board (yes, I have one and refer to it often), is that **the secret to life is giving**.

It is my very personal belief that it is through contribution to others that we find true meaning in life. Therefore, an important aspect of our vision is determining how accomplishing our goal(s) will have a positive impact on others, whether it's family members, spouses, children, or the world at large.

Before moving on, I have a couple of questions for you...

1. Have you ever set a goal and not accomplished it?
2. Or, have you set a goal and accomplished some or most of it but not all of it?

If so you're not alone. I certainly have!

But that's okay. You can't fixate on what you haven't accomplished. Instead, look ahead at the journey to come.

If we fixate on the end goal, and only the end goal, then it can be pretty disheartening not to accomplish this goal. That's not good. If instead we focus on the fact that we are making progress toward our ultimate goal, then we should feel good about what we've done. There is fulfillment in that progress.

You need a little help in that area? Cool. I have some proven strategies to help you set yourself up for success in accomplishing your goals.

50/50 Goals

Let me introduce to you a concept called 50/50 goals...

50% of a goal's success should be based on achieving the quantifiable outcome and 50% on identifying a lesson or skill learned in pursuit of the quantifiable goal that you can apply to your business to improve results in the long run.

Let's say you want to make $100,000 in your first 12 months, but at the end of the year you've made $65,000. First off, congrats! But, if 100% of your success is based on making $100,000, then you've technically failed. You feel discouraged and let down. You curse me for making it sound so easy. Maybe you even drop out of the investment game altogether.

But if you look at things differently... for example, that 50% of your goal is making $65,000 and 50% are the takeaways you can apply to your business moving forward... you are successful! At least you "feel" successful.

By going through the entire process of closing on deals that resulted in a $65,000 payday, you've benefited from the experience gained, lessons learned, relationships created, and new skills adopted. These things will have a lasting positive effect on the business 1, 5 and 10 years down the road. That in itself is a success.

Listen, I am a firm believer in thinking on a macro scale, not a micro scale. In other words, I am planning decades in advance, not just a few months or years down the road. I am committed to the long game. The skills and lessons you learn along the way can be more important than the short-term quantifiable goals, especially early in your career.

Think of the experiences like compound interest, but instead of money you're earning, you're gaining skills. If you learn a skill your first year, it is part of your repertoire forever. If you "only" made $65,000 of your $100,000 goal, but you found a 5-star property manager on one of your deals, that additional team member may earn you more money in the long run than you would have earned had you made the extra $35,000 without finding the property manager.

Following the 50/50 goals concept allows you to approach situations with a "glass half full" mindset or even a "my glass is overflowing" mindset. That's way better than the "glass half empty" mentality.

Two individuals that set the same $100,000 goal but only achieved $65,000 can feel the exact opposite emotions at the end of the year. The syndicator whose success is 100% dependent on making $100,000 may feel awful. Conversely, the syndicator whose success is 50% dependent on making $100,000 and 50% dependent on identifying skills to apply moving forward will feel pretty darned successful.

While the first syndicator is sulking in a corner, the happy syndicator will reflect on their year, analyze what they did right and what they did wrong, determine what they need to do more of and what they need to do less of, and then feel motivated and inspired to reap the improved results by implementing those changes for the coming year. The optimist will, on average, achieve more in life than the pessimist. However, the optimist will make changes more slowly.

If you're the optimist in this scenario, congratulate yourself on what you've accomplished but still identify and make the necessary changes to continue improving over time.

Reframe the way you look at your goals. Don't think of success as being 100% dependent on reaching a specific outcome. Instead, cut that goal in half and focus the other 50% of your efforts on identifying systems, skills, techniques, or lessons learned from the process of working toward the specific, quantifiable goal.

THE ULTIMATE SUCCESS FORMULA

Additionally, whether you're figuring out how to achieve your long-term goal or are focusing on a smaller piece of the puzzle, like raising money or finding deals, there is a common process that you need to follow to attain any outcome. Tony Robbins distilled this process into a 5-step formula he simply calls **"The Ultimate Success Formula."** Since I love Tony and his success formula, I'll share it with you now:

1. Know your outcome
First, know **WHAT** you want. Clarity is power, so you want to be as specific and detailed as you can be. As apartment syndicators, our outcome will be a desired annual income. We want to be as specific as possible, which is why you will determine the exact apartment purchase price and amount of money you need to raise in order to achieve your annual income goal. That way, instead of having a vague goal, you know the exact number of leads and amount of passive investor money you need to attract. Then you can take massive intelligent action (see step 3) to get to that goal.

Tony Robbins says, "Where focus goes, energy flows." Once you define your outcome and make it your main point of focus, you will begin – almost automatically – to take the right steps and identify the right opportunities to achieve that outcome.

2. Know your reasons why
Now that you know your outcome, it's time to formulate your plan of action. But before formulating a plan of action for **HOW** you'll achieve your stated outcome, you need to know the reasons **WHY** you want to achieve it.

Human beings can do amazing things when they have a strong enough why.

What are the reasons behind your outcome? Do you want to leave a legacy? Use your earnings to have a positive impact on the world? Set your children up for success as part of your legacy plan? Whatever the reason is, make sure you understand your reasons consciously and articulate them clearly.

With a strong why comes a strong emotional attachment to your outcome(s). In turn, these emotions will be what allow you to celebrate victories and keep you going when you experience setbacks along the way.

3. **Take massive intelligent action**

After defining the **WHAT** and **WHY**, the **HOW** is to take action. Not a little bit of action. Not a lot of random action. Not sporadic action. But massive, intelligent, and consistent action!

Massive intelligent action is consistently taking the daily steps that, when added together, ultimately lead to the realization of an overall goal and vision.

By defining your overall annual income goal, you can then reverse-engineer the smaller, day-to-day steps required to achieve it. You'll know how much investor money you need to raise, which means you know you'll need at least that amount in verbal interest from passive investors.

You will have an idea of how many deals, or at least the size of the deal, you need to complete. (BTW, for every 100 leads, you will close on one deal, so don't let that discourage you.)

If you're using direct mail, for example, how many marketing pieces must you send to receive the number of leads required to close on an apartment community that would result in you achieving your annual income goal? How many investors will you have to talk to for you to get to the YES? How many networking events will you need to attend and how many online groups will you need to be involved in to keep leads coming in?

The goal here is to build habits and routines that become second nature so you not only take massive intelligent action automatically, but even begin to crave it!

4. **Know what you're getting**

As you begin to take action toward your goal, it is important to analyze and track your progress. If you aren't tracking your results, you won't know if you're on the right path.

A powerful Tony Robbins anecdote is about two different boats starting off at the same point. One boat continues on to the destination while the other veers off by just one degree. A few hours later, the two boats are miles apart. Applied to apartment syndication, if you are slightly off-track at the start of your journey, the longer you go without recognizing the error, the more off course you'll be AND the more effort it will require to get you back on track.

It's a great idea to routinely check in and see whether your massive action is getting you closer to or farther from your money-raising and lead-generation goals.

5. Change your approach
Based on these aforementioned routine check-ins, you may need to make adjustments to get yourself back on course. Or you may see great results with a certain approach for a while, but it may begin to taper off and plateau, dropping you into a rut. When faced with either one of these situations, celebrate the fact that you had the awareness to identify the error(s) and then change your approach.

But don't just take Tony's word (or my word) for the power of this massive success formula. Here are four inspirational examples of people who set out to achieve a certain outcome, faced adversity and barriers, changed their approach... and ultimately reached a level of success far above that which they initially set out to achieve.

Walt Disney: At 22 years old, Walt Disney was fired from a Missouri newspaper for "not being creative enough." One of his early entrepreneurial ventures, Laugh-O-Gram Studios, went bankrupt after only two years. (Walt later credited his time at Laugh-O-Gram as the inspiration to create Mickey Mouse!) Also, he was denied by 302 banks for a loan to start Disneyland because he "lacked originality." Even with this rough start, he didn't give up. By the end of his career, Disney had won a record 22 Academy Awards and was in the process of opening his second theme park, Disney World. Today, the Walt Disney Company holds over $92 billion in assets, with a market capitalization of roughly $150,000,000. Not bad for such a "dullard," huh?

Michael Jordan: Michael was **CUT** from his high school basketball team before going on to win an NCAA championship, six NBA championships, and MVP finals. He once famously said, "I've missed more than 9,000 shots in my career. I've lost almost 300 games. Twenty-six times I've been trusted to take the game-winning shot and missed. I've failed over and over and over again in my life. And that is why I succeed."

Jordan is also a branding wizard. Between his shoes, the highest-grossing basketball film of all time, *Space Jam*, and his part ownership of the Charlotte Hornets, MJ became the first billionaire NBA player in history, with a current net worth of $1.39 billion.

Stephen King: Stephen King is an uber-successful author of horror, supernatural fiction, suspense, science fiction, and fantasy, selling more than 350,000,000 copies of his books, and having many of his books adapted into featured films. This includes the #1 ranked movie on IMDB, *Shawshank Redemption*. But did you know that when he was 20, his manuscript for *Carrie* was rejected by 30 publishers? Yes! One publisher even said, "We are not interested in science fiction that deals with negative utopias. They do not sell."

King actually threw the manuscript in the trash, but fortunately for the world his wife retrieved it and convinced him to resubmit it. Once published, the paperback sold over 1,000,000 copies in its first year alone. The rest is history; Stephen King is now a household name in the horror genre.

Harland "Colonel" Sanders: In 1955, at the tender age of 65, Harland Sanders, a retiree collecting $105 a month in Social Security, attempted to franchise his secret Kentucky Fried Chicken recipe. Sanders traveled the country looking for a restaurant interested in his recipe, often sleeping in the back of his car. After 1,009 rejections, he finally found a taker. By 1964, there were 600 franchises selling his chicken recipe, and by 1976 Sanders was ranked as the world's second most recognizable celebrity. By the time of his death, there were 6,000 KFCs across 48 countries with $2B (that's "billion") in annual sales. That's an amazing success story! Plus, his chicken is still pretty tasty even today!

Why share these stories with you? I want you to see that this formula can be applied in your life. Heck, it should be applied to every step in the apartment syndication process:

1. Define your outcome.
2. Articulate your why and begin taking massive action.
3. Analyze your results and keep doing the things that are working... and try out new things for those that aren't.

My final word on goal-setting is a quote that can be attributed to many successful entrepreneurs and great thinkers:

Success is about the journey, not the destination.

As apartment syndicators, we will spend the majority (99.999999%) of our time on the journey toward our goal(s). You better learn to enjoy that 99.999999%!

PART 1: THE EXPERIENCE

KNOWLEDGE — Chapters 1-4
1. What is apartment syndication?
2. How to Get Started
3. What to focus on

GOALS — Chapters 5-6
1. How do you make money?
2. Set 12-month goal and long-term vision
3. Ultimate Success Formula

BRAND BUILDING — Chapters 7-12 *(YOU ARE HERE)*
1. Why you need a brand
2. Select a target audience
3. How to build a brand

MARKET EVALUATION — Chapters 13-16
1. 3 Immutable Laws of Real Estate
2. Evaluate 7 markets
3. Pick 1-2 Target Markets

PART 2: THE MONEY

BUILD TEAM — Chapters 17-19
1. Find core real estate team members
2. Hire a mentor or consultant

FIND CAPITAL — Chapters 20-24
1. Why will they invest?
2. Build passive investor database
3. Create partnership structure

PART 3: THE DEAL

FIND DEALS — Chapters 25-28
1. Set investment criteria
2. On-market vs. off-market deals
3. How to find your first deal

UNDERWRITING — Chapters 29-31
1. Information needed to underwrite a deal
2. The 6-step underwriting process

SUBMIT OFFER — Chapter 32
1. How to submit an offer on a deal
2. Best-and-final offer
3. Purchase sales agreement

PART 4: THE EXECUTION

DUE DILIGENCE — Chapters 33-37
1. 10 due diligence reports
2. Secure financing from lender

SECURE CAPITAL — Chapters 38-42
1. Create investment summary
2. New investment offering call
3. Secure investor commitments

CLOSE — Chapters 43-44
1. Closing process
2. Notify passive investors

EXECUTE BUSINESS PLAN — Chapters 45-46
1. 10 asset management duties
2. How to sell the apartment

CHAPTER 7

IT'S ALL ABOUT THE BRAND, BABY!

"Think Different."

This two-word, technically and grammatically incorrect slogan from Apple, Inc., in 1997 drastically changed not only the landscape of the technology industry, but also the daily life of every person on Planet Earth. Forever.

In the years preceding the creation of the "Think Different" slogan, Apple was in disarray, to put it mildly. This chaos was due to multiple factors, including the loss of market share to Wintel (a partnership between Microsoft Windows and Intel). Even worse for the Apple brand was the high-profile failure of the billion-dollar Apple Newton project. Obviously something had to change or the company would fail.

Enter the clever "Think Different" advertising campaign. That plus the return of Steve Jobs to the company reversed the brand's negative trend and set the stage for Apple to become the first United States company to boast a valuation of over $1 trillion. Unlike what happened in 1997, Apple is now recognized as the world's most valuable brand.

So, why is this story relevant to apartment syndication?

WHY YOU NEED A BRAND

You will need to build your credibility – also known as building your brand. As a newbie apartment syndicator, you have a credibility problem. Branding will be a part of the solution. When you create a brand that positions you as the expert in apartment investing, you'll stop getting quizzical looks from people you're talking to about investing in your deal.

So, let me ask you something...

What are you known for among your peers and in your sphere of influence? If you are an advertising agency professional, then you are likely known for your skills in advertising. If you are a property manager, then you are likely known for that. If you are a medical device sales professional, then you are likely known for that. In order to shift the perception from where you are now to where you want to be, building your brand is a necessity.

By the way, the advertising agency responsible for the "Think Different" slogan, TBWA/Chiat Day, was in fact my employer prior to my becoming an apartment syndicator! As an advertising agency professional working on Madison Avenue, my responsibilities included working hand in hand with Fortune 500 companies, helping them create and execute on their advertising and marketing strategies. Not only do I understand the power and utility of branding, but I have skillsets that enable me to expand my own *Best Ever* brand, to which I attribute in part my company controlling over $400,000,000 in apartment buildings to date.

NOTE: Branding is an important and necessary step that many apartment syndicators skip or skim over. Big mistake. So pay attention.

Truth is... I didn't begin with the intention of creating a brand. I had recently left my job at the advertising firm and closed on my first apartment syndication. Having lost my six-figure corporate salary, I was in need of a new consistent source of income. While I had four single-family properties, I knew the $250/month from each of these homes could be wiped out with an unexpected move-out or unexpected maintenance issues. You see, it was still early on in the business plan of my first apartment community, so all the profits were going to my investors. I did get a $22,000 acquisition fee, but that would only hold me over for so long before I had to get back out there and take down another big property!

As you can see, I had an immediate financial challenge that needed to be solved. Additionally, I knew that building a large audience of active and aspiring real estate professionals would be beneficial to growing my business as an apartment syndicator. Around this same time, I hired a business coach and mentor, Trevor McGregor.

As I mentioned earlier in this book, I am a huge fan of Tony Robbins. Once I made the decision to hire a business coach, I wanted to find one that followed Tony Robbins' philosophies. So I did a lot of research and went to Robbins' website, where I signed up for a call with one of his Master Coaches. That's how I met Trevor, an outcome-oriented business coach. When I shared with him my financial challenge, he advised me to consider starting a podcast.

I did some more research and discovered the financial advantages of starting a podcast. If I could establish a listener base larger than a few family members and my dog (hi, Jack!), then I could offer advertising spots to real estate companies, which would bolster my income. Pretty exciting stuff!

Thus it was settled – I would create my own real estate podcast.

The obvious first step was what to name the darned thing. Based on my advertising and marketing background, I knew that if I wanted the podcast to gain traction, it needed to stand out from all the thousands of other real estate podcasts out there – most of which are in the iTunes graveyard today.

So, I did more research. A ton. I reviewed all the podcasts on iTunes, looking at the cover art and listening to the podcasts for things I did and didn't like. Maybe the most valuable thing I did was to read the favorable and unfavorable reviews of each of those podcasts. The reviews gave me a very good understanding of what people wanted.

Here's what I learned...

As real estate entrepreneurs, our time is limited. It's not about the amount of information provided; it is more about the meaningful nature of the information. If I could have short, quick-hitting interviews with different real estate professionals who would give their best advice ever, then I'd get to the crux of what people need and want to learn. Or to put it another way, no fluffy stuff, Baby!

Since listeners of the podcast would receive this best advice ever, I came up with the name "Best Real Estate Investing Advice Ever."

I didn't want it to be a mystery as to why you should listen to the show and what you would learn from it. I came across many podcasts with interesting names, but I couldn't figure out what the show had to offer or the format of the show. I was left scratching my head. What was the show about?

That's not the experience I wanted for my listeners. Since I was starting from scratch and no one really knew about me yet, I wanted people to discover my show, see the title, and know that if they listened they would receive the best real estate investing advice from active entrepreneurs in that field.

When Trevor advised me to start a podcast, he told me to look at the EOFire (Entrepreneur On Fire) podcast. Since it was an extremely popular podcast, I decided to mirror my podcast on how it was done. The host calls his listenership "Fire Nation," and each episode ends with a "Fire Round" where the guests rattle off answers to a list of questions. Based on that, I decided to call my listeners "The Best Ever Listeners" and to conclude my interviews with the "Best Ever Lightning Round."

Once I had the title, name of the listener base, and unique format, I was ready to launch. While I was thrilled to have launched, I didn't exactly move quickly. For the first few months, I posted new episodes randomly. I wasn't seeing a massive uptick in listeners and the entire process cost me a few hundred dollars per month, so I began second-guessing my decision. I questioned whether having my own podcast was a good use of my time. Instead of simply giving into my fears and doubts (which are also fears), I decided to post DAILY podcasts for three months. I would re-evaluate at the end of that time.

At that point, if I determined it still wasn't a good use of my time, I would quit. Lo and behold, a few months later, I got my first podcast sponsor! The proof of concept was there, and I was breaking even financially. A month after that, the podcast was generating income! At the end of that three-month period, I decided to not only continue the podcast, but to also continue airing episodes daily. And as of this writing, I've aired a new episode for over 1,500 days in a row, making it the world's longest-running DAILY real estate investing podcast.

I'd like to emphasize something that will really help you, so let's take a quick pause.

I initially released episodes every now and then for the first month or two. It wasn't getting results, so I made a commitment to go ALL IN and do it DAILY for three months. I didn't give up.

When things aren't generating the results we want, yet we know those things have been successful for others, we need to update our commitment or our approach. The same philosophy can be applied to finding investors and finding deals. Remember this. (It's important.)

Ok... and we're back!

As I mentioned previously, I started the podcast for strictly business reasons. I needed the money from advertising. Fast forward to today and I now realize the learning and networking process that goes hand in hand with podcasting has provided exponentially more value to my business than any direct dollar I've received from podcast sponsors.

From a strictly educational perspective, I am benefiting from having conversations with active real estate entrepreneurs every day, probing them for the best, most practical real estate advice they have to offer.

From a broader networking perspective, I am able to get my name in front of real estate professionals while I sleep. As a result, I've sourced apartment deals and private capital, attracted people who are interested in apartment syndication to my consulting business, and formed new, life-long friendships!

Additionally, what started off as a podcast to generate advertising revenue has branched out into a full-fledged *Best Ever* brand that includes:

- Annual Best Ever Conference (www.besteverconference.com)
- Weekly Best Ever newsletter (www.bestevernewsletter.com)
- Best Ever blog (www.thebesteverblog.com)
- Best Ever YouTube channel (www.youtube.com/c/BestEverShow)
- Local Best Ever Mastermind in Cincinnati (www.bestevercincy.com)
- Best Ever books (www.besteverbooks.com)
- Best Ever Facebook community (www.bestevercommunity.com)
- Best Ever Passive Investor Resource page (www.besteverpassiveinvestor.com)

This is pretty exciting stuff for me... and now I get to help more people learn how to do what I do, which is invest in real estate to build a brighter financial future. No kidding. That's mighty rewarding! And talk about credibility...

Now, whenever someone searches my name, they don't just see me; they see this massive and ever-expanding brand. That gives my current and potential passive investors peace of mind, because someone who has consistently posted new podcasts for over 1,500 days in a row and has created various other pieces of online and in-person content over the years is given a higher level of credibility than someone who just has a LinkedIn profile.

On the basis of this evidence, building a brand is an absolute requirement if you want to scale your apartment syndication business. Sure, it takes some time to create and build. But I've extracted the best practices from building my brand that can help expedite the process, which I will outline in subsequent chapters. Keep reading and you will have all the tools you need to create your own brand.

Looking back, one thing I would have done differently was to define a specific target audience for my brand. So naturally, that's the best place for you to start...

CHAPTER 8

YOU HAVE TO AIM BEFORE YOU CAN SHOOT!

Before you construct your brand, you need to determine exactly who your brand will attract. Believe me, the answer isn't "everyone." You need to define a specific target audience. If you don't do this step, you will waste your time. Not understanding your target will result in wasted opportunities and ultimately, money.

When I started my *Best Ever* brand, which began with my podcast, I thought my goal was to be recognized by as many people as possible. The way I figured it, the more people who knew my name, the more business I would receive. So, I focused on offering valuable content to the widest range of real estate professionals. That was a big mistake.

GENERAL VS. SELECTIVE FAME

It wasn't until I read Tim Ferriss' book *Tools of Titans* that I realized this shotgun approach wasn't the most effective method in building my brand and name recognition. In a chapter of Tim's book dedicated to mathematician and economist Eric Weinstein, I was introduced to the concept of 2,000 true fans, which divides "fame" into two categories – general fame and selective fame.

General fame would be the name recognition of a movie star or sports celebrity. A generally famous person is so well known that he/she can't pump gas, enjoy a delicious Chipotle burrito, or buy groceries in public without being recognized and/or harassed by the paparazzi or overly enthusiastic fans. While the prospect of flashing lights and smiling fans seems attractive when you aren't in that position, Eric said that "general fame is overrated." Moreover, I have to assume being recognized so easily and never getting to go out in public without being swarmed would get annoying.

Then there's **selective fame**, which Eric recommends you pursue. He said, "You want to be famous to 2,000 to 3,000 people you handpick."

General, mainstream fame is overrated because it brings more liabilities than benefits, whereas selective fame is the opposite. In Eric Weinstein's chapter of the book, Tim adds, "If you're known and respected by 2K to 3K high-caliber people (e.g., a live TED audience), you can do anything and everything you want in life. It provides maximal upside and minimal downside."

I love this concept, and Tim's words immediately resonated with me. I brainstormed exactly who I wanted my 2,000 fans to be. Since I raise money for multifamily property syndications, I analyzed the characteristics of my current investors to determine their commonalities. Based on the results of this analysis, I established the criteria for my primary target audience:

- **Age**: 35 to 65 years
- **Sex**: Male
- **Location**: Living in or very close to a large city
- **Occupation**: Business owners, C-Suite executives, doctors, dentists, engineers, and real estate investors who used to be active but now want to be passive
- **Other**: Must be accredited investors (refer back to the description in Chapter 1)

Before we go further, I need to make a BIG disclaimer.

The above target audience profile is based on my existing investor database, but not all of my investors fit into these categories. I have many investors who are women and, in fact, one of my largest investors is a woman. Plus, some of my investors are younger than 35 or older than 64. I also have many conversations with couples. I'm simply using general analytics to determine who the primary audience is based on those who have invested the most money and most frequently with me.

As I progressed in my business, I defined a secondary target audience to attract people interested in becoming apartment syndicators. That's because I have a private consulting program to train potential or practicing apartment syndicators. The majority of my content (65% to be precise) is geared toward my primary target audience and the rest (35%) is for my secondary target audience.

How to Select a Target Audience

While it would be easy to simply copy my primary target audience, that's not the most effective approach for you to use. Because I have raised money for over $400,000,000 in apartment communities, I have a very broad range of investors.

When you are starting out, you want your primary target to be hyper-focused and based on your unique background. It should be a group that you already know really well or a network that you're already tapped into. For example, my initial primary target audience consisted primarily of fellow advertising professionals. Thus, if you are in medical sales, your primary target audience will likely be people in medical sales. If you are a part of your college's alumni group, target them.

That said, in some cases, your primary target audience may not be large enough to attract 2,000 true fans. If that is the case, you need to define a broader secondary target audience.

Your secondary target audience should be the group that you want to know really well. Here is where you can either copy my criteria or network with active syndicators in your market to determine their investor demographic so you can copy that.

Ready to determine the characteristics of the people you want as your 2,000 true fans?

Great.

These should be the people who will have the biggest effect on the growth of your business. Following is a questionnaire that will help you determine your target audience!

WHO IS YOUR TARGET AUDIENCE?

Primary
- **Age:** _____
- **Sex:** _____
- **Location:** _____
- **Occupation:** _____
- **Other Criteria:** _____

Secondary
- **Age:** _____
- **Sex:** _____
- **Location:** _____
- **Occupation:** _____
- **Other Criteria:** _____

CHAPTER 9

BUILDING YOUR PERSONAL BEST-EVER BRAND

Once you determine your target audience and your top 2,000 true fans – which means you know the person who will be attracted to your brand – you can then begin to construct the basis of your brand. You need to know this information so you can establish your apartment syndication company and grow recognition for it over time.

HOW TO BUILD A BRAND: THE THREE BASIC COMPONENTS

The basic components you need to create your brand are your:

1. Company name, logo, and business cards
2. Website, and
3. Company presentation.

If those basic branding components just gave your heart a little anxiety jump… all I can say is, "Breathe." It's not hard and every new business start-up has to create these pieces. Plus, I'm here to help. Just follow the steps as they are laid out below.

1. **Company name, logo, and business cards**

When it comes to creating a company name, there are two approaches: including your name or not including your name.

As you begin raising private capital for your deals, investors aren't investing in your business. They are investing in you. That's something you learn over time. If they trust you as an individual, they are more likely to invest. They don't care so much about the name of your company.

Therefore, tying your first name, last name, or initials into your company name can be a powerful branding strategy. For example, I named my first apartment syndication company Fairless Investing. Since people knew me by my last name, that approach to branding worked well for me.

The downside to including your name is that the business becomes dependent on you... forever. As you expand both your business and your brand, it becomes increasingly difficult to be the face of all parts of your company. This discovery came to me a few years into business when my business partner and I created our current business, Ashcroft Capital (ashcroftcapital.com).

Obviously the name of this company doesn't go with my current Best Ever branding or my personal name. It's bigger than me; there are more people at the helm in this company than just me. I'm a part of a team. So the name needed to reflect the expansion of what I've accomplished. The name does a pretty good job of that. Tag lines help, too, because they help you explain to people who land on your site or look at your business card what you do in one short line.

There are pros and cons to each approach, so think about it and use your discretion. In the end, regardless of the approach you choose, the company name should be easy to pronounce and easy to remember. When people (including your investors) talk about your business, they should be able to pronounce the name of your company with relative ease.

Once you decide on your company name, it's time to create a compelling logo. Unless you are a designer, I recommend outsourcing the creation of your logo to a third party. Cost-effective logo creation resources can be found at LogoGarden and Fiverr.com. Have the designers create a few logos; then ask friends or business associates which one they believe is best (e.g., by posting to social media, which acts as an engagement tool and expands your exposure in a fun way). Choose the most popular logo design and stick with it.

Colors and fonts matter, by the way, which is why you want a professional to design your logo. You want to be really happy with it while at the same time not overthink it!

Finally, use your company name and logo in the creation of your business cards. You can purchase inexpensive business cards from LogoGarden, VistaPrint, or countless other online business card and collateral creation sites. If you don't know what "collateral" is, it's all the paper marketing tools you likely won't use in this day and age. But sometimes you may need a flyer or mailer.

2. Website

The next component of your brand is your website. **This is the most important aspect of your brand, so building one isn't optional.** Your website will be the first thing people see when they search for your name or your company name online. It will be your main lead generator and lead-capture source. It will be where you post and offer the valuable content that will make you a trusted and reputable name in the apartment syndication niche. A decent website is something you need to create prior to raising a single dime of private money or forming a thought leadership platform. (I'll talk more about what that is in the next chapter.)

Since your website will be critical to your success, and since creating one is time consuming and requires a lot of creativity, I recommend contracting the work to a third-party source. Fortunately, there are many talented web designers in the world. Again, you can use Fiverr.com or just do a search for "web designer."

Having a custom site created can be expensive, but there are so many template-driven site creation tools online these days there is no need for a costly custom site. There are tools like Wix, Weebly and WordPress that allow you to build your own site. GoDaddy has a "website tonight" option as well as a team waiting to assist you in your build-out needs, and they won't break the bank either. You will need to pay for the domain name, the sub-domain names (these aren't seen by the public and don't show up in searches, but they are domains that point to your main site), and monthly hosting. The longer the term, the lower the hosting cost. Go for the 3-year plan and the price drops dramatically, but you will need to pay in full up front. If you don't have much of a budget, just choose the monthly for now and work your way up.

If you have the budget to have a custom site created, go for it. Depending on where you are starting (from a financial perspective), it may make more economic sense to invest the time to create your own and have a professionally created site done later.

If you like Wix, GoDaddy, Weebly or any of the other make-your-own-site companies available to you, rest assured that each company offers a step-by-step guide to creating and designing a beautiful, yet simple website from scratch. At first you just need something simple that helps to credentialize you as the apartment syndicator in your local area. It's a great idea to include a blog. If you aren't a great writer, that's okay. You can hire one.

As your business begins to grow, along with your bank account, you can hire a professional designer to build a more advanced website. Use sites like Fiverr, UpWork, or ELance to find a reputable web designer. Better yet, ask for referrals from associates. Costs can range from a few hundred dollars to thousands of dollars, depending on who you hire, their level of experience, and their understanding of your niche, as well as the complexity of your site. The old rule of keep it simple applies. You want the site to be easy to navigate and highly informational with a clear call to action (CTA) to get in touch with you, plus friend you and follow you everywhere.

3. Company presentation
Another important element of your brand will be your company presentation. Others will call this a pitch book, but I hate that name. We never pitch anything. We identify challenges and offer solutions. That's how you should think, too. YOU PROVIDE SOLUTIONS.

Your investors want to preserve and grow their capital. You offer them an opportunity to do so through participating with you in your real estate deals.

As you have conversations with potential investors (more on this in Chapter 22), your company presentation will be their introduction to your business. Therefore, the company presentation, which is best created in PowerPoint, where it can be a downloadable asset, must contain all the information a passive investor would need in order to determine whether or not they are interested in investing with you and trust you enough to give you their money to use in your deals.

There are five different components of the company presentation I currently use when initially speaking with prospective investors. Aside from being a guide to creating your own company presentation, the following overview will give you an introduction to the entire apartment syndication process.

If you are confused by anything you read below, don't be alarmed. We will dive deeper into the details in later chapters.

Section 1 – Meet Our Team

This section includes a brief biographical history of the people on your team. If it is just you, think of who helps you in your business. Include your assistant(s), but make sure to give their write-ups a real estate investing spin.

As I explained before, you should have previous real estate experience and/or a solid business reputation before launching your syndication career. If you have real estate investing or related experience, include those statistics in your biography. If you have previous business experience, include your business accomplishments.

Here is an example of a bad biography:

> *Joe Fairless has invested in real estate for over three years. He is currently the host of a successful real estate podcast. In his spare time, he is involved in various extracurricular activities and charitable organizations.*

Conversely, here is an example of a good biography:

> *Joe Fairless controls over $400,000,000 worth of real estate in the Dallas-Fort Worth area and Houston. He is the host of the world's longest-running daily real estate investing podcast, "Best Real Estate Investing Advice Ever," which generates almost 350,000 monthly downloads. Joe is also on the Alumni Advisory Board for Texas Tech University and the Board of Directors for Junior Achievement in Cincinnati.*

Additionally, your team should include a consultant or board member who has a successful real estate track record. Their biographies should be included in this section of your presentation.

Section 2 – Why Apartments?
The purpose of this section is to prove to the potential investor that apartments are the best asset class in which to park their money for solid returns. Through graphical representation, show that apartments are an advantageous asset class. Depending on the current apartment market, you can include all or a combination of the following:

1. **Risk vs. returns**
    - How returns reaped from investing in real estate compare with the returns of other investment vehicles, like stocks, bonds, mutual funds, retirement accounts, and REITs. Specifically, you should discuss the benefits of investing in apartment buildings and complexes vs. other types of properties.
    - This comparison generally looks at the total number of down years (negative returns) and up years (positive returns) of each.
    - Unless there is a huge change to the economy, real estate will have the highest number of up years and the lowest number of down years compared with stocks and bonds.
2. **Taxes**
    - Investing in apartments will lower your taxable income through depreciation. Generally, the depreciation will exceed the investor's annual distributions, so they won't have to pay taxes until they receive their proceeds at sale.

3. **Home ownership**
   - Talk about how the rate of owner-occupied units (i.e., the percentage of owner-occupied units) is trending downward.
   - As the percentage of owner-occupied units decreases, the percentage of renter-occupied units increases. Renters are your "customers," so the more renters the higher the demand for apartments.
4. **Population**
   - Discuss how the overall population is increasing.
   - More people means more people looking for places to live!
5. **Number of renters**
   - The number of renter-occupied units is increasing.
   - The same logic for the owner-occupied unit rate applies for the rate of renter-occupied units. An increasing number of renter-occupied units means there is a high demand for apartments (assuming that the apartment vacancy rate is decreasing or remaining static).
6. **Apartment vacancy rates**
   - Bring up questions such as how does today's apartment vacancy rate compare with the vacancy rate last year? Five years ago? A decade ago? Is the rate trending downward or remaining static?
   - The apartment vacancy rate will paint a picture of the overall demand for apartments. A high or increasing vacancy rate is not a good sign, while the opposite means that the demand for apartments is high and/or increasing.
7. **Demand**
   - The combination of all of the factors above tells the story of apartment demand. But there are various

other factors that will or won't point to the same conclusion.
- Supply requirements: How many units need to be constructed to keep up with future projected demand? Do you know? If not, do your research.
- Economic impact: What is the total number of renters? How much do they contribute to the economy? How many jobs are generated due to apartments? If the economy is highly dependent on the continuation of the apartment industry, that points to a strong apartment market for the foreseeable future.
- The renter demographic is dominated by non-families. If, as research and studies indicate, people are starting families later and the number of families is decreasing over time, these factors point to a strong demand for apartments.
- Immigration growth: Immigrants have a higher propensity to rent and typically rent for longer periods of time than established citizens. A high percentage of the population growth being due to immigration is a positive sign for apartment demand.

It is quite clear that the evidence pointing to apartments being the best investment asset class will vary from market to market and year to year. Therefore, use data points that are relevant to the current apartment market conditions and continuously update this section as trends ebb and flow.

Section 3 – Our Investment Strategy
Next, provide the prospective investor with an overview of your investment strategy. Address four potential questions your investors will ask about your strategy. I've included how my company answers these questions, which you can use as a guide but will

need to adjust based on your business plan and investment strategy (which you will learn about and define in later chapters).

1. **Our Target Market**

    My business targets Tier 1 markets with strong apartment fundamentals. Tier 1 markets/cities have a developed, established real estate market. These cities tend to be highly developed, with desirable schools, facilities, and businesses. Cities and markets classified as Tier 1 are New York, Los Angeles, Chicago, Dallas, Boston, San Francisco, and Washington D.C. You will begin the market selection process in chapter 13 and will want to include the following market information in this section to support/reinforce your reasoning behind its selection:
    - **Employment drivers**: Strong employment drivers, like a low/decreasing unemployment rate, new businesses, increasing job numbers, and job diversity, provide stable rent income and lower the risk of the investment by keeping occupancy rates high.
    - **Supply constraints**: The ratio of the number of rental units coming onto a given market to the number of units rented in the same period (referred to as the absorption rate) is a useful tool for monitoring whether the supply is keeping up with demand. Additionally, future population growth in the market should be sufficient to absorb the scheduled future supply.
    - **Submarket information**: This must have high barriers to entry and population growth sufficient to absorb scheduled future supply.
    - **GDP growth**: Avoid markets that are nearing a potential bust (decreasing GDP) and are currently experiencing low cap rates.

- **Multifamily cap trends**: In order to achieve 8% annual returns, the economics of the metro area must be very strong, yet the cap rates of Class B product are ideally 5% or greater. But in reality, cap rates are not the only variable to consider since they don't factor in your value-add business plan.
- **Multifamily rental trends**: Growing rents serve as an important indicator of a healthy and stable economy with lower associated risk of investment.
- **Multifamily occupancy trends**: Healthy occupancy rates signal a growing population that is outpacing the current supply of new apartments.

2. **How We Source Our Deals**

As a value-add investor, your focus is to identify underperforming properties that have a potential value-added component. That could be implementing a ratio utility billing system (RUBS) program, putting in place professional management, investing money into units to generate market rent, improving landscaping, or any number of other tactics:
- Generally, you will follow the 100:30:10:1 process for sourcing deals.
- You want to have a continuous stream of opportunities. On average, for every 100 opportunities, you'll perform more detailed underwriting on 30. Of those 30, you'll submit offers on 10. Of those 10, you will acquire 1.

3. **How We Analyze Deals**

Our underwriting process includes five steps.
1) **Select a submarket location**: Proximity to employment drivers and quality of competition
2) **History of property**: Year of construction, as well as demographic and ownership history

3) **Condition of property:** Exterior deferred maintenance and interior vintage and quality
4) **Competition:** Rental comparison and sales comparison
5) **Business plan that creates the best ROI**: Interior and/or exterior renovation, repositioning demographic of tenants, and complete rebranding

4. **How We Structure Our Deals**

    Here are my company's investment criteria (you will set your own investment criteria in Chapter 25):
    - The property must be at least 100 units.
    - We purchase using long-term debt at a 70% to 75% LTV.
    - Our target investor returns are 8% or more on an annual basis, as 8% is the preferred return we offer to limited partners.
    - We plan on a 5- to 10-year hold, depending on the business plan, with a 5-year IRR target of 14% or higher to the limited partners.

Section 4 – Our Roles

This section outlines the responsibilities of your team (general partners) and the investors (limited partners).

1. **Limited Partners (LPS)**
    - Provide the equity for the project
    - Mortgage approval (case-by-case basis)
2. **General Partners (GPS)**
    - Find opportunities
    - Review opportunities and determine which to submit offers on
    - Make and negotiate offers
    - Coordinate with professional property inspectors

- Secure the best financing option for property
- Coordinate with attorneys to create LLC and partnership agreements
- Travel to the subject property's location to perform due diligence and market research
- Hire and oversee the property management company
- Perform additional asset management duties, including lender conversations, overseeing and executing the business plan, and ongoing investor communication

Section 5 – Our Process

For simplicity, we outline our seven-step process for buying an apartment complex:

1. Our team finds a property that is projected to meet the goals of our investors.
2. Our team makes an offer and negotiates a purchase price.
3. The offer is accepted and the deal is shared with our investors.
4. Our team performs more detailed due diligence on the property, which includes reviewing the utility bills and bank statements, on-ground research, and inspections.
5. Our team renegotiates the offer based on the results of the due diligence (if applicable).
6. Legal documents are created by the attorney and signed by both our team and our investors and the mortgage is approved with the signature of a loan guarantor (who is a 3rd party or a member of the GP).
7. The deal is closed.

Please note, if you need to provide an investor with the GP/LP responsibilities and the outline of the apartment syndication process, the likelihood that that individual will actually invest soon is low because they probably need more time to get familiar with this structure. You'll likely target this "less sophisticated" investor on your first few deals and will remove this segment as you gain more experience and attract more knowledgeable investors. Lastly, I recommend concluding the company presentation with a sample deal. Either use one of your previous deals as an example or, if you haven't completed a deal, use one of your mentor's, business partner's, or other team member's previous deal. This section should highlight the financials of the deal from the perspective of the limited partner. It should include the same information that is provided in the "Case Studies" section of the investment summary, which you will learn about in Chapter 39.

Start the process of building the basis of your apartment syndication brand by creating a company name and designing a logo and business card. At the same time, build your initial website. Using the information included in the company presentation outline above, generate a company presentation using PowerPoint.

At this point, you'll have the information required to create all of the company presentation sections with the exception of section 3, Part 1 (Your Target Market) and the sample deal. Once you've selected and evaluated your target market (beginning in Chapter 13) and learned about the investment summary in Chapter 39, you can complete the company presentation.

CHAPTER 10

THE ROAD TO SELECTIVE FAME

After you determine your ideal target audience and as you build the foundation of your company, you need to determine how you will attract your 2,000 true fans. I have found that the most effective way to accomplish this is by creating a thought leadership platform. It is my belief that if you want to achieve massive levels of success in apartment syndication, having a consistent thought leadership platform is a must.

WHAT IS A THOUGHT LEADERSHIP PLATFORM?

A thought leadership platform is an interview-based online network where you consistently offer valuable content to your loyal following free of charge. In doing so, you will position yourself as an expert in the field. You become the go-to source for investing advice and wisdom while obtaining your own customized real estate education at the same time. As a result, your platform will enable you to create and cultivate new relationships with potential investors, team members, and business partners. Be sure to reinforce your relationship with those who already know you. Engage with them in various ways. A great way to accomplish this goal is to create a strong social media presence and answer questions on those pages. It's also a great idea to share valuable content with this base via email. (At this point you are selling nothing; you are simply sharing great information they can use, like videos and articles you have created or those created by people you respect in the industry.)

Essentially, the purpose of the thought leadership platform as it applies to apartment syndications is to stay top of mind with and be credible in the eyes of the people who are relevant to your business in a way that is scalable, as well as to create your own customized education program. So, we are taking this deep-dive into branding because your thought leadership platform is the key to attracting team members, business partners, and passive investors.

Where do you begin?

SELECT YOUR THOUGHT LEADERSHIP PLATFORM

As I've already mentioned, my initial thought leadership platform was a podcast. Once the podcast was established, I created additional platforms to complement the podcast and expand the reach of my brand. I started an in-person mastermind group, created a weekly newsletter, launched a YouTube channel with tips for raising money and buying apartments, began posting daily blog posts to my website, hosted an annual in-person real estate conference, and have authored three books at the time of this writing.

I didn't, however, wake up one morning and think to myself, "I am going to start a podcast, YouTube channel, newsletter, blog, and mastermind group and write a book today." I took it one step at a time, creating and establishing one platform before launching another. Therefore, pick one platform, focus your time and efforts on its growth, and use it as your launching point.

There are numerous ways to become a thought leader in the apartment syndication niche, but the best platforms to start with are:

1. YouTube channel
2. Podcast
3. Blog
4. Newsletter
5. Facebook group

Why are they the best? Because most of them, with the exception of the blog and newsletter, have a built-in audience. Why start from scratch, speaking to zero people, when you can start speaking to people who are already on the platform.

The reason I included a blog and a newsletter is that if you have a full-time job, your employers might not like (or even allow) you hosting a podcast, YouTube channel, or Facebook group. The blog and newsletter are more private yet serve the purpose of creating a platform.

To determine which of these platforms to initially pursue, perform a simple experiment. Examine the list provided above and ask yourself, "What would I enjoy or prefer doing?"

Do you enjoying writing and/or dislike hearing yourself speak? Consider starting a blog or creating a weekly newsletter.

Do you enjoy speaking with people, but are camera shy? Start a podcast.

Do you enjoy sharing your thoughts, but the idea of doing so in public sends a shiver down your spine? Launch a YouTube channel.

Regardless of which platform you select, if you have a Facebook page, you should create a Facebook group that you can use to promote new content, and record Facebook Live interviews.

Perform this exercise and fill in the blank with your selection of a thought leadership platform: _____
_____.

THREE KEYS TO A SUCCESSFUL THOUGHT LEADERSHIP PLATFORM

Once you select a platform and prior to developing a structure, in order to set yourself up for success and to minimize the learning curve, you should adhere to the proven tactics practiced by owners of already successful thought leadership platforms.

After researching the strategies of the top thought leaders in the business realm and personally producing over 1,500 podcast episodes, hundreds of blog posts and YouTube videos, and multiple books, I have discovered that there are four keys to becoming a successful thought leader: (1) interview-based, (2) consistency, (3) ability to tie into a large, built-in audience, (4) uniqueness.

1. Will you interview real estate professionals?

The main objectives for creating a thought leadership platform are education, to increase your credibility, and to network with potential team members, business partners, and passive investors. The best way to achieve these objectives is through an interview-based thought leadership platform.

With an interview-based thought leadership platform, you will speak with people who are active and already successful in real estate investing and/or apartment syndications. If you conduct one interview a week for two years, for example, that's over 100 conversations or "classes" that go towards your education, as well as over 100 networking opportunities to find potential team members or business partners.

At the same time, you are positioning yourself as the go-to resource for the best information and strategies for real estate investing and/or apartment syndications. As your audience and reputation grow, you'll attract better, more successful guests, which in turn can increase your audience, reputation, and quality of business opportunities. Also, as your reputation grows, you will attract a greater number of passive investors, because you are seen as a credible expert in the apartment syndication industry who can execute a business plan effectively.

2. How often will you publish content?

If you want to create a loyal following, consistency is critical. Your audience needs to know when to expect another piece of content. If you post content sporadically, you won't build rapport with your listeners, which means you will struggle with retaining listeners. Pick a schedule for releasing new content and adhere to it unfailingly. The only exception is when you reach the point where you will increase the frequency at which you release new material. If you increase your frequency, that's fine. Just don't decrease it.

We all have our favorite forms of entertainment, whether it's viewing our favorite TV show or watching our favorite sports team. There is a reason all forms of entertainment are offered on a consistent basis. The NFL hosts games every Sunday. TV shows usually air on a weekly basis. Some entertainment types, like movies or the MLB and NBA, are on an infrequent basis, but the schedule is available months or years in advance. Regardless, the followers and fans know exactly when to expect their entertainment, resulting in their anticipation and loyalty.

The same idea applies to your thought leadership platform. Your followers should know when to expect your next piece of valuable content. Is it every Tuesday or every Thursday? Is it bi-weekly? Monthly?

Following this schedule may be challenging at first. You won't have the momentum or habits from consistently posting content for an extended period of time. That means you want to plan your thought leadership platform out at least a few weeks in advance on an ongoing basis, and a few months in advance when starting out. Create an editorial calendar of sorts!

For example, if you are launching a podcast and you commit to posting a new episode once per week, before airing your first episode you want to have at least 5 pre-recorded episodes in the queue. Then, as long as you record one new podcast a week, you will always be planned out 5 weeks in advance. This tactic is extremely important if your thought leadership platform is a podcast, because this will increase your chance of being featured in the "New and Noteworthy" section on iTunes. (Some podcasters I've known create far more than 5 episodes ahead of airing them. To be in the "New and Noteworthy" section of iTunes, the more you release quickly the better.)

Determine how often you will create and post content for your thought leadership platform. Based on that frequency, create a content calendar and begin brainstorming and scheduling content.

3. What larger platform will you tap into?

There is no reason to start from scratch with your thought leadership platform. Tap into a larger platform and leverage their existing audience. BiggerPockets, the world's largest real estate blogging platform, boasts nearly 1 million members. iTunes has over 70 million monthly podcast listeners. Over a billion people use YouTube. And over 80% of the U.S. population has a social media profile.

After creating a piece of content, post it to a large platform, and then share it on your social media profile. But do not expect quick results. I didn't see a substantial growth in podcast downloads for over a year, and I was posting on a daily basis. That's why consistency is so important. Keep it going!

4. How is it unique?

If you create a generic thought leadership platform, you will have average results.

Every single human being on this planet is unique in some way. You are a human and are therefore unique. I'm not talking about your toenail-collecting fetish (seriously, keep that to yourself). We all have different backgrounds, areas of expertise, personalities, passions, and interests. Your aim is to tap into your uniqueness and let that shine through in your content.

Tim Ferriss says, "Be unique before trying to be incrementally better." I agree wholeheartedly!

Have you identified your unique talents? If you haven't, or if you want to verify that you are correct, or if you want to learn how to cultivate your unique talent, then complete the following four-step exercise, which is a variation of an exercise I learned from Perry Marshall's book *80/20 Sales and Marketing*.

It will help you identify your strengths and create a plan to improve upon your existing gifts and talents:

- o **Step #1** – Create a list of five friends or colleagues who've known you for at least one year.
- o **Step #2** – Ask them to provide you with the answers to these two questions: (1) What is my unique ability? (2) What do I naturally do better than most people?
- o **Step #3** – Categorize the responses to determine what talents they all mentioned, what talents most of them mentioned, and what talents at least two of them mentioned.
- o **Step #4** – Using all of the responses you gather, create a single paragraph that outlines your unique talents. This is your "gifted zone" and will give you a clear idea on where you should be focusing your energy.

After you determine your giftedness zone, you can put your unique spin on the thought leadership platform you create.

For another level of uniqueness, incorporate your area of expertise into your thought leadership platform. For example, if you have a background in construction, you can create content with hands-on tips from your personal experience or interviews with owner operators or fix-and-flippers. If you're transitioning from a career in direct sales, offer content on applying different sales techniques you've acquired over the years to real estate investing. If you're a marketing executive, focus on providing marketing tips for finding deals or residents.

With the combination of your unique talents, background, and area of expertise, you shouldn't have an issue with structuring your thought leadership platform in a personalized way.

Complete the four-step unique capabilities exercise. Then use the results to incorporate your unique talents and gifts when structuring your thought leadership platform.

CHAPTER 11

ENTERTAIN WHILE EDUCATING

Who is more famous, LeBron James or Mrs. Stacy?

Oh, you don't know Mrs. Stacy?

Mrs. Stacy was my kindergarten teacher! While this wonderful woman was an amazing educator, you have no idea who she is. As a result, you said LeBron James is the more famous of the two. That's because people prefer to be entertained than to be educated, which is why you don't know who Mrs. Stacy is and why she is paid significantly less than LeBron James and other famous entertainers.

Taking this into consideration, when structuring your thought leadership platform, it is important to brainstorm about how you will entertain while you inform. For example, on my podcast, I always include intro and outro music. Rather than have the same format for each episode, I change it up on the weekends with a "Follow-Along Friday," "Sticky Situation Saturday," and "Skillset Sunday." I end each weekday episode with a "Best Ever" lightning round.

The BEST way to determine whether you are entertaining while informing is to ask yourself the following question before you put out the piece of content:

"Will my target audience love this so much that they will feel compelled to share it with their friends?"

If you believe they will share it, then that is the ultimate validation of your content. Then, after posting, track which content is being shared the most. This helps you in optimizing your approach.

FIVE-STEP PROCESS TO DEVELOP YOUR THOUGHT LEADERSHIP PLATFORM

Keeping this in mind, along with the four keys to success I outlined in the previous chapter (interview-based, consistency, tying into a larger built-in audience, and uniqueness), here is a five-step outline for developing the structure of your thought leadership platform:

1. What is the goal?
Why are you creating a thought leadership platform? In Chapter 6, you set a 12-month goal and a long-term vision. So, how will a successful thought leadership platform support those outcomes?

Start by writing out a list of your thought leadership goals, remembering to make them specific and quantifiable. Then condense that list down into a paragraph or two. This will be the mission statement for your thought leadership platform.

For example, the purpose of the thought leadership platform could be to find deals, find private money, and help you effectively execute on the business plan. If that fits what you are aiming for, your mission statement might be "I will research apartment owners in my target market, invite at least one per month to be an interview guest on my podcast, build a relationship with them, and ultimately purchase their apartment communities in the future. By interviewing active real estate professionals once a week, including these owners, my target audience will get to know me faster, resulting in a higher level of trust and confidence in my ability to successfully invest their money. When I stick to interviewing one real estate professional per week, which equates to 52 per year, I will grow smarter. In turn, this will help me execute on my business plan."

In regard to investors getting to know you faster, I frequently have new investors say they feel like they already know me because of my podcast. Don't underestimate the power of a thought leadership platform and its ability to directly impact your apartment syndication goals!

2. Who is the target audience?
You've already determined your primary target audience in Chapter 8. You should now be able to structure a thought leadership platform to focus exclusively on that demographic. However, you may want to define a secondary target audience as well.

For example, individuals who may not meet your target demographics at the moment, but who may in the future. Or people who are one or more degrees of separation away from your primary target demographic. Or potential team members. Or people who can benefit your business in some other way, like becoming a client or bringing you deals. For example, as I mentioned before, my secondary audience is individuals who want to become apartment syndicators. (Hey, that's you! That's why 35% of my content is directed at that audience.)

Determine your exact target demographic and add that description to the end of your mission statement. For example, "Sixty-five percent of my content will be directed at my primary target audience, who are 35- to 65-year-old males who are accredited investors; 35% of my content will be directed at my secondary target audience, who are individuals who want to become apartment syndicators."

3. What is the name of your platform?
Once you've created a goal and determined a target audience, you can create a name. For example, the name of your podcast or Facebook group.

Create three to five names that accomplish both of these objectives. Then, similar to how you picked a logo, ask for feedback from your circle of influence to select the most appealing option.

4. Why will they come?
Unfortunately, "If you build it, they will come" doesn't apply here.

This step will be one of your main drivers for success. Why will anyone follow your platform? If you cannot answer this question, your followers or lack thereof won't be able to either.

The answer to this question should be reflected in your thought leadership platform's description. Why does your target audience NEED the information you will provide? What solutions to THEIR problems can you provide on your platform? What's in it for them? How will they benefit? Why will they become a loyal follower of your content and not the thousands of other real estate platforms in the marketplace? Finally, what qualifications do you have that make you the go-to person for this information?

For example, the description for my podcast is "Are you ready for the best real estate investing advice EVER? Welcome to the world's longest-running DAILY real estate investing podcast. Join Joe Fairless as he talks to successful real estate professionals and they give you their best advice ever with none of the fluff. Joe controls over $400,000,000 in real estate but started with $0 in 2009. He went from buying single family homes worth $35,000 and moved up by raising money and buying large apartment communities with investors. He has made mistakes, money, and friends along the way. So click play now and see why this is one of the top investing shows in iTunes!"

5. How will it flow?
What will the specific structure of your platform be? Will the content be your own or will it be valuable information presented in an interview form? How often will you create content? How long will it be? How will it start and end? Will each piece of content be unique or will it follow a standard template?

For example, my podcast flow is as follows:

- Briefly introduce the guest.
- I ask the guest to provide more information on their background and what they focus on.
- For the next 10 to 25 minutes, I ask them questions related to their given field. If they are investors, I focus on specific deals they've completed or are in the process of completing. If they are NOT investors, I ask questions to extract skill sets and information that could be relevant to investors. (This information is designed to help listeners.)
- I ask the money question: What is your best real estate investing advice ever?
- I ask the guest questions for the Best Ever Lightning Round: What's your Best Ever book? Best Ever deal? Biggest mistake? How can Best Ever Listeners get in touch?
- I conclude by summarizing the information provided by the guest.

You will find that as you produce content, the flow will evolve depending on what is or isn't working. But first you need a well-thought-out starting point so that you come out of the gate strong and professional rather than amateurish.

Now Let Me Address Your Objections

If you are wincing right now at the prospect of starting a thought leadership platform, just as I said in regard to using other people's money, I hear you! It's a commitment. But so is working 9am to 5pm for 20 years at a job you hate. Which commitment do you want to pursue?

This will be the foundation for growing your own business. Your platform will serve to educate others and build the credibility you need so you can attract passive investors who you will help achieve their financial goals... and yours!

Another objection I hear often is that you don't have the time (because you have a full-time job) or the money (because you have no job) to start a thought leadership platform. My response to that is, "How have similar excuses served you in the past?"

GULP.

Let me just say that if you are unwilling to take action or make positive change, you will continue to see the same results (or lack thereof) that you've always gotten. So, here's the deal. Instead of listing reasons for why you can't do something, brainstorm ways of how you can prioritize your time differently, which will ultimately lead to different results.

Here are a couple solutions.

If you don't have a job, money might be a challenge. But there are too many free website-building tools and social media outlets for me to agree that having no money is actually a hold-up for you on creating your platform.

As long as you have a functioning laptop or cell phone and access to the Internet, you have the tools to begin and manage a thought leadership platform. As you grow and begin generating income, either through the platform or your syndication business, you can purchase fancier equipment to optimize your content. But don't use "I don't have a great microphone or an HD webcam" as an excuse to not get started. My first couple podcast episodes were recorded on a phone! An app called Call Recorder and regular headphones is all I had, so I used those tools as effectively as I could.

If you have a full-time job and claim that you don't have the time, all I can say is, "Okay... sure." (In other words, is that really true?) It boils down to how you manage your time. After all, we all have the same 24 hours in a day. You aren't at your job from dusk to dawn, are you?

To strengthen my case, let's take a look at social media.

At present, the average daily usage of social media is 135 minutes. That's 945 minutes per week, 3,780 minutes per month, and 49,275 minutes per year. In other words, the average person spends over twenty 40-hour work weeks on social media per year! Let's say you are one of them. What if you were to reduce your social media usage by 20%? You would have an additional 30 minutes per day to spend on something productive, like a thought leadership platform. The same logic can apply to TV, movies, video games, sleeping in, and going out to the bar. (If you start your platform on social media, instead of watching funny cat antics videos, put that time into building your group page and platform.)

Okay, fine. Maybe you have a full-time job and are 100% efficient with the rest of your time. Then another strategy is to use part of your full-time income to hire team members to manage the platform. When I first started out, I didn't have a full-time job, so I did everything for the podcast myself. I found the guest, interviewed the guest, edited the audio, inserted intro and outro music, uploaded the audio to Libsyn, formatted the podcast on my website, and notified the person that their interview was live.

Once my podcast was established and I focused more time on my syndication business, I hired team members to perform all of the tasks with the exception of the interview.

Finally, you could create content outside of work hours. For example, I have clients who do a weekly podcast while having a full-time job. They interview people on Saturdays, late at night or early in the morning.

Ultimately, the choice is yours.

Many will choose not to do this stuff and that's okay, because that provides an opportunity for those of us who do. That's just how the world works. Some do; some don't.

My suggestion to you is to be one of the ones who do. I think YOU will be one of those people because you're reading this book and have already shown a level of commitment that is higher than that of most people.

CHAPTER 12

MANUFACTURING A MASTERMIND

In addition to launching a thought leadership platform, you need to start a Meetup group. It's pretty easy and can put investors directly in your path. Go to www.Meetup.com and name your group around your brand.

More work? Sure, if you call building out your deal flow and finding passive investors work. I choose to call that Money Time. (Actually, I just made that up, but you get the picture!)

My question to you is "How badly do you want to be at the next level in your finances?" That will dictate how much upfront work you are willing to do.

If you think I'm asking too much, go back to your goals and review what inspires you and what disgusts you. Then come back to this chapter. If that didn't do the trick, then revise your goals and make them more compelling.

I have interviewed more than a thousand business and real estate entrepreneurs on my podcast, and one of the most valuable pieces of advice I continue to receive concerns the why and how of starting an in-person Meetup group.

From a business development standpoint, the educational benefits, relationships formed, and potential for direct monetization have been instrumental both to the growth of the investors who attend my meetings and to how those meetings positively impact the continued growth of my business. In fact, having my own Meetup group has been so successful for my business that I require my consulting clients to start their own in-person Meetups within their local markets.

How to Create a Meetup Group

The advent of the Internet has given us the capability to connect with like-minded strangers more easily than ever before. While forums, blogs, and social media allow you to join any number of virtual communities, other platforms promote the formation of in-person communities. One such outgrowth I take advantage of is Meetup groups. You see, it's not just that I have my own, but also that I attend other people's group meetings. (It's called networking.)

No matter how mainstream or obscure your interests might be, there's a Meetup group for you. Meetup.com, one of the more popular networking sites, boasts a membership of over 32 million people participating in over 288,000 Meetup groups across 182 countries.

Interested in joining a community of psychic vampires? Guess what? There's a group for you. Want to relive a cherished childhood freeze tag experience? Yep. There's a group for you, too.

Of course, as an apartment syndicator, you're not as interested in meeting vampires or playing freeze tag. You want to leverage popular Internet advancements to scale your business. Since online-generated meet-your-fellow-man groups are a relatively new concept, and monetized meetups even more so, many people don't know how to get started.

The truth is that starting a Meetup group can be nerve-racking – especially if you're an introvert. This anxiety will be the number-one enemy that keeps you from scheduling your first event. My Best Ever advice to you is to avoid spending an inordinate amount of time planning and structuring the perfect event. Instead, simply focus on starting the group.

A successful Meetup group can be pretty informal. For example, one investor I interviewed on my podcast, Anson Young, has been hosting a Meetup for more than three years with very little structure. Once a month, Anson and about 70 other investors meet at a local beer hall. For three hours, they just drink beer and talk real estate. There's no agenda or scheduled speaker. It's just good old-fashioned networking, a time set aside in a relaxed atmosphere for investors to chat and solve any problems they're facing, team up on real estate projects, and, most important, learn from each other's mistakes and successes.

Even so, in just three years, Anson has earned six figures directly from partnerships and relationships formed at that Meetup. That's a return of nearly $1,000 per hour. Who would have thought drinking beer with friends could be so profitable?

Starting a Meetup group like Anson's at a local bar is an easy and informal option, but maybe you'd like it to be a little more structured. I created a Meetup that's much more structured than Anson's. It is broken into five parts:

- **Presentation**: Each meeting begins with a short presentation from an active real estate professional or attendee.
- **Opportunity sharing**: Attendees have the opportunity to share deals with the group – maybe they're trying to sell a deal or find a partner, or have questions on a deal under contract.
- **Business updates**: Each person provides a 60-second update on the latest news and information in their business.

- **Open floor**: I allot the remaining time, about an hour, for networking, closing deals, sharing information, and forming business partnerships.
- **Goal setting**: Before heading home, each attendee posts their goal for the month to our private Facebook group.

Overall, the meeting typically lasts two hours.

I run my group on a monthly basis. You would be wise to do the same, with your primary objectives being to educate and build relationships – efforts that indirectly result in more deals, more business partnerships, and more money in the long run. But if you want an even more direct avenue to financial gains from your group, create a rock star-level Meetup – like real estate entrepreneur Taylor Peugh – and turn the group into a deal-generating machine.

Taylor hosts a Meetup FOUR times a week!

Three are dinners and the fourth is a lunch. About 30 to 40 unique investors attend each Meetup, which means Taylor networks with 100 to 150 real estate entrepreneurs every week. The result? Every rental property, every wholesale deal, and the majority of the fix-and-flip projects he negotiates stem directly from someone he met at his Meetup. For Taylor, a Meetup group isn't just a space to educate and build relationships; it's the main source of his investment gains.

Want to replicate Taylor's success?

Here's the agenda for his Meetups:

- **Check-in**: At check-in, attendees must answer: "What are you doing right now that will move you forward in the next 30 days?"
- **Recognition of wins**: Each person describes what they accomplished personally, or in their business, that week.

- **Needs and wants**: Attendees have the opportunity to ask for anything they need. For example, "I need a plumber," or "Does anyone know a good CPA?"
- **Property pitches**: This is where Taylor makes his money. Anyone who has an active deal can present it to the group to see whether anyone has an interest in buying, partnering, or funding it.
- **Open floor**: The end of the dinner/lunch is an open Q&A session where attendees can ask any questions they want. (That's really exciting for attendees, because they get the chance to have all their questions answered. It's great for Taylor because he gets to be perceived as the expert he really is. That's called a win-win!)

Hosting regular Meetup group events is one of the best ways to create valuable relationships, learn about real estate from those active in the field, and find deals and create partnerships that generate wealth in the short and long term.

I provided three Meetup examples above, ranging from monthly, informal beer hall gatherings to powerhouse groups that meet four times a week. In reality, the sky's the limit. There are an infinite number of ways you can structure your Meetup group. Do it and make it your own!

If you have time to attend a Meetup event then you have the time to host one. Once you do, you will quickly understand that the benefits are disproportionately greater in having your own group than in simply attending those hosted by other investors.

PART 1: THE EXPERIENCE

KNOWLEDGE — Chapters 1-4
1. What is apartment syndication?
2. How to Get Started
3. What to focus on

GOALS — Chapters 5-6
1. How do you make money?
2. Set 12-month goal and long-term vision
3. Ultimate Success Formula

BRAND BUILDING — Chapters 7-12
1. Why you need a brand
2. Select a target audience
3. How to build a brand

MARKET EVALUATION — Chapters 13-16 *(YOU ARE HERE)*
1. 3 Immutable Laws of Real Estate
2. Evaluate 7 markets
3. Pick 1-2 Target Markets

PART 2: THE MONEY

BUILD TEAM — Chapters 17-19
1. Find core real estate team members
2. Hire a mentor or consultant

FIND CAPITAL — Chapters 20-24
1. Why will they invest?
2. Build passive investor database
3. Create partnership structure

PART 3: THE DEAL

FIND DEALS — Chapters 25-28
1. Set investment criteria
2. On-market vs. off-market deals
3. How to find your first deal

UNDERWRITING — Chapters 29-31
1. Information needed to underwrite a deal
2. The 6-step underwriting process

SUBMIT OFFER — Chapter 32
1. How to submit an offer on a deal
2. Best-and-final offer
3. Purchase sales agreement

PART 4: THE EXECUTION

DUE DILIGENCE — Chapters 33-37
1. 10 due diligence reports
2. Secure financing from lender

SECURE CAPITAL — Chapters 38-42
1. Create investment summary
2. New investment offering call
3. Secure investor commitments

CLOSE — Chapters 43-44
1. Closing process
2. Notify passive investors

EXECUTE BUSINESS PLAN — Chapters 45-46
1. 10 asset management duties
2. How to sell the apartment

CHAPTER 13

TIME FOR TARGET PRACTICE!

As you launch and grow your thought leadership platform and establish your apartment syndication brand, you will want to begin the process of selecting and evaluating a target market – the primary geographic location in which you will focus your search for potential investments.

The proper selection of a specific target market is necessary for many reasons. If the target market is undefined, your deal pipeline will be unmanageable. It would be silly – and could even be deadly to your business – to attempt to screen apartment deals from the more than 19,000 cities located in the United States.

If the target market is too large, whether it encompasses the entirety of a single massive city (e.g., New York City) or it's a combination of too many small to medium-sized cities, it will be impossible for you to gain the level of understanding you need to make educated investment decisions.

Conversely, if the market is too small, you'll have issues finding deals that meet your investment criteria.

That said, the size of the target market is only one variable.

A well-known and widely accepted dictum in real estate investing is that "it's all about location, location, location." That's because you can have the exact same apartment in two markets that have drastically different rents, resident quality, and asset value. The same can be said about two submarkets within the same market, two neighborhoods within the same submarket, or even two parallel streets within the same neighborhood. Therefore, you must perform an analysis at multiple levels BEFORE sourcing apartment deals, which I will outline in chapters to come.

The long and short of it is that once you understand a target market on multiple levels of analysis, you can then summarize your findings by creating a market study document. This will be used later in the process of buying the property and securing commitments from investors (see more on this topic starting in Chapter 38) to convey your knowledge and reinforce your selection of the market in which you are investing.

ized di jomp # CHAPTER 14

NARROWING IT DOWN TO THE TOP SEVEN MARKETS

While I recommend that you analyze the market in which you think you want to invest prior to looking for apartment deals, that's not the approach I used for my first two apartment deals.

Initially, I was interested in the Tulsa, Oklahoma, market for relationship reasons. Being within driving distance of Dallas/Fort Worth, the Tulsa market is close to family. Additionally, a friend introduced me to a few real estate professionals with whom he had relationships, so I already had an established, built-in network in that market. However, I struggled to find an apartment deal that penciled in financially and that I could acquire using creative financing (creative financing isn't a requirement, but that's just what I was looking for at the time).

Eventually, a broker presented me with an opportunity located in Ohio. The numbers looked good and there was a way for me to creatively finance the deal using a master lease. Using this approach, I qualified the deal first and then the market. At the time, I looked at the number of Fortune 500 companies located within a market, because I assumed a billion-dollar company would perform adequate due diligence prior to moving their headquarters to a market. (Not the most scientific approach nor is it a best practice to only look at Fortune 500 companies.)

You have to understand that I was just starting out as a real estate investor and didn't have a book like this to guide me through the step-by-step process. Fortunately, you do... you lucky dog. We'll get into specifics on the best practice and approach in a bit. For now, keep reading.

My next deal involved a slightly different situation.

You see, I was presented with an opportunity in Houston, Texas. The deal came from my now business partner, whom I met through a mutual friend. This man had identified a deal, but he didn't have the money to close it. Again, the deal came first before I formally evaluated the market. However, I lived in Houston for a year as a toddler, grew up in Dallas, and went to school at Texas Tech University. That meant I had many relationships with native Houstonians and I had also visited the area many times before this deal came along.

At that time, I was by no means an expert on the market, but I was very familiar with it. My partner had already formally analyzed the market, and I looked at Houston businesses and industries as well. Everything looked good and we moved forward with the deal.

After purchasing a second apartment community in Houston, we made a conscious effort to diversify outside the city. On this occasion, we proactively analyzed many markets across the United States using the evaluation method I will outline in this and subsequent chapters. We landed on Dallas-Fort Worth as a market where we've purchased over 4,000 apartment units to date in various submarkets across the city.

Obviously, after reviewing the apartment opportunities in Ohio and Houston, I would have passed on the deals if, after evaluation, the markets didn't meet my qualification standards. However, I was fortunate enough to come across two deals that passed both the financial and market evaluations. Pretty exciting stuff! But I just as easily could have stopped at the financial analysis without even looking at the market, or I could have wasted a lot of time and effort underwriting the deals just to learn that the market was a disqualifier. If the latter situation continued to repeat, I would still be analyzing deals to this day! That's why *it is vital to qualify the market first, and only then should you begin sourcing and analyzing deals.*

I'm proud to tell you that today my company has a formalized step-by-step process for evaluating new potential markets, which I recommend you follow.

Initially, I recommend selecting and focusing on one target market. Two tops. Then, as you gain experience and success, you can expand to multiple target markets.

How to Select Seven Potential Target Markets

First, let's break down your potential selections into two categories: (1) the city in which you currently reside, and (2) all other cities. If the prospect of managing a project from a distance isn't attractive, by default your target market will be where you live. But if, after analysis, your city has suboptimal market conditions or the investment opportunities are slim, you'll have to look elsewhere.

If you are fearful of investing in out-of-state properties, you still need to include other cities in your market evaluation... even if it's for the practice alone. For the initial market evaluation, you will analyze at least seven potential target markets. One of those markets can be the city in which you currently reside.

But how do you select the other six?

One market should be within a 1- to 2-hour drive (or 3-hour drive if you are in a state like California, Texas or New York), because you may live in a market that doesn't have a lot of value-add apartment communities or apartment communities in general (think rural America or the Northeast).

Two or three markets should be areas with which you have some level of familiarity. Maybe you have childhood or college friends, family, or relatives who live there. Maybe it's where you grew up or went to school. Or maybe it's a location you've visited on multiple occasions. This way, you won't have to start from scratch.

The remaining two or three markets should be areas about which you have at least minimal knowledge and that pique your curiosity. One simple method for finding these markets is to Google "top apartment markets in the U.S." However, there are detailed commercial real estate reports and surveys that are created by different companies about the condition and trends of the real estate market. Even if you're going to select target markets at random or use the Google approach, I still highly recommend reading these reports for a behind-the-scenes look at the overall real estate economy.

The six reports I use are:

1. **Marcus & Millichap's Annual U.S. Multifamily Investment Forecast:** This gives you an analysis of the economic and political factors that have effects on the multifamily niche's forecast for the coming year and provides a ranking of major U.S. real estate markets using a number of economic factors.

2. **CBRE Biannual Cap Rate Survey:** This provides you with an analysis of cap rate and return data for major U.S. markets for all real estate niches and asset types, including multifamily. Remember that cap rates and the return (NOI) determine an asset's value.
3. **Integra Realty Resources (IRR) Annual Viewpoint Commercial Real Estate Trends Report:** When you want detailed, data-driven reports on overall commercial real estate trends based on the current economic and political landscapes, for each commercial niche including multifamily, and specialty reports for the current property types that are on the rise... this is a good resource!
4. **Zillow Annual Consumer House Trends Report:** This report gives you an overall analysis of the different consumers in the real estate process, including the buyers/renters, lenders, and sellers. This report provides you with an overall snapshot of the consumer of today and what they are looking for when selecting a place to rent.
5. **RCLCO Quarterly State of the Real Estate Market:** This resource is dedicated to real estate developers, investors, the public sector and non-real estate companies, and organizations seeking strategic and tactical advice regarding property investment, planning, and development.
6. **PwC Annual Emerging Trends in Real Estate:** This is a compilation of more than 800 interviews and 1,600 survey responses regarding the emerging trends in the real estate industry from the top real estate professionals in the country.

Use a quick Google search to locate each of these documents. They are all free as of the publication of this book. Read through the different reports and resources, then decide what makes sense for you and what doesn't. Use them to determine which two or three markets you will add to your list.

Now you're ready to fill in the blanks below with the seven markets you will evaluate. I've put together a prompt for each to make it easy for you:

1. Home Market: _____
2. Market within a 1- to 3-hour drive: _____
3. Market you're familiar with most: _____
4. Market you're familiar with a little: _____
5. Market you're familiar with a little/piques your curiosity: _____
6. Market that piques your curiosity: _____
7. Market that piques your curiosity: _____

These are the seven markets you will initially evaluate. But, by all means, you can evaluate more. I chose seven because it's great practice!

THE THREE IMMUTABLE LAWS OF REAL ESTATE INVESTING

Before you begin evaluating these markets, it's important to understand that there won't be a "perfect" market. Investors have made money in every market across the country at every point in time throughout the last 50 years. But the actual market means nothing if you cannot execute on the business plan and if you fail to stick to the **Three Immutable Laws of Real Estate Investing** that allow you to thrive in any real estate market, no matter what's happening in the current economy.

The first of these three laws is **buy for cash flow, not appreciation** – in particular, natural appreciation – because it is completely out of your control. Natural appreciation fluctuates up and down based on what's going on in the overall real estate market and economy. Conversely, forced appreciation is the bread and butter of value-add investors like me. Forced appreciation involves making improvements to the asset that either decrease expenses or increase income, which in turn, increases the overall property value.

Many investors, past and present, buy for natural appreciation… and it is a gamble. Eventually, they all get burned – unless they're extremely lucky. Buying for natural appreciation is like thinking you'll get rich at the casino by playing roulette and only betting on black. Yeah, maybe you can double up a few times, but sooner or later the ball lands on red or green and you lose it all.

It's best to buy for cash flow (on value-add opportunities). When you buy for cash flow (as long as you have a large supply of renters), you won't care what the market is doing. In fact, if the market takes a dip, the demand for rentals will likely increase!

The second law of real estate investing is secure long-term debt. This law is straightforward – the debt secured should have a loan term that is longer than the projected hold period. For example, if the business plan is to sell after five years, the loan term should be longer than five years.

You shouldn't run into this problem if you are getting a commercial loan from a bank or an agency loan from Fannie Mae or Freddie Mac, as they will offer loan lengths of up to 12 or more years. However, if you are pursuing a creative financing strategy, you may have the opportunity to negotiate terms that expire before the end of your business plan. Don't be tempted. Similarly, a bridge loan (a short-term loan usually used to cover the purchase price and renovation costs before securing permanent longer-term financing) may offer loan term lengths of as low as six to 12 months. In these cases, make sure you have the ability to purchase loan extensions.

Securing long-term debt in tandem with committing to buy for cash flow, not natural appreciation allows you to avoid being forced to sell or refinance the property at a loss in the event of a downturn in the market.

The final law is **have adequate cash reserves.** When you don't have adequate cash reserves and an unexpected issue arises, you can't cover the expense. Then, you may need to do a capital call, asking your investors for more money which reduces their overall returns. If the expense is too large or the issue significantly reduces the economic occupancy rate, you may not be able to distribute the projected returns to your investors. Even worse, you may not be able to continue covering the debt service, which means you may be forced to sell or give the property back to the bank.

To mitigate this risk, I recommend creating an upfront operating account fund that is approximately 1% to 5% of the purchase price at closing and having an ongoing operating budget of at least $250 per unit per year in reserves, making sure that you account for this expense when underwriting a deal (more on underwriting in Chapter 31).

If you stick to these *Three Immutable Laws of Real Estate Investing*, your investment portfolio will not just survive, but it will thrive in any real estate market and under any economic conditions.

Your big takeaway here?

Don't spend an excruciating amount of time selecting the "perfect" target market. You will have much more success following these three fundamental "laws" with a team that executes the business plan incredibly well in a bad market than the other way around.

CHAPTER 15

GET READY TO HIT THE TARGET

As I told you in a previous chapter, as an apartment syndicator you will use a multifaceted approach when evaluating any market. On the opposite page is a helpful flow chart for a visual representation of the steps required to select and analyze a real estate market(s).

SIX-STEP MARKET EVALUATION PROCESS
Step 1: Record Demographic and Economic Data and Step 2: Interpret Data by Determining Market Insights
When performing the first level of evaluation (demographics and economics) for your seven potential markets, you will record data for seven factors:

1. Unemployment
2. Population
3. Population Age
4. Job Diversity
5. Top Employers and Businesses
6. Supply and Demand
7. Miscellaneous

In the following sections, I outline the data required for each of the seven factors and why each was selected, what to look for

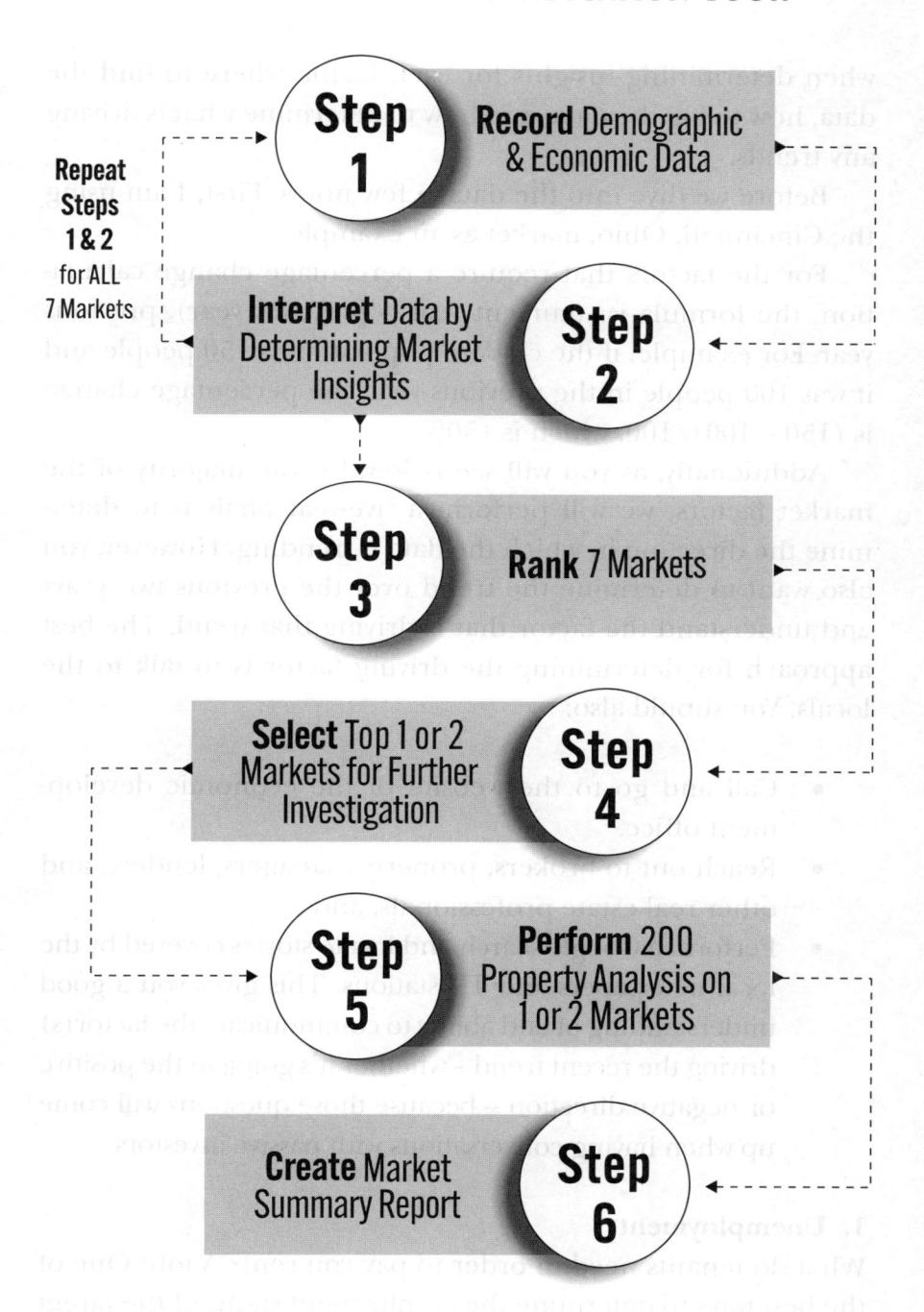

Step 1 — **Record** Demographic & Economic Data

Step 2 — **Interpret** Data by Determining Market Insights

Repeat Steps 1 & 2 for ALL 7 Markets

Step 3 — **Rank** 7 Markets

Step 4 — **Select** Top 1 or 2 Markets for Further Investigation

Step 5 — **Perform** 200 Property Analysis on 1 or 2 Markets

Step 6 — **Create** Market Summary Report

when determining insights for each factor, where to find the data, how to log the data, and how to determine what is driving any trends.

Before we dive into the data, a few notes. First, I am using the Cincinnati, Ohio, market as an example.

For the factors that require a percentage change calculation, the formula is: (current year − previous year)/previous year. For example, if the current population is 150 people and it was 100 people in the previous year, the percentage change is (150 − 100)/100, which is +50%.

Additionally, as you will see below, for the majority of the market factors, we will perform a five-year analysis to determine the direction in which the data is trending. However, you also want to determine the trend over the previous two years and understand the factor that is driving that trend. The best approach for determining the driving factor is to talk to the locals. You should also:

- Call and go to the website of the economic development office,
- Reach out to brokers, property managers, lenders, and other real estate professionals, and ...
- Perform a Google search and locate stories covered by the local newspapers and TV stations. This gives you a good understanding of and ability to communicate the factor(s) driving the recent trend – whether it's going in the positive or negative direction – because those questions will come up when having conversations with passive investors.

1. Unemployment

What do tenants need in order to pay you rent? A job! One of the best ways to determine the employment status of the target market's population is to track unemployment data.

Specifically, you want to calculate the unemployment change over a five-year period. This will require you to obtain the unemployment percentage for the city for the last five years.

A decreasing unemployment rate is ideal. A low, stagnant rate is acceptable. A high and/or increasing rate is unfavorable.

This data can be found on the Census.gov website under the "Selected Economic Characteristics" data table. Example – Cincinnati, Ohio, Unemployment Data:

2011 % Unemployment	7.4%
2012 % Unemployment	7.7%
2013 % Unemployment	8.3%
2014 % Unemployment	8.5%
2015 % Unemployment	8.2%
5-year % Unemployment Change	**10.8%**

Insights: Based on this employment data, one can conclude that the unemployment rate in Cincinnati is up nearly 11% compared with five years prior. However, the rate is currently trending downward, going from 8.5% to 8.2%.

2. Population

The target market's population and population growth/decline is one of the factors that indicates an expanding or dying market. This is important to understand as apartment syndicators, because our number-one focus is people! People are our customers.

To determine whether the market's customer base is growing or declining, calculate the population change for both the target market city and the metropolitan statistical area (MSA). You need the population data for the last five years for the market.

An increasing population is ideal. A stagnant or decreasing trend is unfavorable, especially if apartment supply is on the rise.

Both the city and MSA population data can be found on the Census.gov website. The city data is located in the "Annual Population Estimates" data table, and the MSA data is located in the "Annual Estimate of the Resident Population" data table.

Example – Cincinnati, Ohio, Population Data:

2012 MSA Population	2,128,439
2013 MSA Population	2,136,296
2014 MSA Population	2,146,784
2015 MSA Population	2,155,392
2016 MSA Population	2,165,139
5-year MSA Population Growth	**+1.7%**
2012 City Population	296,794
2013 City Population	297,444
2014 City Population	298,100
2015 City Population	298,654
2016 City Population	298,800
5-year City Population Growth	**+0.7%**

Insights: Both the city and the MSA populations are on the rise – 0.7% and 1.7% respectively. However, looking at the previous three years of city data, the population growth has almost come to a halt.

3. Population Age

Someone in their 20s will be attracted to an entirely different type of apartment than someone with a small family or someone that is approaching retirement. Therefore, another factor to analyze is the population and population growth/decline of a variety of ages.

You will accomplish this by calculating the population change for different age ranges. This will require the population age data for the most current year and the five previous years.

The increase or decrease of the proportion of people in specific age ranges will dictate the property types that will be in the most demand. For example, an increasing population of 25- to 34-year-olds will put luxury apartments with nicer amenities in higher demand, while an increasing retirement age population will put assisted living facilities in higher demand.

This data can be found on the Census.gov website under the "Demographic and Housing Estimates" table. Example – Cincinnati, Ohio, Population Age Data:

Age Range (years)	2010 % of population	2015 % of population	% change
15 to 19	8.0%	7.1%	-11.3%
20 to 24	9.7%	9.8%	+1.0%
25 to 34	16.5%	17.7%	+7.3%
35 to 44	12.2%	11.3%	-7.4%
45 to 54	13.8%	12.1%	-12.3%
55 to 64	10.0%	11.7%	+17.0%
65+	11.1%	11.4%	+2.7%

Insights: Based on Cincinnati's population age data, one would conclude that the largest population increases are for the 55- to 64-year-old and the 25- to 34-year-old age ranges. The largest population decrease is for the 45- to 54-year-old and 35- to 44-year-old age ranges. Apartment communities that attract retirees (i.e., assisted living facilities) and singles/small families (i.e., luxury apartment communities or communities with amenities for young children/families) are the investment types to pursue in the Cincinnati market.

4. Job Diversity

Detroit is a perfect example of why analyzing a market's job diversity statistics is critical. The Detroit market was dominated by the auto industry in the 1970s and 1980s. However, a few years after Chrysler and GM filed for bankruptcy, the city itself followed suit. The outcome for that market wasn't good. Therefore, before investing in a market, determine whether a specific industry is responsible for a large percentage of jobs. Determining a market's job diversification will require the employment data for the different industries for the most current year.

A market with outstanding job diversity will have no single industry that employs more than 25% of the employed population; 20% is even better. If a certain industry is dominant, like you once found in Detroit, the market would struggle or even collapse if that industry were to be negatively affected.

However, a lot of markets will have one industry that makes up 25% or more of jobs. This isn't a deal-breaker. It's about how much trust you have in that job sector, which is determined by looking at the top employers or businesses and your research (i.e., talking to locals, reading local articles).

This data can be found on the Census.gov website under the "Selected Economic Characteristics" table. Example – Cincinnati, Ohio, Job Diversity Data:

Civilian employed population 16 years and over	136,182
Agriculture, forestry, fishing and hunting, and mining	0%
Construction	3%
Manufacturing	10%
Wholesale trade	2%
Retail trade	11%
Transportation and warehousing, and utilities	5%
Information	2%
Finance and insurance, and real estate and rental and leasing	7%
Professional, scientific, and management, and administrative and waste management services	14%

Educational services, and health care and social assistance	27%
Arts, entertainment, and recreation, and accommodation and food services	12%
Other services, except public administration	5%
Public administration	3%

Insights: For Cincinnati, 27% of the employed population work in one industry – education services, and health care and social assistance. If the industry as a whole were to take a hit, a large portion of jobs would be in jeopardy.

5. Top Employers or Businesses

If a certain industry is dominant in a market, analyzing the top employers and businesses allows you to determine whether the majority of those jobs are provided by one or two companies, or whether the risk is spread across multiple companies.

To do so, determine who the top 10 employers are in the market.

Similar to job diversity, a market with one company that employs the majority of the city is unfavorable. Also, understanding who the top employers are will allow you to track any developments within that company (e.g., are they creating a new facility, cutting jobs?).

This data can be found by Googling "(city name) + top employers." Example – Cincinnati, Ohio, Top Employers or Businesses Data:

1	Kroger - 21,646
2	University of Cincinnati - 16,016
3	Cincinnati Children's Hospital - 14,944
4	TriHealth - 11,800

5	Procter & Gamble - 11,000
6	UC Health - 10,000
7	GE Aviation - 7,800
8	Mercy Health - 7,500
9	St. Elizabeth Healthcare - 7,479
10	Fifth Third Bank - 6,882

Insights: Based on the top 10 employers and business data, 6 of the top 10 companies are in the educational services, health care, and social assistance industry. While the job diversity data is concerning, the top employer data tells us that at least the jobs aren't concentrated in one or two companies, thus alleviating some of the risk.

6. Supply and Demand

Understanding the state of supply and demand in a market will allow you to gauge the overall strength of the apartment niche. Too high of a supply or too low of a demand will impact the amount of income an apartment community can generate, which – in turn – will impact the overall value of the asset.

To determine the market's supply and demand, you want to analyze the five-year rental vacancy rates and median rental rates in the market, as well as the year-on-year change in the number of building permits created for commercial properties (five or more units).

These three factors are strongly correlated. As vacancy increases, median rents and new building permits should decrease... and vice versa.

Low or decreasing vacancy rates and increasing median rents are ideal. A high vacancy rate that is decreasing is also a positive sign indicating the market may be turning around. A stagnant vacancy rate is okay, too. An increasing vacancy rate and/or a decreasing median rent is unfavorable.

BEST EVER APARTMENT SYNDICATION BOOK

On its own, the number of five or more unit building permits won't tell us much. However, a huge red flag to you would be when you see an increase in the number of permits in combination with an increasing vacancy rate and/or a decrease in median rents.

All supply and demand data can be found on the Census.gov website. The vacancy data can be found under the "Selected Housing Characteristics" table, the median rent data can be found under the "Financial Characteristics" table, and the building permit data can be found by locating the MSA annual construction page. You will select the data table for the most current year. Example – Cincinnati, Ohio, Supply and Demand Data:

2011 Rental Vacancy Rate	15.2%
2012 Rental Vacancy Rate	14.1%
2013 Rental Vacancy Rate	11.8%
2014 Rental Vacancy Rate	10.9%
2015 Rental Vacancy Rate	9.7%
5-year Rental Vacancy Rate Change	**−36.2%**

2012 Median Rent	$630
2013 Median Rent	$640
2014 Median Rent	$653
2015 Median Rent	$649
2016 Median Rent	$662
5-year Median Rent % Change	**5.1%**

5+ Units Permitted in 2015 (MSA)	1036
5+ Units Permitted in 2016 (MSA)	1665
YoY 5+ Units Permitted % Change	**60.7%**

Insights: Based on this supply and demand data, one could conclude that Cincinnati has a strong apartment rental market. The city has seen a large increase in building permits. However, the five-year vacancy rate is down a whopping 36.2% and the median rental rate has increased by 5.1% over that same period.

7. Miscellaneous

Finally, you want to research other characteristics relevant to the strength or weakness of a market. Examples of information to locate include, but are not limited to:

- Landlord vs. tenant friendly: Each state has different laws in regards to whether the landlord or tenant is favored. Factors to determine which party is favored are things like how quickly a landlord can evict a tenant that is in violation of their lease, the eviction process in general, the grace period a tenant has to pay their rent before receiving an eviction notice, how much time in advance the landlord must give a tenant notice prior to entering the tenant's unit, the security deposit return process, security deposit limits, and which party is favored in court proceedings.
- Property taxes: This is one of the largest expenses associated with apartment communities. States vary significantly in regard to property taxes. Generally, northeastern states have the highest property taxes, while the southern states (with the exception of Texas) have the lowest.
- Upcoming construction: Do a quick Google search of your target market and see whether there are any new offices and retail centers that are slated for construction. Upcoming construction equals new jobs! Those workers need housing.
- Ranked on a "top markets" list: Do another Google search of your target market and see whether it is included on any "top markets" list.

Now it's your turn...

Obtain and log the data for the seven factors outlined above for your seven potential target markets. I recommend generating an Excel spreadsheet using the following data table as a formatting guide:

	Market A	Market B	Market C	Market D	Market E	Market F	Market G
Unemployment							
Population							
Population Age							
Job Diversity							
Top Employers							
Supply/Demand							
Misc.							

Step 3: Rank the Seven Markets

After logging the data for all seven potential target markets, analyze and compare markets and determine one or two best/ideal markets that you will evaluate further. One simple method is to rank each of the seven markets 1 to 7 for each of the factors. For example:

	Market A	Market B	Market C	Market D	Market E	Market F	Market G
Unemployment	1	4	2	3	7	5	6
Population	3	6	1	4	2	7	5
Population Age	4	3	5	1	2	6	7
Job Diversity	1	5	2	4	6	7	3
Top Employers	7	4	6	3	5	2	1
Supply/Demand	3	6	4	5	1	7	2
Misc.	1	5	3	2	4	7	6
Total	20 (1st)	33 (6th)	23 (3rd)	22 (2nd)	27 (4th)	41 (7th)	30 (5th)

Based on these rankings, Market A and Market D are the winners. Or are they...

Before picking the top two markets, you need to know which factors are the most important. All seven factors should not be given equal weight. Some are worth more and others are worth less. I break the factors into three tiers, with Tier 1 being the most important:

1. Tier 1: Supply/Demand, Job Diversity
2. Tier 2: Top Employers, Population, and Unemployment
3. Tier 3: Age, Miscellaneous

Based on this tiered system, a revised ranking data table would look like this:

	Market A	Market B	Market C	Market D	Market E	Market F	Market G
Tier 1 Ranking	1st	6th	3rd	5th	4th	7th	2nd
Tier 2 Ranking	3rd	5th	1st	2nd	5th	5th	4th
Tier 3 Ranking	2nd	4th	4th	1st	3rd	6th	6th

Step 4: Select Top One or Two Markets for Further Investigation

Based on these new rankings, which market would you select? If it were me, I would select Market A, because it has the highest Tier 1 ranking. Markets C and G come in a close second. So, in order to determine which one to select as my second market, I would review the market insights for the Tier 1 (and maybe Tier 2) factors.

But, as I mentioned in the previous chapter, I don't want you to spend hours and hours picking your target markets. As long as you hire the right team members (more about that in Chapter 19) and follow the *Three Immutable Laws of Real Estate Investing*, you will have success in any market!

What are/is your markets/market?

BEST EVER APARTMENT SYNDICATION BOOK

1. _____
2. _____

Step 5: Perform "200-Property Analysis" on One or Two Markets

The next step in the evaluation process is to gain a more detailed understanding of your one or two target markets. You will accomplish this by finding and logging information on actual (yes, real) properties in those markets. I recommend a total of 200 properties between your one or two target markets.

The purpose of this exercise is to become an expert on your market. It is also an introduction to finding and reviewing deals (more on this in Chapters 27 and 31). This is not just an academic exercise. In fact, later on in the process, you will use this database of properties to conduct a marketing campaign, so one of these properties could very well be your first deal!

In order to do the 200-property analysis, you will need to create a spreadsheet that allows you to record data for the following 17 factors for each property:

1. Market Name
2. Property Name
3. Property Address
4. Submarket/Neighborhood
5. Total Units
6. Rentable Square Footage
7. One-Bedroom Rent
8. Two-Bedroom Rent
9. Three-Bedroom Rent
10. Year Built
11. Who Pays Utilities?

12. Value-add?
13. Source
14. Owner Name
15. Owner Address
16. Appraised Value
17. Year Purchased

A "shortcut" to completing this exercise would be to pay CoStar (a commercial real estate information and marketing provider), a similar service, a title company, or a broker with whom you have built a relationship and have them perform this exercise for you by providing you the data via their database.

That said, you can do it manually too, using the following five-step process:

Step One
Find properties by using Google to search "city name + apartments," which presents you with a long list of websites (Apartments.com, Craigslist, Zillow, LoopNet, Rent.com). You should be able to locate the information required on most of these sites, but I have found that Apartments.com tends to have the most complete data for my needs.

From your Google search, click on the link for Apartments.com. You should then be presented with a map of your target market scattered with icons denoting apartments in that market on the left and a list of the top apartment buildings available for rent on the right.

On your spreadsheet, record the name of the first city you are evaluating in the column titled "Market Name."

Step Two
Click on an apartment building in your market, which should bring you to a screen with detailed property information.

On your spreadsheet, record all available data for the specific property, including property name, address, neighborhood, total units, rentable square footage, rents, year built, who pays utilities, and the source link.

Since you are a value-add investor, you want to determine whether that asset has any value-add opportunities. But how do you do that without visiting the property? Well, that's where your resourcefulness comes into play.

One strategy is to look at the pictures. Do the interiors look outdated? If only one picture is listed, that is also an indicator that the interiors are outdated. Because if the interiors had been recently updated, the owners of the apartment would list a bunch of pictures to highlight the renovations.

Another strategy is to determine whether the owner pays the utilities (water, trash, sewer). That indicates an opportunity to implement a RUBS program, billing a portion of the utilities back to the tenants and increasing the income as a result.

What if you can't locate a required data point? For example, maybe the rental data is missing and, in its place, it reads "Call for Rent." The solution is simple and, in my opinion, fun. Pick up the phone and call the number listed! Simply tell them you are performing a market survey and ask them for the remaining information.

Step Three
Obtain the property owner's information by going to the market's county website. You can locate the county website through a simple Google search of "city name + county website (or county auditor)." Most county websites should have an online property search tool. Look up the property (likely by address).

On your spreadsheet, record the owner name, owner address, appraised value, and year purchased.

Step Four

Repeat Steps 1 to 3 for 200 properties. Yes, I know this is an arduous process. But, as I've mentioned multiple times, anytime you run into a challenge, it's time to review your goals – what inspires and disgusts you – and get to work!

Additionally, no two streets are the same in a real estate market. As such, this process can save you and your investors from years of headaches because of acquiring an asset on the wrong street or in the wrong neighborhood. Additionally, you will be marketing to this list of properties later on in the process.

Trust me. When you acquire a deal from this list of 200 properties, you will thank me!

Step Five

Steps 1 to 4 can be performed regardless of whether or not you live in the target market. However, this final step will differ if you live in or outside your target market, because you will now practice analyzing a property in person!

If you live in your target market or the drive is manageable, then print out your Excel spreadsheet of properties and schedule a full or half-day to view properties in person. At the property, you will want to perform the following tasks:

- Take a general picture of the property.
    - Why? Because you will be viewing a lot of properties, so this main image will be your visual reminder.
- Take another picture of something noteworthy.
    - Example: Large green spaces, fresh landscaping, newly paved driveway, and/or interesting monuments or signage. Be creative here.

- Why? Because when you eventually begin reaching out to the owners to see whether they're interested in selling, you can bring up this noteworthy item during the conversation. (I know... clever, right?)
- Look for any signs of distress and take pictures of anything noteworthy.
  - Example: Uncovered pool in the winter, pool closed for the summer, poor landscaping, peeling paint, old roofs, and old HVAC systems.
  - Why? Signs of distress signal a potential value-add opportunity and/or a motivated seller.
- Drive around the property and look at the surrounding points of interest.
  - Why? This in combination with viewing multiple apartments gives you a great feeling for and understanding of the neighborhood.

If you live outside of your target market, you have a few options:

- Find a local partner, send them your list of properties, and have them perform the in-person analysis. Depending on who this person is, you may want to pay them for their time.
- Depending on your target market, you may be able to perform a partial version of the in-person analysis using the Google Street View function.

Once you have advanced further through the apartment syndication process, you will likely begin reaching out to the owners and local brokers to aid you in purchasing properties. For now, the goal is to (1) practice finding properties, (2) practice logging all of the relevant information required to qualify a deal,

(3) understand what to look for when reviewing properties in person and (4) become comfortable with and knowledgeable about your local market.

The final step in the process is to create a market summary report for your one or two markets, which is the subject of the next chapter.

Chapter 16

Describe the Target

After performing both the high-level, data-driven and property-level, on-the-ground analyses, it's time to create a survey report for an overall synopsis of your specific market. The main purpose of this report is to reinforce the reasons you selected the market and to proactively provide that information to your investors. Also, the process of creating this report will help solidify your understanding of the market.

How to Create Market Summary Reports

There are two main structures you can follow when creating a market summary report: (1) a Top 10 List or (2) a Detailed Market Overview.

1. Top 10 List

Your Top 10 List, as the name implies, is a list of the top 10 reasons to invest in a market. The 10 market characteristics you highlight will depend on the market and the specific strengths you identified during your evaluation process. Further investigation may be required. Highlights to consider, based on the seven market factors from the previous chapter, are:

1. Unemployment: New businesses moving to the area
2. Population: Population size and how it compares with other cities/MSAs in the nation

3. Age: Significant demographic shifts
4. Job Diversity: The largest industry (if below 25%); recent or planned economic developments
5. Top Employers and Businesses: Top companies
6. Supply and Demand: Future real estate/development/ overall economic outlook
7. Miscellaneous (but could also be included in one of the six other categories):
   - Top colleges and universities
   - Being ranked on any "top market" list (e.g., named #1 place for recent college graduates, top suburb in the state)
   - List of awards/acknowledgments that market has received
   - Commuter characteristics

You want to review the market insights discovered during your initial evaluation and use those to create a Top 10 List. Then, use Google to locate important information that you may have missed. Simply search "city name + real estate market" and scan the results for articles and news articles on the state of the real estate market.

For an idea on how to word the highlights on your Top 10 List, here is an example of the Top 10 Reasons to Invest in Baltimore, created by one of my apartment syndication clients:

1. Baltimore has, in recent years, seen tremendous economic growth, ranging from Port Covington, one of the largest urban renewal projects in America, to Harbor Point, a 27-acre mixed-use waterfront project developed by Beatty Development for Exelon Corporation, totaling about $10 billion invested by private and public organizations. **(Job Diversity highlight)**

2. Baltimore, home to top companies such as Under Armor, Pepco, Morgan Stanley, T. Rowe Price, The Johns Hopkins Hospitals, and the University of Maryland Medical Institutions, serves as a hub for a highly educated and talented workforce. **(Top Employers and Businesses highlight)**
3. Twelve universities call Baltimore home; the influx of students not only helps the student housing and/or rental market, but also builds on the talent pool, as most of the students stay in the region after graduation. **(Unemployment and Population Age highlight)**
4. Baltimore ranks 18 out of 25 top markets for rentals across the U.S. **(Supply and Demand highlight)**
5. The city is witnessing a demographic shift, as the millennial population has increased 16% over the last 5 years. **(Population Age highlight)**
6. With about 2.7 million people living along the 1,000 miles of beautiful shoreline, Baltimore is the 20th largest city amongst the 382 MSAs in the U.S. **(Population highlight)**
7. Due to previous unrest in Baltimore, many investors (mostly out of state) have been bearish on the city's outlook. Luckily, in-state investors have taken the opportunity to leverage on the decreased inflow of out-of-state capital. **(Supply and Demand highlight)**
8. Baltimore has received numerous awards, such as:
    a. 1st in the U.S. for innovation and entrepreneurship
    b. 1st in state education system
    c. 1st U.S. hospital – Johns Hopkins
    d. 2nd best for tech jobs
    e. 2nd hotbed city for high-tech growth
    f. 6th for least costly city in which to conduct business
    (Job Diversity highlight)

9. More than 900,000 people commute into Baltimore every day from the surrounding Baltimore County. In addition, 200,000 people commute on a daily basis from Washington, DC, and Virginia to Baltimore. **(Misc. highlight)**
10. Baltimore, a diamond in the rough, continues to be a strong market for multifamily development in the U.S. **(Supply and Demand highlight)**

As you can see, the most effective way to highlight a certain market characteristic is to provide the actual data, and then follow that up with an explanation as to why that data point contributes to a strong apartment market.

Additionally, once you find an opportunity, you can use each of these highlights as talking points to support your decision to invest in that particular market.

Exercise: Using the results from your market evaluation, create a Top 10 List market summary report.

2. Detailed Market Overview

If you want to blow your investors away or if you have one larger investor whom you want to have invest in your deal, you can skip the Top 10 List and/or, in addition to the Top 10 List, create a more in-depth market overview report instead.

The detailed overview will contain, at minimum, the following six sections:

1. **Top Five Key Assets**: This section should list out what are the top five key points about the market. You can either pull these from your Top 10 List or create this section using the key information from the other sections in this report. If you are sending this report to investors for a specific deal, this section should highlight important information that's relevant to the property.

2. **Employment Information**: This section will summarize the employment data for a market. Examples of information to include are how the number of jobs in the city compares with the surrounding submarkets, top industries and companies, labor demographics, employment data, and related employment data.
3. **Economic Information**: This section will highlight recent or planned economic or real estate growth. Examples of information to include are companies moving to the area, new jobs created, retail development, commercial development, mixed-use development, and real estate price trends.
4. **Education Information**: This section will highlight education data relevant to apartment investing. Examples of information to include are colleges and universities, their student population and ranking, and/or notable school districts.
5. **Awards, Recognitions, and Achievements**: This section will list out any awards won by the city, market, and local businesses/industries.
6. **Map**: This section will feature a map of the market that includes markers to illustrate points of interest, which include anything you mentioned in sections 2 to 5. Once you have your first deal, you will include that on the map. As you begin to build your portfolio, you can also include properties currently under your control to show investors that you're already established in the market. The free mapping tool I use is Zee Maps.

I followed this market summary approach when I was presenting an opportunity to one of my larger investors. It was located in Richardson, Texas – a submarket of Dallas. Chris was interested in being the only investor in the deal. I created and sent him a detailed market summary report and he was blown away. To date, he has invested approximately $20 million with our company, and I am certain he did so (at least in part) because of the following market summary:

ABC Apartments Top Five Key Assets
1. Located in Richardson, Texas, which is the second largest employment center in the Dallas/Ft. Worth metro area. Richardson has an unemployment rate of 3.6% (compared with 5.2% for the U.S.)
2. X miles away from the $1.5 billion ongoing development at City Line, which is currently at over 3 million square feet of office, restaurant, and retail space
3. X miles away from Richmond College, which has a total enrollment of 20,000 students, and X miles away from the University of Texas at Dallas, which has a total enrollment of 27,000 students
4. X minute drive to downtown Dallas
5. Richardson is 3rd best real estate market, 3rd best city to live in, and 5th happiest mid-sized city in America

Employment Information
Richardson is the second largest employment center in the Dallas/Ft. Worth metro area and includes a diverse range of businesses. The city's four largest employers represent three separate industries: (1) Financial services/insurance, (2) Telecommunications, and (3) Public education.

Richardson is the home of the Telecom Corridor, a more than 25 million-square-foot technology business center that accounts for over 130,000 jobs. It is headquarters to more than 5,700 companies, 600 being technology companies, including top companies such as AT&T, Alcatel-Lucent, Ericsson, Verizon, Samsung, Texas Instruments, and Metro PCS. Richardson is also home to the BlueCross-BlueShield of Texas HQ in the health care industry, and a State Farm Insurance Regional Hub in the insurance services industry, which are Richardson's 3rd and 1st largest employers respectively.

Richardson serves as a hub for the well-educated and diverse labor supply, with 50% of the adult workforce having an undergraduate or advanced degree. Due to its strategic local and superb transportation infrastructure, about 80,000 to 130,000 daytime workers (over 60%) come from outside the city limits.

Richardson has an unemployment rate of 3.6% (compared with 5.2% for the U.S.) and 3.09% job growth in last 12 months (compared with 1.59% for the U.S.).

Economic Information

In recent years, Richardson has seen extensive revitalization and tremendous economic growth:

- **Business/Corporate Sector**
    - State Farm Insurance recently moved into a $1.5 billion mixed-use, transit-oriented development.
    - Real Page, a software company, recently leased a 400,000-square-foot corporate HQ facility and is currently renovating.
    - Geico Insurance relocated 1,600 employees to Richardson at the end of 2015.
- **Retail Sector**
    - Over the past 10 years, 25 centers have been redeveloped or remodeled and 7 new centers have been constructed or expanded.
    - Most notable is City Line and City Line Market, which is a $1.5 billion development of more than 3 million square feet of office, restaurant, and retail space.

- The University of Texas at Dallas has recently broken ground on a 370,000-square-foot retail and housing center.
- **Transit-Oriented/Mixed-Use Developments**
  - Richardson has five recently completed transit-oriented/mixed-use developments and one currently under construction.
  - Notable past investments include:
    - Brick Row – $140 million multifamily and townhome complex
    - Port Eastside – $90 million multifamily, office, and retail complex
    - AMLI Galatyn – $35 million upscale apartment development
  - The development currently under construction is Palisades Village, an 80-acre, $700 million luxury apartment development.

Overall real estate prices in this market increased 23% in 2015, with an estimated additional 5.5% increase by the end of 2016.

Education Information

Richardson has five colleges and universities, including the University of Texas at Dallas, with an enrollment of 26,792 students, and Richland College, with an enrollment of over 20,000 students.

The influx of students helps the student housing and rental market, and also builds on the employment talent pool.

Awards, Recognitions, and Achievement

Richardson ranked 3rd in Wallet Hub's "2016's Best Real-Estate Markets" Report and was named "America's 3rd Best City to Live In" according to 24/7 Wall Street.

Other notable achievements include:

- 5-star accredited Chamber of Commerce
- Texas City Management Association City Council of the Year
- Triple A Status, which is the highest possible rating available for credit worthiness, from both Moody's and Standard and Poor
- 5th happiest mid-sized city in America
- Texas Award for Performance Excellence for the Methodist Richardson Medical Center

Exercise: Using the template provided above, create a detailed market overview for your one or two target markets.

PART 2: THE MONEY

PART 1: THE EXPERIENCE

KNOWLEDGE — Chapters 1-4
1. What is apartment syndication?
2. How to Get Started
3. What to focus on

GOALS — Chapters 5-6
1. How do you make money?
2. Set 12-month goal and long-term vision
3. Ultimate Success Formula

BRAND BUILDING — Chapters 7-12
1. Why you need a brand
2. Select a target audience
3. How to build a brand

MARKET EVALUATION — Chapters 13-16
1. 3 Immutable Laws of Real Estate
2. Evaluate 7 markets
3. Pick 1-2 Target Markets

PART 2: THE MONEY

YOU ARE HERE

BUILD TEAM — Chapters 17-19
1. Find core real estate team members
2. Hire a mentor or consultant

FIND CAPITAL — Chapters 20-24
1. Why will they invest?
2. Build passive investor database
3. Create partnership structure

PART 3: THE DEAL

FIND DEALS — Chapters 25-28
1. Set investment criteria
2. On-market vs. off-market deals
3. How to find your first deal

UNDERWRITING — Chapters 29-31
1. Information needed to underwrite a deal
2. The 6-step underwriting process

SUBMIT OFFER — Chapter 32
1. How to submit an offer on a deal
2. Best-and-final offer
3. Purchase sales agreement

PART 4: THE EXECUTION

DUE DILIGENCE — Chapters 33-37
1. 10 due diligence reports
2. Secure financing from lender

SECURE CAPITAL — Chapters 38-42
1. Create investment summary
2. New investment offering call
3. Secure investor commitments

CLOSE — Chapters 43-44
1. Closing process
2. Notify passive investors

EXECUTE BUSINESS PLAN — Chapters 45-46
1. 10 asset management duties
2. How to sell the apartment

CHAPTER 17

YOUR CORE APARTMENT SYNDICATION TEAM

As I mentioned in Chapters 10 and 12, one of the main reasons for launching a thought leadership platform and starting a Meetup/mastermind group is to establish yourself as an apartment syndication expert in your local area. In the process, you will attract and interact with many real estate professionals, both followers and interviewees. Your reputation and the relationships formed, along with your ability to effectively communicate your apartment investing and market knowledge, will enable you to begin the process of building your real estate team.

Your core real estate team will consist of a real estate broker, accountant, property management company, mortgage broker, real estate attorney, securities attorney, and mentor/consultant.

One way to find candidates to bring onto your team is to look at the real estate professionals you have met through your thought leadership platform and Meetup/mastermind group(s). However, based on both my apartment syndication business and my clients' similar businesses, one of the most effective ways to locate high-quality team members is through referrals. Further, one of the best sources for obtaining qualified referrals is through a consultant or a mentor.

Let me explain...

CHAPTER 18

TO BE MENTORED OR NOT TO BE MENTORED...

At this point, you may be saying, "Joe, why the heck do I need a mentor? I got this, man!" Well, by "mentor," I mean a paid consultant to provide you with guidance along your apartment syndication journey. The thing here is that unless you are really seasoned, you're going to need a mentor. Heck, even seasoned professionals tend to have mentors when they want to stay relevant.

However, that's just my opinion.

Ask another successful apartment syndicator for his or her opinion on hiring a mentor and you're not likely to receive the same answer twice. One syndicator will swear by mentors, saying it's impossible to reach the highest levels of success without one. Another will say that mentors are unnecessary and not worth the money. Yet another will have an opinion of mentors that is somewhere in between the two extremes.

My personal philosophy is that I find truth in all of these opinions, because like most things in apartment investing... hiring a mentor depends. It depends on your expectations of a mentor. It also depends on why you want to hire a mentor in the first place. The decision is ultimately up to you. Let's go over the four main things you can expect to get out of a relationship with the right mentor.

1. A mentor should demonstrate expertise on how to do what you're wanting to do. The mentor should not only have experience in apartment syndications, but be active in the field as well. A good mentor is someone who has a successful track record as an apartment syndicator and is still completing deals to this day. A poor mentor is someone who has never syndicated a deal or someone who has stopped syndicating, even if they have a long list of clients who are actively and successfully syndicating deals. If you decide to go the mentor route, do not hire someone unless they have experience and are an active syndicator. Period.
2. You should expect a mentor to provide you with a step-by-step system for how you can replicate their success. While there is an overall process to syndicating an apartment deal, there is only so much that can be covered in one book. A mentor will provide you with a system, but will also be able to help you navigate the many gray areas along the way.
3. A mentor should be an ally that you can call upon to talk to only about yourself and work out any problem you might be facing in a deal. Since you are paying this person, you don't have to feel guilty about being the center of the conversation. You don't even need to be interesting. You can and should talk about whatever it is you need to at the moment. On the other hand, if you are not paying a mentor, you will likely feel guilty for always calling on them or talking about yourself without giving anything in return.
4. The fourth thing you should expect from a good mentor is connections. Since the mentor should be active in real estate investing, specifically as a syndicator, they will have relationships with all the movers and shakers in apartment syndication. Therefore, they should

connect you with team members relevant to growing your business.

There are two main things you should NOT expect when hiring a mentor:

1. A mentor will not be your savior or your knight in shining armor. Do not expect to hire a mentor and POOF have all of your problems solved. Yes, the mentor should offer expertise, provide a step-by-step process, be an ally, and provide connections, but you will still be required to take action. Moreover, the best mentors, rather than being your knight in shining armor, should give you the tools and knowledge for you to become your own savior! That means you need the baseline knowledge outlined in Chapter 3 before even entertaining the idea of hiring a mentor.
2. You cannot expect a "done for you" program from your mentor. If you find a mentor who indeed does offer such a program, run! If a mentor promises you anything that doesn't require any work on your part, run! The problem with a "done for you" program, assuming it truly is and is not just a scam, is that you're not learning anything. You are not building the foundation of knowledge required to sustain a business. Even if you are able to attain a high level of success using one of these programs, it is unstable and likely unsustainable. Once you lose that program, you lose your progress as well.

WHEN ARE YOU READY FOR A MENTOR?

You are ready to hire a mentor when you have defined a specific outcome you want to achieve by hiring a mentor. Know exactly what it is you want to get out of the relationship. At this point in the syndication process, you need team members, and the right mentor will have the connections with the right people in the industry. But that's not all a mentor is good for.

Do you want immediate access to expert apartment syndication advice if you happen to run into a gray area that isn't covered in this book? Do you need an unbiased person with whom to speak without feeling guilty for only talking about yourself? Do you need an experienced, active apartment syndicator on your team so you can leverage their proven track record and credibility to raise money from passive investors? If you said yes to any of these questions, a mentor can be your ideal solution.

Conversely, do you want a mentor because you were told you were supposed to have one? Do you want a knight in shining armor who will do all the work for you? Do you want a "done for you" program so that you can sit back, relax, and enjoy the returns? These are wrong reasons to hire a mentor.

One of the challenges that I came across when I was starting out, and one you will likely come across, is a lack of credibility. Having an experienced mentor who in turn connects you with experienced team members can offset your lack of experience in the eyes of your passive investors and the seller.

Obviously, you can fulfill any of the above-mentioned needs and outcomes through other parties. But nowhere else can you fulfill them all in one fell swoop than with the right mentor!

The other challenge you will face in finding a mentor is a lack of alignment of interests. This is something important to understand and we will discuss the solution to this problem in more detail in Chapter 23.

So, for now, based on what a mentor can offer, are you interested? If so, there is really only one effective way to find a mentor – word-of-mouth referrals. That is the only way that I have found to verify the legitimacy of a mentor. That's also where your thought leadership platform comes into play. With your interview-based thought leadership platform, you are speaking with – at minimum – one active real estate entrepreneur each week. You shouldn't have much difficulty getting a handful of referrals for mentors. While this isn't my focus with this book, visit www.BestEverAptProgram.com to learn more about my apartment syndication mentorship program.

While each mentor referred has had their legitimacy verified, always double check to make sure they align with the expectations outlined above. Are they active, successful apartment syndicators? Do they have step-by-step systems, as opposed to a DFY (done for you) system? If so, and if you feel comfortable speaking to them, move forward. If not, find someone else.

Even if you find a rock star mentor who provides you with referrals of people they work with, you still need some sort of screening process to determine whether they are the best fit for your exact needs. Like any business that needs to hire a new employee, you must conduct interviews to fill these roles. (In the long run, this saves you time, money, and pain.)

CHAPTER 19

HOW TO BUILD YOUR ALL-STAR TEAM

No one reaches success on their lonesome... at least not after the initial phase where you're trying to do everything yourself. You need a team to get you where you want to go as an apartment syndicator!

But how do you find these all-star players?

The truth is that the interview process will differ for each team member because each team member will fulfill different responsibilities. Also, during the interview, if candidates are serious professionals, they will be interviewing you as well. If they are stellar performers, they will have many investors vying for their business. Your interview preparation should not just include creating a list of interview questions to ask these candidates, but you also need to be prepared to answer potential questions. That means you really need to know your stuff.

After completing a round of interviews, review the responses and referrals. Then select the ideal team member.

As I mentioned in Chapter 17, your core real estate team will consist of a real estate broker, accountant, property management company, mortgage broker, real estate attorney, securities attorney, and mentor/consultant.

The first team member you should bring on is a mentor. After that, through referrals from either your mentor or your thought leadership platform, you will find a real estate broker and a property management company with which you want to work. Those are the three team members you need to bring on prior to looking for deals.

Finally, again through referrals either from your mentor or from your thought leadership platform, you can bring on an accountant, mortgage broker, real estate attorney, and securities attorney. This can happen while you look for deals.

Hiring Real Estate Brokers

One of the real estate professionals you want as a part of your real estate team is a real estate broker. A great one sends you deals and, more specifically, sends you off-market deals. However, like all good relationships, it must be reciprocal. Most likely, the real estate broker will have countless investors asking them for deals. Therefore, when approaching a conversation with a new real estate broker, it is important to realize that they are interviewing you as much as you are interviewing him or her.

So, what are the best practices for approaching these real estate broker conversations/interviews?

First, let me give you the questions you need to ask a real estate broker. Next, let me outline how you can win him or her over to your side by portraying yourself as the ideal candidate to fulfill their need... because you are a serious, credible investor who will close a deal. Finally, I am giving you a list of questions the broker may ask and that you should be prepared to answer.

1. Questions to Ask the Real Estate Broker

When interviewing a real estate broker, you need to know your outcome for the conversation. Since you are an apartment syndicator, your main goal should be to determine the broker's level of experience and success with apartment communities that are comparable to your investment criteria (which you will set in Chapter 25).

To accomplish this goal, here is a list of 12 questions to ask during the interview:

1. What is your transaction volume?
2. How many successful closes have you experienced in the last year?
3. How long have you been working as a real estate broker and how long have you focused on apartments?
4. How many listings do you currently have?
5. How do you find deals?
6. Do you offer both on-market and off-market deals?
7. What stage is the local apartment market in?
8. What is your specialty?
9. How do you structure your fees?
10. Is there anything in particular that you do differently than other real estate brokers in the market?
11. Will you please provide references?
12. What haven't I asked you that I need to know?

Ideally, you want to find a real estate broker that will send you an endless supply of off-market apartment deals. However, don't bank on this, especially in the beginning phases of the relationship. That said, after you've proven to the real estate broker that you're the real deal, successfully closing on a few deals, it will become more and more likely that you will be the first person he or she calls with a new off-market opportunity. As with all good relationships, trust is built over time.

A final qualification of a real estate broker is that they must be local to your target market.

2. Winning Over the Real Estate Broker

Again, when interviewing a real estate broker, it is important to realize that they are interviewing you, too. Put yourself in their shoes and ask yourself, "What are they looking for when deciding whether or not to bring on a new client?"

Since real estate brokers are paid a commission at the sale of a property, their number-one motivator is to close on a deal as quickly and as easily as possible. They don't like tire kickers, wannabe investors who waste their time asking a bunch of questions but never close on a deal. Their ideal client is an investor who has a proven track record and funds required to close on deals. So, if you don't have previous investing experience, verbal commitments from passive investors, and the ability to qualify for financing, these will be your top challenges.

To win over a real estate broker during a conversation, you need to sell yourself and your business, and build rapport without being pushy or over-confident. What relevant experience do you have that will convey to them that you are serious about closing deals? Have you successfully completed projects in a non-real-estate-related field? Have you started a business in the past?

If you are struggling to come up with relevant experiences, this is where having a reputable team comes into play. Sell your team members. Talk about your real estate mentor's or consultant's real estate experience. (I told you having a mentor will come into handy!) If you've already found a property management company, tell them about the number of apartments the company manages. Bring up any other relevant relationships you've formed.

Along with asking the real estate broker business questions, to build rapport you need to get to know something personal about them. Find out something that's important to them and bring it up with genuine interest next time you meet. A quick way to accomplish this is to ask one of my go-to questions, after having already established yourself. Ask the real estate broker, "What's been the highlight of your week?"

Finally, I recommend preparing an opening statement. If you already have a deal in mind, you can say, "I'd like to discuss making an offer on ABC apartment." Or, another example would be, "I am working with ABC Property Management and will be buying a property in (city name) in the next few months." The purpose of the opening statement is to grab the attention of the real estate broker, to come across as a serious investor, and to address their "want" – which is to close on an apartment – from the start.

After your introductory conversation or meeting with a real estate broker in person, they might still be uncertain about your ability to pull the trigger on a deal. Therefore, you must make a continuous effort to prove, without a doubt, that you are the real deal.

One tactic is to offer the real estate broker a consulting fee. To show that you are serious and that you respect their time, offer to pay them an hourly fee ($150 to $200 per hour), even if you don't find a qualified deal.

Another tactic is to get in your car and drive to the real estate broker's recent apartment sales. For example, create a list of their 10 most recent apartment sales and visit the properties in person. Follow a similar approach to the one I outlined in Chapter 15 for performing the in-person analysis of apartments in your target market. After reviewing the 10 properties, follow up with the real estate broker, telling them which properties meet your investment criteria (which I outline in detail in Chapter 25) and why. In doing so, you are not just portraying yourself as a serious investor but giving the real estate broker an idea of what type of apartment you are interested in acquiring as well.

The third tactic is to provide the real estate broker with information on how you will fund a potential deal. As an apartment syndicator, you are raising money from accredited investors. Explain how many people have expressed interest or have verbally committed to investing (more on how to find passive investors in Chapter 21). Since you will be securing a loan, tell them about the mortgage brokers you've already spoken with. Anything else related to the funding of the deal should be communicated to the real estate broker to qualify yourself as a credible investor who has the financial capabilities to close a deal.

Last but not least, be diligent in constantly following up with the real estate broker. More deals are lost due to poor follow-up than I can count! Whenever you perform a task that brings you closer to completing a deal, notify the real estate broker. A simple email will suffice. For example, if you have a conversation with a lender, provide the real estate broker with their contact information and the outcome of the meeting. For example, say, "I met with XYZ Lending. I told them about my business plan and my source of equity and they told me that I will qualify for a loan."

Once you've found a qualified property management company, send the real estate broker their information and background. Before sending out a direct mailing campaign, as well as when you start receiving phone calls from interested owners, notify the real estate broker. Overall, qualifying yourself in the eyes of an experienced real estate broker boils down to putting forth strategic, although not necessary, effort and continuous communication with relevant information. Of course, the consulting fee is the cherry on top.

3. Questions You Need to Be Prepared to Answer

Don't expect the broker to simply answer your questions, chat about their business and personal life, and then get up and walk away. If they are seriously interested in bringing you on as a new client, they will want to ask you questions. You need to proactively brainstorm questions they may ask and have ready-made answers.

Here is a list of 11 potential questions an interested real estate broker will ask you during the interview:

1. Who is your property management company?
2. How many units do they manage?
3. Are they local?
4. Have you (or someone on your team) purchased an apartment building before?
5. What type of deals are you looking for? (This is where you tell them about your investment criteria, which you will define in Chapter 25.)
6. What markets are you looking into?
7. How will you fund the deal?
8. How did you find me?
9. Will you sign an exclusive agreement with me so I can get you the best deals? (I do not recommend doing this, because it will lock you into one real estate broker, which means you are limiting your lead generation pipeline.)
10. What are your expectations?
11. Can I see biographies of you and your partners?

Hiring a Property Management Company

One of the most important members of your team is a property management company. A property manager will obviously manage the apartment for you upon closing, but a great property manager should offer additional services. They should advise on attractive or struggling neighborhoods within your market, offer locations of prospective properties based on your business model, and even provide a pro forma on prospective properties based on how they would manage them.

You should work on finding a property management company concurrently with your search for a real estate broker.

Similar to real estate brokers, a relationship with a property management company goes both ways. An accomplished management company will have other investors swarming over them for business. Therefore, this must be taken into account when preparing for an interview, because you are being analyzed as well.

What follows are the best practices for approaching these property management interviews.

First, I give you a list of questions you need to ask, followed by an outline for winning them over, and finally, a list of questions you should be prepared to answer.

1. Questions to Ask a Property Management Company

Prior to conducting your interview, you need to define an outcome. Or, in this case, a few outcomes. Similar to the outcomes of speaking with a real estate broker, your first objective is to find the right property management company that fits your style, business plan, and budget; your second objective is to prove that if they bring you on as a client, you will satisfy their business needs.

To accomplish the first objective, here is a list of 26 questions to ask during the interview:

1. **How long have you been in business?** A relatively newer property management company might not have enough experience managing certain sizes or types of apartment communities/buildings. Generally, the longer they've been in business managing value-add apartment communities the better.

2. **What geographic area(s) do you cover?** The property management company must be local to your target market. But you also want to know whether your target market is their sole focus, or whether they are focused on other markets across the country as well. The latter isn't a disqualifier, but it may signal a lack of understanding or a lack of manpower in your target market.
3. **How many units do you manage?** Compare the number of units a property management company manages with the number of units that other local companies you are in contact with manage. If they are the largest one in the market, that means they are likely highly trusted and effective. But if they are too large, you might not get the level of service that you desire; if they are too small, they might not be capable of managing certain sized projects. However, I wouldn't go with a property management company that manages fewer than 1,000 units.
4. **How many properties does each regional office manage?** Similar logic to the response to question number 3.
5. **How many do you own yourself?** If the property management company owns their own apartment communities in your target market, it could be a conflict of interest. Think about it this way... if your property and their property have similar vacant two-bedroom/one-bathroom units, which one are they more likely to fill first? However, when starting out, don't automatically disqualify a firm that owns its own portfolio, because there could be the potential to joint venture.
6. **Do you specialize in or concentrate on a particular class of property?** You want a property management company that specializes in value-add apartment deals (or

whatever investment strategy you decide to pursue). If they specialize in multiple asset classes, ask them what percentage of their portfolio is value-add apartments.

7. **What kind of due diligence services do you provide? What is the potential cost if the deal doesn't close?** As you will learn in Chapter 34, the property management company should be heavily involved in the due diligence process. Generally, they will provide these services for free, but you still want to confirm whether they will (1) help during the due diligence process, (2) do it for free, and (3) charge extra if you don't close on the deal.

8. **Do you take on value-add properties?** You want a property management company that has experience successfully taking value-add apartment communities through the full cycle, which includes the acquisition, renovations, and sale.

9. **Can you describe your process for managing a moderate property renovation?** How is the status of the work tracked? Who manages the contractors? How are invoices tracked and verified against bids? Who approves the work before the contractor is paid? What fees do they charge for renovation/CapEx costs?

10. **What are some of the names of nearby properties that your company is currently managing?** Visiting these properties will allow you to confirm the types of apartments they manage and see how these properties are being maintained.

11. **What special training do your managers receive from your company?** Again, not a deal-breaker. But if you are looking at multiple property management companies, this information could sway your decision one way or another.

12. **How do you manage a property's online reputation?** Most prospective residents perform their apartment searches online, and one of the first things that they will see is the apartment's ranking. As value-add investors most if not all of the properties we purchase will have lower than average online rankings. So, you want to know what steps the property management company will take to maximize the online reputation of the apartment after acquisition.
13. **Who will be my point person?** Ideally, your point person is the site manager and not an employee of the site manager.
14. **What do you see as the site manager's duties?** The main responsibilities of the site manager include managing unit turnovers, managing the implementation of the business plan, managing maintenance requests and repairs, and maintaining a clean environment. No tenant wants to live in an unkempt building.
15. **Can I interview and approve the site manager?** Again, not a deal-breaker. But if you are looking at multiple property management companies, this information could sway your decision.
16. **What kind of relationship do you want your site manager to have with the owner?** How often does the site manager contact you? Is it on a consistent schedule (e.g., once a week, biweekly, or whatever schedule you request)? What types of updates will they provide during the renovation period and thereafter? On which types of maintenance issues will they require your approval? How accessible will they be? If you call them, will they tend to pick up every time, and if not, how quickly will they follow up with you?
17. **Will you provide a written management plan?** This is referring to a renovation plan and a marketing plan. You

need to know how long the renovations are expected to take when underwriting the deal. But you also want to know whether they will create and provide you with a written plan for how they will maximize occupancy, and whether they will set goals for the leasing agents.

18. **What percentage do you charge as a management fee?** If you are looking at a property with over 100 units, the property management fee will likely range from 3% to 5% of the collected revenue. But if you start off by focusing on smaller apartment buildings, the fee will be higher. You also want to know on what criteria the fee is based. Is it a percentage of the gross rents or collected income (which includes the other income)?

19. **What is included with the monthly management fee?** You want to understand whether the management fee is all inclusive or whether they charge one-time fees for other services, like leasing fees, vacancy fees, set-up fees (i.e., to set up a new tenant in their system), late fees, maintenance fees, lease renewal fees, and eviction fees.

20. **Which property management software do you use?** There are a few out there, and it's a good thing to know, though it's certainly not a deal-breaker. You just want to be sure they do use management software so they can track everything properly and provide you with accurate reporting.

21. **How much time do you typically take to do a make-ready?** Timelines can range from 12–24 hours to 7–10 days to prepare a unit for rent once the former resident moves out. Of course, the longer it takes to turn over a unit, the more money you lose.

22. **Can tenants pay with auto-withdrawal/automatic payments? What other methods are available to them?** You want to make sure that the rent payment method aligns

with your resident demographic. If the residents don't have bank accounts, there has to be a way for them to pay their rent. If that means money orders, you need to know what the property management company can do when it comes to managing the rents.

23. **Do you require me to list the property with you upon its sale?** Some property management companies can have a clause in the contract which requires you to list the property with them when you are ready to sell.
24. **Will you give me your cell phone number?** You want a direct line of communication to your property manager, regional and national office should you need to get in contact with them.
25. **What are some of the reasons we should use your company?** This allows the property management company to distinguish themselves from other companies in the market.
26. **Can you give me contact information for three current clients who have buildings/communities like mine?** Have a conversation with these clients, asking questions about the property management company's quality of service.

Armed with these questions you should do just fine as an apartment syndicator and lock down the best property management company in your market. Next I'll share with you how to win over the property management company!

2. How to Win Over the Property Management Company

Again, when interviewing a property management company, remember that they are interviewing you, too. They want to be confident that if they bring you on as a client, you will satisfy their business needs.

Since property management companies are typically paid a percentage of rental income, their main motivator is to have a client that will close on a deal. At the same time, they don't want a client with unrealistic expectations of the services they will offer, or to not get fairly compensated.

Besides finding a property management company to bring onto your team, your other objective is to have them commit to letting you send them potential deals and giving you their expert advice. This can be a life saver (and time saver... money saver).

At the very least, you want the property management company to confirm your underwriting assumptions. They will only agree to this if you are able to prove that you are capable of fulfilling their wants by conveying that you are a credible investor who is serious about closing on a deal. Therefore, prior to asking whether you can get their feedback on prospective deals, you need to prove YOUR worthiness. Hopefully this doesn't involve them asking for you to offer up your first-born child. Instead, they will ask you a series of questions, which I'll go over in the subsequent section. You don't have to wait. You can be proactive during the conversation by selling yourself, your relevant experience, and/or your team.

Follow the same process in this part of the process that you used to sell yourself to a broker. For your opening statement to a property management company, you might say, "I'm buying a property in (city name) and am in the process of making offers" or "I'm working with ABC broker and will be buying a property in (city name) in the next few months." Then tell them, "I've done my initial research on you and would love to learn a little more about your company."

You need to get their attention by conveying that you are interested in doing business with them first. Then you can ask about sending them prospective deals and getting their feedback.

3. Questions You Need to Be Prepared to Answer

To qualify you as an investor, an interested property management company will pepper you with questions. Here is a list of seven potential questions you should be prepared to answer during the interview:

1. Who is your broker?
2. Have you (or someone on your team) purchased an apartment building before?
3. What types of properties are you looking for? What markets/neighborhoods are you looking in?
4. How did you find me?
5. Are you currently working with any other property management companies?
6. What are your expectations for a property management company's duties and obligations?
7. How do you underwrite deals? (I dedicate an entire chapter to underwriting – Chapter 31)
8. Can I see biographies of you and your partners?

HIRING AN ACCOUNTANT

Taxes can be very complicated, especially in this line of work as an apartment syndicator. A 2010 report by the Internal Revenue Service's Taxpayer's Advocate Office found that the tax code contained 3.8 million words. A 2012 version of the report put the number of words at 4 million. That's five times as long as the Bible! You want to take advantage of as many tax deductions as possible, so hiring a certified accountant is a must.

Moreover, if you don't want to have a stress-induced heart attack in the next 5 to 10 years, I also highly recommend hiring a bookkeeper. (Okay, that's being dramatic, but you get my point. Hiring a bookkeeper is a really good idea.) Preferably your accountant can also fulfill the role of a bookkeeper.

When you're on the hunt for a good seasoned accountant, first and foremost you want to make sure they already work with clients who are doing what you are doing... apartment investors, or more specifically, apartment syndicators. Therefore, the first question you should ask in an introductory email or phone call – to avoid wasting anyone's time – is "Do you currently work with other apartment syndicators?"

If they don't know what an apartment syndication is, then that's obviously an indicator that they don't work with syndicators.

If they know what apartment syndication is, but they haven't yet worked with any syndicators, that's not necessarily a deal-breaker. However, I would recommend finding someone else, because you don't want them learning the ins and outs of apartment syndication on your dime. You want an accountant who already knows the types of tax deductions you can take and knows the apartment syndication business model.

If the accountant does know what apartment syndication is AND they currently represent syndicators, then you can move forward with an interview with the purpose of the gaining an understanding of their tax-saving strategies.

Here is a list of eight questions you should ask:

1. **How are your fees structured?** Get an understanding of exactly how you will be charged. Will there be fees for each time you call in? Can you give them a quick call every now and then and not be charged? Do their fees include the tax return at the end of the year or is that separate? Do they charge a monthly retainer just so you have the right to call them and have conversations? How do they structure their bookkeeping fees?
2. **Who will be my point person?** When you sign up for their services, with whom will you be engaging? Will it

be someone right out of college, a partner, or a mid-level accountant?

3. **How conservative or aggressive are you with the tax positions you are willing to take?** Additionally, does the conservative/aggressive nature of the accountant align with your desires? If taking aggressive stances, how will that be communicated to you for you to understand and accept? You may rely on the accountant to prepare your tax returns, but when you sign your tax return, ultimately you are taking legal responsibility for what appears on that paperwork.

4. **Do you offer a secure portal to transfer sensitive files back and forth?** Tax documents contain a lot of personally identifiable information (social security numbers, adjusted gross income). Stolen identifies can wreak havoc on your personal and professional lives for years. A secure portal for information-sharing purposes is a must.

5. **How proactive are you with tax planning and how do your tax planning services work?** This is a straightforward question. You want an accountant who is proactive.

6. **Are you able to file tax returns for all state and local governments in the country?** This seems like a no-brainer question, but ask it anyway.

7. **What do you expect in your clients?** Expectations should be set early and communicated clearly. That way you avoid surprises.

8. **May I have some references?** No matter how great the interview goes, always ask for references so you can make sure they are legitimate. Don't leave it at that. You're not done performing your due diligence. Follow up with the references to ask about the accountant's quality of service and to confirm that they provided you with honest answers to the eight questions above.

If you previously experienced a failed relationship with another accountant, be upfront with prospective accountants about why it failed.

Finally, the accountant doesn't need to be located in your local market, or even in the same state for that matter. It is helpful, but not necessary. It's important that the accountant be available for regular in-person meetings. For example, I meet with my accountant in person on a monthly basis, and you may want to do the same. However, you may be comfortable with not meeting with your accountant until tax season, or you may prefer to conduct monthly meetings over the phone instead. That part is up to you and your comfort level.

FINALIZING YOUR ALL-STAR TEAM

As I said at the beginning of this section, additional professionals you need on your team are a mortgage broker, a real estate attorney, and a securities attorney. However, if you've properly screened your real estate broker, property management company, and accountant there is a high probability that the rest of your team can be found through referrals (likely from your existing team members).

After getting the nod from your current team members, you'll still want to meet for interviews to confirm that your new team members will align with your business goals and have experience with apartment syndications.

The real estate broker, property management company and real estate attorney must be local to your target market. A local accountant is helpful but not necessary. The mortgage broker and securities attorney do not need to be local to the market.

Another invaluable "team member" that will help you shorten the learning curve and automate parts of your business in order to free up more of your time so that you can focus on the money-making activities is technology! A great resource that highlights the best real estate technologies currently available is *Investor Hacks! 20 Essential Tools for Real Estate Investors* by Seth Williams.

Finally, after surrounding yourself with a team of expert real estate professionals, you will start the process of finding and priming your passive investors. Are you getting excited?

PART 1: THE EXPERIENCE

KNOWLEDGE
Chapters 1 - 4
1. What is apartment syndication?
2. How to Get Started
3. What to focus on

GOALS
Chapters 5 - 6
1. How do you make money?
2. Set 12-month goal and long-term vision
3. Ultimate Success Formula

BRAND BUILDING
Chapters 7 - 12
1. Why you need a brand
2. Select a target audience
3. How to build a brand

MARKET EVALUATION
Chapters 13 - 16
1. 3 Immutable Laws of Real Estate
2. Evaluate 7 markets
3. Pick 1-2 Target Markets

PART 2: THE MONEY

BUILD TEAM
Chapters 17 - 19
1. Find core real estate team members
2. Hire a mentor or consultant

FIND CAPITAL
Chapters 20 - 24
1. Why will they invest?
2. Build passive investor database
3. Create partnership structure

YOU ARE HERE

PART 3: THE DEAL

FIND DEALS
Chapters 25 - 28
1. Set investment criteria
2. On-market vs. off-market deals
3. How to find your first deal

UNDERWRITING
Chapters 29 - 31
1. Information needed to underwrite a deal
2. The 6-step underwriting process

SUBMIT OFFER
Chapter 32
1. How to submit an offer on a deal
2. Best-and-final offer
3. Purchase sales agreement

PART 4: THE EXECUTION

DUE DILIGENCE
Chapters 33 - 37
1. 10 due diligence reports
2. Secure financing from lender

SECURE CAPITAL
Chapters 38 - 42
1. Create investment summary
2. New investment offering call
3. Secure investor commitments

CLOSE
Chapters 43 - 44
1. Closing process
2. Notify passive investors

EXECUTE BUSINESS PLAN
Chapters 45 - 46
1. 10 asset management duties
2. How to sell the apartment

CHAPTER 20

WHY WOULD SOMEONE INVEST WITH YOU?

Before setting out to find passive investors, you must first answer the question "What's the primary reason people will invest in YOUR deals?"

You already knew "who" will invest with you when you created your target audience in Chapter 8. However, what is the "why"? It may be different than you think.

Before raising $1,000,000 for my first syndication, I thought the primary reason people would invest in my deals would be based on the return structure I offered. Everyone just wants to make a lot of money, right?

Well, I was dead wrong.

Of course, returns are a necessary part of the equation, but returns can be provided by any number of competent syndicators or through any number of investment strategies.

Instead, I discovered that an investor's determining factor is trust. They will only invest with you if they trust you as a person and trust you as a business person.

How to Gain Trust from Potential Investors

To raise money, the question you need to reflect on is "How do I gain trust from potential investors?"

From my personal and professional experience, trust is created in three important ways:

1. Time

It takes time to establish a relationship with investors. For your first syndicated deal, you likely won't attract investors who haven't known you for at least a couple years. You just don't have the track record yet. Once you're established, it will be easier to get new friends and business contacts to invest with you, because they will see that you've successfully hit or exceeded your return projections on your deals.

The more expertise you have, the shorter amount of time you need to know the investors. For my first $1,000,000 raise, I had known all of the investors for 2 to 10 years. The more experienced I became and the more deals I completed, the shorter that window of time to raise capital. In fact, after growing my portfolio to over $400,000,000 I am at the point now where I attract investors from word-of-mouth referrals from current investors. Plus, my deals have waitlists!

2. Expertise

The more expertise you demonstrate, the easier it becomes for you to raise the money you need for deals. But there's a big caveat. You must demonstrate the expertise in a way your potential investors can understand. It doesn't matter how much you know. It's more about what's relevant to your investors and how you communicate that information to them.

What I mean by this is that you need to speak in a different language to one person vs. another. A sales professional likely needs the information communicated differently than an engineer. The same logic applies for the small business owner, the seasoned passive investor, and the person who has never invested in real estate before. The key to your success is in recognizing how to communicate the information to each investor based on their unique background, understanding, and needs.

Moreover, you can display expertise without having done that specific thing for which you are raising money. That's what I did for my first money raise. Here's the story...

When I raised money for my first deal, I didn't have prior apartment investing experience. But I did have relevant experience in real estate from purchasing four single-family homes and teaching a real estate class. That experience, combined with my aligning myself with more seasoned team members, allowed me to qualify with investors in the expertise category.

You'll also gain expertise, build credibility, and even find investors from your thought leadership platform. Because of my podcast activities, something interesting happens upon the first meeting with investors. During my first conversations with potential passive investors a great majority of them say, "I feel like I know you well already, because I've been a long-time listener of your podcast."

That's great news!

Investing your time and maybe some money in a thought leadership platform is like purchasing an express lane ticket at Universal Studios. Sure, you could wait in line and still get to experience the ride, but it will take longer and, as a result, you won't get to enjoy as many rides. But when you purchase the express pass, you get to bypass the standby line and you also get to enjoy more rides! Similarly, investing your money and time into a thought leadership platform will help you find more deals and build more relationships at a faster pace than "waiting in line" like the majority of other aspiring apartment syndicators who don't have a thought leadership platform.

3. Personal Connection

The thought that people only invest with their analytical mind is bogus. We invest with emotion first; we analyze later. The key then becomes to establish a solid personal connection with potential investors.

Help yourself. Learn what they care about and see whether you can align with that thing in a genuine way. Don't know what they care about? Here is my go-to question, which I mentioned earlier: "What has been the highlight of your week (or weekend)?"

That simple question helps to uncover a few topics that are top-of-mind for them. They might say "making a business transaction," which will tell you that it's important to focus on the numbers and profitability more than other factors. Or they might say, "finally being able to get away with my family." That tells you that time is precious to them and perhaps you should focus on the "passive investment angle" with this type of person.

Ideally, to form a personal connection you want the investor to lead the conversation. You're simply there to answer any questions they might have, not give them an in-depth presentation on the benefits of passively investing in apartment syndications. Every investor you speak with will have a unique need, which means that there is a unique benefit of apartment syndications that can fulfill that need. Your goal is to identify that need and tailor all of the information you offer to that specific need.

In short, get good at having really good conversations!

Now all your bases are covered. You know that people will invest in your deals if they've known you for at least a couple years (especially relevant early on in your career), you've demonstrated your apartment syndication expertise, and you've formed a personal connection with potential investors. Now it's time to start finding potential passive investors.

What are you waiting for?

Get out there and start communicating!

CHAPTER 21

How to Find Passive Investors

At this point, you may be thinking...

"But, Joe, I don't have the right network to raise money, so what should I do?"

Five Ways to Find Passive Investors
If you can connect with this situation, or if you are simply looking to increase your network of potential passive investors, here are five proven solutions:

1. Build a Thought Leadership Platform
The more effort you put into building your thought leadership platform, the more relationships you will form. You will be transmitting to the world that you are a syndicator who is raising money from passive investors to purchase apartment buildings. As you grow and build a credible reputation, you will begin to attract interested parties.

I recommend creating an "INVEST WITH US" landing page on your website so that these interested parties can easily get hold of you. As a guide, you can check out my landing page at www.InvestWithJoe.com.

2. Join and Participate in BiggerPockets

Online communities, like BiggerPockets, that focus on real estate education tend to attract investors who are actually looking for opportunities. You aren't allowed to explicitly advertise deals or ask for money, except on the BiggerPockets Marketplace, which requires a paid membership, but you can convey the same message by posting valuable content – on the blog and in forums. A good "hack" is to post content that is based on your podcast or other thought leadership platform. Remember to create a strong, appealing biography page that includes a link back to your website. Those viewing your profile will always know that you're an apartment syndicator that raises money for deals.

3. Attend Meetup Groups and Consider Starting One of Your Own

Another method by which you can build relationships is through Meetup groups. You want to attend Meetups in your area and start your own group so you can host networking events. You aren't explicitly advertising for deals or for money, but rather are focused on building relationships.

In-person Meetup groups, or even conferences and other business events when approached correctly, can be one of the best places to form lifelong business relationships. To get the most out of an event, it's important to go in with a plan. Overall, there are two main approaches: the broad approach or the hyper-focused approach. Do you hand out as many business cards and have as many quick conversations as possible? Or do you spend time with one entrepreneur each day with the goal of forming a personal connection that results in a mutually beneficial relationship?

Every entrepreneur has his or her preference, and I'm sure people have achieved success with both approaches. However, from my experience of attending countless real estate events, here is the three-step approach that I have found to be the most effective.

STEP 1: Create one new relationship. Between the broad and hyper-focused approaches, I find the latter to be the most effective. At real estate-related events, I go in with the outcome of building one friendship per day. I don't see how many business cards I can hand out. I don't try to meet as many people as possible. I focus on creating one solid, personal relationship. If it's a multiday event, I build one relationship per day. As long as I leave the conference with my new friend, I consider it a success regardless of the immediate business outcome.

STEP 2: Ask personal questions. By approaching people attending real estate events in this manner, you are playing the long game, taking the time to actually learn about what this person has going on in their life from both a business and a personal perspective. The majority of the conversation should be focused on your learning about their goals, and most important, why they are attending the event. That last part is the most important, which is to ask them what they want to achieve by attending the event.

STEP 3: Follow up with those people you met at the event on LinkedIn and add value. When the conversation ends, I typically take some quick notes on how this person answered questions. (Usually they will attend events to overcome a challenge they face in their business.) When I get home after the event, I send them a colleague request on LinkedIn along with a personal message where I attempt to add value to their business.

This follow-up is very important. I don't just add them as a colleague. I take it one step further and send them a personal note based on their outcome for attending the event. In my message, I attempt to provide them with a solution to the challenge they said they are currently facing. If I cannot help them myself, or if we aren't in comparable phases in our businesses, I will connect them with someone else in my network.

The reason for this personal note where I proactively add value is to stand out in a sea of basic colleague requests. Also, if I go back to their profile years later, I will remember how I met them and what we talked about. I meet so many people that I usually forget how I initially met someone. This personal note technique acts as my external memory bank. LinkedIn keeps track of messages that people send back and forth all the way back to the message sent with the initial colleague request.

4. Volunteer
Find a nonprofit organization that aligns with your values, interests, and beliefs. Then put your best foot forward as a volunteer. Make sure that it's something you'll honestly enjoy doing. The main purpose is to give back. However, your secondary, business-related goal is to become a board member. It is likely that the other board members are going to be affluent. That is, a high net worth individual who is friends with other high net worth individuals. Once you've become a fellow board member, these individuals will likely be more interested in building a relationship with you outside of volunteering. They will want to learn more about your personal and/or business goals. This is a perfect transition into discussing your apartment syndication business.

The key to truly bonding with the board members is to NOT expect anything else in return than building a relationship. Your main goal isn't to attend your first board meeting and ask the members to invest in your apartment deals. The goal is to contribute to the organization by doing something that you genuinely enjoy. Then, slowly and organically, get to know other volunteers and board members.

Volunteering and becoming a board member is a long-term approach. However, it is an approach that I have successfully implemented, so I know it works. By volunteering for causes I believe in, I was able to build relationships with others that shared my beliefs, which resulted in millions of dollars in apartment investments. I am a board member for the nonprofit organization Junior Achievement in Ohio, as well as for the College of Media and Communications at Texas Tech University.

5. Build Personal Connections

As I mentioned earlier, the majority – if not all – of the investors on your first deal will be people you already know. These are family members, work colleagues, players on your intramural sports team (yes, I have investors whom I met while playing flag football), college friends, and anyone else with whom you have an existing relationship.

Create a list of all of your personal connections. Categorize each person based on how you know them. The goal is to get one person from each category to say, "Yes, I am interested in investing." Then, you can name drop that person to the rest of the individuals within their category if they give you permission. Human beings are social creatures. Therefore, if I know someone else who is interested in doing something, I am much more likely to do it, too.

"Oh, Joe is interested in investing? I know he's a smart, fiscally responsible guy, so I'll take a look at this, too." It's just how humans behave. So why not leverage human nature to build social credibility?

As an example of the people who could invest in your deals and where/how you could meet them, here is a list of the 12 investors on my first deal:

1. Advertising colleague: $311,000
2. Advertising colleague: $150,000
3. Texas Tech Alumni Advisory Board: $100,000

4. Brother's friend: $50,000
5. Brother's friend: $50,000
6. Advertising colleague: $32,000
7. New York City roommate (whom I found through Craigslist): $25,000
8. High school friend: $25,000
9. Flag football team: $25,000
10. High school friend's boss: $25,000
11. College roommate: $25,000
12. Texas Tech Alumni Advisory Board: $25,000

Between those 12 investors, I raised $843,000. The remaining equity, $317,500, came from brokers who were given 25% ownership. Total raise was $1,160,500.

Another really good book that offers practical tips, tactics, and strategies for raising private money is *Raising Private Capital* by Matt Faircloth.

Exercise: Using the five methods outlined above, create a spreadsheet and build an exhaustive list of potential passive investors. This is your passive investor database. For each individual, you want to log the following information in your spreadsheet:

- *First name*
- *Last name*
- *How we met*
- *Current investor (Y/N)*
- *Amount invested*
- *Estimated investment potential in next deal*
- *City*
- *State*
- *Address*
- *Email*
- *Notes*

BEST EVER APARTMENT SYNDICATION BOOK

Before speaking with these individuals, the basic information you really need is their name and email address. The additional information can be obtained during your introductory call, which will be discussed in the next section.

CHAPTER 22

THE COURTING PROCESS

The next step is to set up introductory calls with your list of potential passive investors, which can be accomplished easily enough using a fancy technology called email.

The purpose of the first email is to get the potential investor to agree to speak with you on the phone. Below is a template to follow. It's something that has worked really well for me. However, it shouldn't be used verbatim. It is just a guide.

Customize your email based on your understanding of and relationship with this person. For example, if you have a formal or business relationship with the individual, write the email using more formal language. If the person is a friend, make your email more informal.

Email Subject: Catch up on (Date/Time)?
Email Body: Hi XXX,
First off, I hope you're having a wonderful week and that (fill in with a personal reference about them, like "your job is going well at GM, your kid is doing well in basketball, or whatever...").

I'm writing to let you know that I've evolved my business to incorporate investors into the deals I do. As you might know I've (fill in with your personal experience in real estate). And, after doing that, I realized it makes sense to have a small number of people I know join me in the best deals I come across.

I'd love to meet with you and learn more about your financial goals to see whether I can help you reach them. It would be great to catch up, too.

Are you free (fill in date/time suggestions)?

Either way, I wish you the best and am looking forward to staying in touch.

(Your name)

(Company name and address/phone)

This template assumes that you have previous real estate experience to leverage. However, if that's not you, another approach you can implement is:

I'm writing an article for my blog about the lessons business professionals, such as yourself, have learned as they've evolved their careers. I'd like to include some of the lessons that you've learned in this article.

Schedule a phone call to interview them for the blog article. Refer to it as an article, because it will be more enticing. Then tell them that you will add them to your email list so that they will be notified when the blog article is live. This is a long-term play, because now that they are on your email list, you will send them an email when you have a new investment opportunity.

Once you have confirmed a date and time for the call, in a follow-up email, you want to attach a copy of your company presentation (which you created in Chapter 9). Here is the email template I use, but – again – personalize it accordingly.

Email Body: Hi XXX,
We are scheduled for (fill in with date/time).
   In the meantime, I've attached the (fill in with your company name) company overview to give you some background on my company.
   I'm looking forward to our conversation and will speak with you (fill in with date/time).
(Your name)
Attachment: Company Presentation

Before going into the specifics of what questions to ask during the call, here are three tips on the high-level approach to the conversation.

First, take a ton of notes. Every call that I do, I have a Word document open with the individual's name at the top and the date of the conversation listed below the name. During the conversation, I write out bullet points of what was discussed. That way, next time we have a conversation I can open up their Word document, see what we previously discussed, and bring up anything relevant on the current call. This approach is powerful, especially because you will be having repeat conversations with these individuals. Never underestimate just how impressed they will be that you remember them and what's going on in their lives. That happens simply because you bothered to take notes and by you bringing up information from previous conversations.

Second, this is a conversation, not a presentation. You might want to instantly dive into your PowerPoint presentation, but that automatically sets you up to lose. Instead, it should be a conversation about getting to know about the other person, identifying what their ideal investment looks like, and answering any questions they may have. That is why you send them your company overview prior to the conversation. This allows them to learn about your business so you don't have to go through it all – slide by slide – on the call.

Finally, since the purpose of the call is to get to know them and their investment goals, they should do the majority of the talking. Be an excellent listener! A great rule of thumb is for you to speak only about 30% of the time and listen 70% of the time. This goes for in-person meetings, too. You want them to feel like the most interesting person in the room. Become a great listener and make the conversation about the other person.

The only exception is if the person is obviously wanting you to lead the conversation. If that's the case, take the lead. However, the majority of the time, and I've had over 1,000 of these conversations, they'll do most of the talking. The more they talk, the more you're set up for success, because you learn more about them and their goals. That's like a golden ticket. When you know about their goals, you can match them up with an investment solution based on what is the best fit for them, which could mean them passively investing in your business or you introducing them to someone else.

So, with those three tips in mind, there are two main categories of questions you will ask the investor on the call:

1. What is your background?
Lead off the conversation by asking about their background – both personal and business. You want to learn about their investing background but getting to know them on a personal level and building rapport is equally important. Ask them, "What's been the highlight of your week?" or "What's the best thing to happen to you since the last time we chatted?"

Spend as long or as short on their background as you need to build rapport. Remember, if we like and trust someone, then we want to spend more time with that person. If we want to spend more time with them, then it's more likely that we will do business with them.

Also, you are deciding whether you want to partner with them as much as they are deciding whether they want to partner with you. It may not seem like that when you are starting out, but as you begin to grow you will become more selective with the investors you bring on board.

2. What are your investment goals?
After learning their background, transition into asking questions about their investing goals. My favorite question is "What does a good passive investment look like to you?"

First, this question lets it be known that you are only taking on passive investors. If someone wants a more active role, this question is a polite way to eliminate them (at least for now). But it also allows you to understand what is important to them. I've heard all sorts of responses, like "I want alignment of interest," "I want X% return," "I don't want to lose money," and "I want to be comfortable with you and the team that's calling the shots."

Based on their goals and what is important to them, you can focus your conversation with a potential investor on explaining the aspects of your apartment syndication business that will fulfill those needs.

You also want to determine what type of deal – if any – the investor prefers and how much money they might want to invest. I've found that the best approach is to ask, "if I find something that I think you'll be interested in, what would be the range of investment you're looking to do?"

I've found that these conversations can be as short as 8 minutes and as long as 30 minutes. After building a relationship over email with one such investor, I had an 8 minute conversation during which I learned about the investor's background. He asked, "What do you have?"

I responded with, "I happen to have a deal, and I'll share that information with you." He invested $100,000 in my deal!

Sometimes it's fast like that... or it could be a 30-minute conversation where a potential investor asks a lot of questions yet don't invest in the end. Which leads us to the next section...

CHAPTER 23

HEY, I OBJECT!

In Chapter 2, I explained that for you to become an apartment syndicator, you need either previous success in the business world or success in another real estate niche, and preferably both. However, regardless of how much you've achieved in business or real estate, you will still likely face objections from your investors. For example, if your background is in business, they may say, "Well, I see that you have prior success working for a larger corporation, but that doesn't make me feel any more comfortable giving you my money to invest in real estate."

Or, if your background is in a non-apartment-related real estate niche, they may say, "It is amazing that you've flipped all those properties, but you haven't done anything in the multifamily realm. I don't want to be your test subject."

How do I know?

I heard these things when I was starting out in syndication!

Aside from responding with "Just trust me," how do you overcome these objections? Especially since these objections are valid. Education, previous business experience, or non-apartment real estate experience is important, but if you haven't completed an apartment deal before, potential investors may hesitate. Therefore, to overcome these objections, like I said in a previous chapter, leverage the experience of your team and have alignment of interest with your investors.

How to Have Alignment of Interest with Your Investors

At this point you may think I sound like a broken record on this topic, but it's important, so I'm saying it again. Team members who will help you turn your lack of experience into a strength, as well as create alignment of interest, are a property management company, a real estate broker, and/or a local owner/mentor. However, the team member and the role they play in the deal results in varying degrees of alignment of interest. In fact, there are four different tiers of alignment of interest, with the lowest tier bringing the least alignment of interest and the highest tier bringing the most alignment of interest.

Tier 1 Alignment of Interest: In regard to the role in the project, the least valuable is simply finding a qualified person to partake in the project. While this does help with your lack of apartment syndication experience, it does not create an alignment of interest because they do not have their own skin (i.e., money) in the deal, nor are you providing them with equity in the deal.

Tier 2 Alignment of Interest: Bring on a qualified team member and provide them with a small piece of equity on the general partnership. Similarly, for the property management company in particular, you can ask them to reduce their property management fee by 1%. In return, you will provide them with a bonus at the sale of the property that is double or triple the amount of money they lost from the reduced property management fee. You get both the experience and the alignment of interest, because they are financially incentivized to ensure that it is a good deal and that it operates efficiently. However, they still do not have their own money in the deal.

Tier 3 Alignment of Interest: Bring on a qualified team member, provide them with a small piece of equity, and have them invest their own money in the deal. The alignment of interest is higher because now they have their own skin in the game.

Tier 4 Alignment of Interest: The most valuable is when you bring on a qualified team member, provide them with a small piece of equity, they invest their own money in the deal, and they bring on their own passive investors who invest in the deal. The alignment of interest is the highest in this tier because they have not only their own skin in the game, but their investors' skin to consider, too.

Also, if a team member is signing on the loan in any of the previous four scenarios, the alignment of interest increases substantially, as they would be personally liable if the project were to fail.

In regard to the team members, not all three will result in an equal amount of alignment of interest. The one who promotes the most alignment of interest is the property management company, because they are overseeing the day-to-day operations of the deal. The next highest is a local owner/mentor, because they have experience successfully completing apartment syndications. The real estate broker results in the least alignment of interest, because they won't have an ongoing role in the day-to-day operations. You can see that a property management company that invests their own money in the deal results in a greater level of alignment of interest than a local owner/mentor investing their own capital in the deal. Plus, a property management company and a local owner/mentor investing their own money in the deal results in a higher level of alignment of interest than a broker investing their own capital in the deal.

Another tactic in overcoming objections by potential investors is to leverage the experience of your mentor, an experienced syndicator who has already done what you are trying to accomplish. An applicable Tony Robbins' quote is that "success leaves clues." What he means by this is that you aren't the first person to ever live. Nor are you the first person to invest in or raise money for apartment communities. Therefore, you don't have to start from scratch. Instead, after you've found the best of the best in their given field as apartment syndicators, you can follow the breadcrumbs they've left behind so you can replicate their success. Their experiences can help you along the way, and you can leverage that experience to get the deal done, and to gain that credibility and alignment of interests that your investors are looking for. This alignment won't just help you with finding passive investors. It will also help you when you move forward to secure financing from a lender (Chapter 37) or during a best and final offer call with a seller (Chapter 32).

THE 49 COMMON INVESTOR QUESTIONS

In fact, you should expect objections from your investors and proactively address them before they even come up in the conversation. In addition to the lack-of-experience objection you will ultimately come across, there are 49 common objections – or questions – that I have experienced after having more than 1,000 conversations with potential investors. I've broken the objections into two categories: team-related and business-related questions.

Below, you will find each of the questions along with the thought process for formulating an answer. For each question, write out how you would answer it **before** entering into conversations with an investor. Don't recite the information provided below verbatim, because you need to base the questions on your unique situation.

Team-Related Questions
1. How much money will you have in the deal?
    - If an investor knows you have your own capital in the deal there is an extra level of alignment of interest. By not having your own money in the deal, you aren't exposed to the same level of risk as they are. Conversely, if you are on the limited partner (LP) side (i.e., you invest your own money in the deal), you will have the investors' best interests in mind, because if the LP loses money you lose money, too.
    - Starting out, you may not have any of your own capital to invest in the deal. If that is the case, as I mentioned in the previous section, you can create alignment of interest by having a qualified team member invest in the deal, having them bring their own investors to the deal, and/or having them sign on the loan.
    - You can also allocate a portion of your acquisition fee to investing in the deal.
2. How many of your investors have invested in multiple deals?
    - Having investors continue to come back to invest in future deals is a signal to potential investors that you have a proven track record of meeting and/or exceeding your projected returns. If you have done deals in the past, even if it's only one, mention how many investors have come back to invest in another deal. This happens more often than you might think, because this is a relationship-based business!
    - Obviously, if this is your first deal, you won't be able to leverage this fact to your advantage. Instead, you will focus on other factors to attract potential investors.
3. Do you have family and/or friends that invest in these opportunities?

- If you have family members investing in your deals, say yes and share a bit about it.
- As far as friends go, if I have a relationship with someone – even if I don't know them well or have known them for a short time – and they invest (which is technically all of my investors), I consider them a friend.
- Instead of just saying that you have friends investing in your deals, talk about your relationship with them. How did you meet them? How long have you known them? How has your relationship evolved over time? It may not seem relevant but maintaining relationships over an extended period of time with people who trust you enough to invest in your deals speaks volumes to your character. (Think about how you feel when you hear someone has had long-term friendships that have lasted the years. There is an immediate trust factor, isn't there? You think, "Hey, this must be a great guy or gal to have maintained friends like that.")

4. How many investors do you have in a typical deal?
    - It depends on the size of the equity raise, which is different for each deal.
    - Explain what the average investment size is (for my deals, it's $175,000), but that it will go up over time as investors reinvest.
    - Generally, returning investors will invest more. For example, I have an investor who invested $100,000 and $250,000 for two deals, and then invested $4 million, $6 million, and $6 million on deals three, five, and six. While this is an exception and not the norm, it is possible for an investor to make that large of a jump after investing in a successful deal.

5. What is your experience?
    - Before becoming an apartment syndicator, you should have a proven track record in real estate and/or business. Additionally, before you start reaching out to investors, you should have an experienced team.
    - Leverage both your previous experience and your team members' experience to convey your ability to successfully acquire and operate an apartment deal.
6. There are a number of apartment syndicators in your market. Why should an investor invest with your company?
    - The three main ways to differentiate yourself from other syndicators is through alignment of interest, transparency, and trust. I've given and will give plenty of examples for how to convey these three factors to your investors. Keep reading.
    - Identify and promote your unique skillsets. For example, I have a client who has 33 years of engineering experience. His company's tagline is "Engineering Conservative Deals." When speaking with investors, he talks about all the ways he uses his engineering background to offer conservative deals.
    - You can give back in the form of charity. But if you follow this approach, make it crystal clear that it will not impact investor returns because it is your personal money or money you make on the deal. Also, by having a thought leadership platform you are giving back by educating the greater real estate community.
7. How do you know your business partner?
    - They don't really care how you met your business partner. They want to know whether they are in good hands.
    - Explain how you met your business partner but, more important, why you selected them. Elaborate

on the partner's skillsets and how they complement your skillsets, which will set the deal up for success.

8. Where did your business partner work before?
   - Use the same logic from question 7 to formulate your response.
   - Your business partner should have past success in the apartment syndication field, because that's why you brought them on in the first place.
   - Their credibility, in combination with your and your team's credibility, will provide the investor with the confidence to trust you with their money.

9. Have you ever taken a deal full cycle?
   - If you haven't, explain that you've surrounded yourself with an expert team that has a proven track record of successfully taking deals through a full cycle.

Business Plan-Related Questions

10. Is the investment in a fund or in an individual asset?
    - Tell the investor that they will always know what they are investing in, which are stand-alone, individual apartment assets. Unless, of course, you are doing a fund, in which case you tell them that.

11. Do you currently have any deals under contract?
    - If you just put a deal under contract, mention that fact and invite investors to the new investment offering conference call (which I will outline starting in Chapter 40).
    - If you have a deal under contract and are well into the due diligence phase, mention how much money you've already raised (total dollar amount) and the amount you still need to raise (a percentage). For example, for a $10 million raise where you already have $5 million in commitments, you would say that you've already raised $5 million and have 50% remaining.

12. How do taxes work with this investment?
    - Assure them that you will provide your investors with a Schedule K-1 tax form at the beginning of the year.
    - As for the tax benefits, have them consult with their accountant for specifics. But, generally, investors are attracted to real estate because of depreciation. Most likely, the depreciation will be greater than the distributions paid out that year. In such cases, the investor won't pay taxes until they receive the proceeds from sale of the property. At that point, they will pay capital gains tax.
    - Some groups don't pass the depreciation onto the LP, but you should because it will be a selling point for your company.
13. What type of financing do you typically do with these assets? Rates, terms, loan-to-value (LTVs), and is it a recourse vs. non-recourse loan type?
    - The type of financing is determined on a case-by-case basis. However, you should still be able to describe your general financing structure (which you will learn about in Chapter 37).
    - Overall, the type of financing will be selected based on which option will maximize investor returns while minimizing risks.
14. How frequently will I get paid?
    - This is something you need to decide early on. Will you provide distributions on a monthly, quarterly or annual basis? My company prefers monthly distributions, but it is ultimately up to what you can deliver.
    - Talk to your property management company, which will likely be responsible for distributions, about what they are capable of delivering.

15. Can you walk me through the typical investment from an investor's point of view?
    – In Chapter 9, you created a company presentation, which should outline the details of your investment strategy. You're ready for this question!
    – Tell them about the preferred return percentage, profit splits, target total return and IRR, and the expected hold period.
16. Why should I invest in apartments?
    – The reasons you invest in apartments are outlined in your company presentation. Historically, there is less risk and better returns with real estate investments than with stocks and bonds, decreasing homeownership, increasing overall population, and an increase in renters and decrease in apartment vacancy rates.
    – That said, if they are asking this question, they probably aren't going to invest in your deal. It will take them some time to get comfortable with this asset class. That's where your thought leadership platform comes in – to educate people about the benefits of passively investing in apartment syndications.
17. Why did you decide to pursue this type of business model?
    – You are a value-add investor.
    – Generally, there are three business models – turnkey, distressed, and value-add. Turnkey has lower risk with lower upside potential. Distressed has higher risk with a higher upside potential. Value-add offers the best of both worlds (lower risk, high upside potential) without the drawbacks.
18. I want something that is low risk, so what are the major risk factors in investing in apartments?

- The deal, the market, and the team are the three major risk factors. There are a lot of bullet points below each of these, which will be outlined in the Private Placement Memorandum (PPM).
- To address these risk factors, conservatively underwrite deals, properly evaluate your target market, and hire qualified, experienced team members.
- Additionally, follow and align with the ***Three Immutable Laws of Real Estate Investing***: buy for cash flow, secure long-term debt and have adequate cash reserves.

19. Can you provide me with the worst-case scenario for the typical investment from an investor's point of view?
    - The worst-case scenario is we lose all your money. Then, we do a capital call, so you put more money in the deal and we lose that, too. This is not likely, but this is an investment and like all investments there are risks.
20. How long do I have to keep my money in the deal?
    - This depends on how long you and your team determine that the project will last. For my company, that is usually five years.
21. What happens if I want to use my invested money for something else? Can I pull it out?
    - The process for how/whether an investor can pull their money out of the deal will be outlined in the PPM. Generally, investors can sell their shares with the written consent of the general partner. They must find a qualified buyer who must be approved by the general partner.
22. How are you finding deals?
    - You will learn that there are many ways to find apartment deals in Chapter 27. If you've done a deal in

the past, tell investors how you found the one on the table currently.
23. What markets are you currently focused on?
    – You've already selected one or two target markets. Explain why you selected those target markets. If you come across a deal in a market that shares those characteristics, you'll pursue that deal in that market.
24. Do I have to submit my financials to anyone?
    – Not if the general partnership does a 506b offering; tell them yes if it is a 506c offering (learn more about what these two offerings are in Question 36).
25. Who owns the property?
    – Generally, the asset is owned by an LLC set up by the general partnership, and the investors buy shares of the LLC.
26. Who manages the property? Is it a third-party management company or do you do your own management?
    – The asset will be managed by a property management company that has a proven track record.
    – Give the investor some statistics on the property management company. How many doors do they manage? How long have then been managing apartments? Have you worked with them in the past?
27. What happens if the project fails?
    – While you don't expect the project to fail, the unexpected could happen. As with any investments there is risk in real estate investment. They will be presented with all the risks associated with the deal prior to committing capital to a specific deal. However, always make sure you address all potential risks upfront by conservatively underwriting and performing detailed due diligence, qualifying the market, and partnering with experienced team members.

28. What type of reserves are typically established with each property to shield investors from any potential capital pitfalls?
    - When underwriting a deal, you will include an operating budget and contingency budget to cover unexpected dips in occupancy, as well as higher than projected renovation and operating expenses, and lower than projected rent premiums.
29. What are my responsibilities?
    - The investor's sole responsibility is funding the deal. Also, if one of your investors agree to be a loan guarantor, they will need to sign on the loan.
30. What are your responsibilities?
    - Your team is responsible for finding deals, reviewing and qualifying deals, making and negotiating offers, coordinating with professional property inspectors, finding the best financing options, coordinating with attorneys to create the LLC and partnership agreements, traveling to the subject property's market to perform due diligence and market research, hiring and overseeing the property management company, and performing additional asset management duties, including lender conversations, overseeing the business plan, and ongoing investor communication.
31. How much of a role do you personally take in overseeing the acquisition and management of the asset?
    - You are responsible for overseeing the entire acquisition and ongoing management of the asset.
    - Your specific duties are outlined above in question 30 (and in greater detail in Chapter 45).
    - Take time to talk about how your team is qualified and who does what.

BEST EVER APARTMENT SYNDICATION BOOK

32. Do you guarantee a return?
    – No. You don't guarantee a return.
33. What happens if you can't make the projected cash flow?
    – Ideally, your projected returns are higher than the preferred return offered to investors. That way, if you don't achieve your projected returns, you can still distribute the full preferred return. However, if you are unable to distribute the full preferred return, it depends on what was agreed to. Usually, the distributions accrue until they can be paid out, with the sale of the property being the absolute latest. Of course, if the property loses money, they won't be paid out.
34. What does my money go toward?
    – What the money goes toward will be listed in the "Sources and Uses" section of the PPM.
    – Categories includes closing costs, renovation costs (which the lender might prefund or provide in draws, depending on the type of loan you secure), operating account funding, debt origination fee, the fees paid to the general partner (which are outlined in Chapter 5), and the loan down payment.
35. How do you make money?
    – Refer to Chapter 5 for a list of the various fees you can charge. All fees will be outlined in the PPM.
36. What is the minimum investment?
    – There will be a minimum investment amount based on the type of investment offering. For my company, we currently have a first-time minimum of $50,000 and $25,000 for returning investors but this will likely go up.
    – If you do a 506c offering, which means you can advertise your deals to the public, the minimum will

be much lower. You can cast a wide net, advertising online and in print in order to bring in as many accredited investors as possible (who may invest as little as $5,000), and hope to grow over time. If you are doing a 506b offering, which means you need to have a pre-existing relationship with your investors, you want a minimum investment amount. My company has set our minimum investment to $50,000, because the opportunity costs to focus on an investor who will invest less than that is too high.

37. How does the process work after you find an investment?
    - Once you place a deal under contract, the investors will be notified about the new opportunity and the date and time of the new investment offering conference call. During the conference call, the investor will learn about the business plan and more specifics on the deal. After the call, interested investors will verbally commit to invest in the deal and sign the required documentation to officially commit to the deal (we use DocuSign).
38. What are you doing about the market correction that's coming?
    - As you learned in Chapter 14, when buying apartments be sure to follow my **Three Immutable Laws of Real Estate Investing:** buy for cash flow, secure long-term debt, and have adequate cash reserves.
39. What contingency plan is there for these properties if we go into another recession?
    - Refer to the answer to question 38.
40. Are there any other asset classes that you focus on?
    - You might focus solely on apartments or you might focus on other asset classes at the same time (e.g., mobile homes, self-storage, single-family residences).

41. Is everyone notified at the same time when you have a new opportunity?
    - This also depends on your strategy. My company will notify all investors on our private email list at the same time when we have a new opportunity. Other investors may email their returning investors first. It depends on your preference.
42. Who will be my point person?
    - You will be the point person. You pride yourself on transparency and your communication timeliness. The investor will receive ongoing communications from you and any questions or concerns can be directed to you.
    - Or you might have another person, like an admin, who will be the point person.
43. Can I invest with an LLC?
    - Yes. Have them ask their CPA on how to invest with an LLC. You cannot advise them on how they should invest.
44. What type of reporting do your investors receive?
    - You will send recap emails.
    - The updates will include occupancy rates, unit renovation updates, and details on your rental premiums, capital improvement projects, relevant market updates, and resident events.
    - I provide recap emails each month and send out the financials on a quarterly basis.
45. What other questions do you typically get from investors?
    - Well, here's an entire list of questions potential investors will ask. Feel free to pick some questions from this list that they didn't ask.
46. From your perspective, as an educated and/or experienced investor, what other questions should I ask that I haven't already?

- Refer to the answer to question 45.
47. If I want to talk to other investors/references, is that something that you can arrange?
    - Yes. Be prepared to give references, so ask your investors beforehand.
48. If I want to invest, what would be the next steps?
    - The next steps are to add them to your private email list. Let them know that they will be notified if you have an opportunity.
49. Do you have any tips you can pass on to me as someone who is investing for the first time?
    - Focus on risk mitigation and conservative opportunities. Explain my Three Immutable Laws of Real Estate Investing (buy for cash flow, secure long-term debt, and have adequate cash reserves).

If these questions don't come up during pre-deal conversations, you aren't off the hook yet. Most – if not all – of these questions will come up as you are securing commitments after putting a deal under contract (more on securing commitments starting in Chapter 38).

CHAPTER 24

LAYING THE GROUND RULES

While investors' main motivation will be to NOT lose money, they are still highly motivated by the prospect of making a great return on their investment. That's why they'll ask a lot of questions about your payment structure during initial conversations. Hey, it's important stuff to know.

So how do you structure the deal?

THE TWO TYPES OF INVESTORS

The way you structure a deal with your investors will depend on the deal itself, but will also be based on your goals and those of your investors. The two main ways to structure a syndication partnership are with equity investors or debt investors.

Equity Investors – Equity investors participate in the upside of the deal; their capital remains in the deal until the conclusion of the business plan at sale. Usually, equity investors are offered a preferred return on their investment. The preferred return typically ranges from 2% to 12% annually, based on the experience of the general partnership, their team, and the risk factors of the project, as well as the investment strategy (which you will learn about in the next chapter).

For example, on a development deal or a highly distressed deal, the general partnership may offer a 12% preferred return. However, since the deal will likely have a lower or no return during the development or construction period, the preferred return would accrue during that period and be paid out to the investors in one lump sum or incrementally after the property is stabilized. Since these types of deals have more risk, the preferred return is higher. We'll get into this a bit deeper in a few pages. Just keep reading.

Here's the deal: You don't need to offer a preferred return to investors at all and, instead, could just do a profit split. However, I like to have a preferred return because it shows alignment of interest, since the equity investors receive a return before the general partners do.

Once the preferred return is hit the remaining profits are usually split between the equity investors and the general partners – 50/50 to 90/10 limited partner/general partner profit splits. A variation on the profit split is to include return hurdles, using return factors like internal rate of return (IRR) or cash-on-cash return. For example, on a recent deal we purchased, we had an IRR hurdle. In this deal, the equity investors are to receive an 8% preferred return and 70% of the remaining profits up to 13% IRR. Once the 13% IRR hurdle is passed, they are to receive 50% of the remaining profits. Usually IRR hurdles won't come into effect until the sale of the deal because the IRR is 0% until the equity investors get all of their initial investment back.

Equity investors are the most common type of investor in apartment syndication. And the most common equity investor structure is an 8% preferred return with a 70/30 LP/GP split.

Debt Investors – Debt investors receive a predetermined interest rate on a predetermined schedule (monthly or quarterly) and are paid that interest rate until the end of the term, at which time they will receive their initial investment amount back in full. The syndicator can pay back the debt investor after a refinance or by securing a supplemental loan. A supplemental loan is a financing option that is secured on top of the existing financing on the property that is typically available 12 months after closing the initial loan, assuming the value of the property has increased.

Compared with equity investors, debt investors do not participate in the upside of the deal, but they can receive a higher ongoing return and receive their initial equity back at an earlier date. For example, you can offer a debt investor a 12% interest rate for three years, at which point you refinance the property and return 100% of the investor's capital.

It is very difficult to return 100% of the capital back to the debt investor if they are bringing 100% of the capital. But, if they are bringing a portion of the capital to close (for example, they bring 50% and you bring 50%) or if you negotiate a longer loan length (for example, five to seven years), then you may have the ability of returning all of the capital to the debt investors through a refinance or supplemental loan.

Another drawback of debt investors is that you are saddled with that debt until you pay them back completely. If you don't, they get the property. In contrast, equity investors are not debt collectors. They are in for the long haul, good or bad.

Debt investors are the way for you to make the most money. Once you've returned all of the capital back to the debt investor, you have sole ownership of the deal.

If you take the debt investor route, you need to find a deal where you can increase the property value such that you can distribute the interest rate and return 100% of the capital to the debt investor after the agreed upon number of years. If you do, in the end you will have 100% ownership of the apartment.

THE STRUCTURE DECISION TREE

To create your limited partner compensation structure, follow the decision tree and the instructions below.

Do you have equity investors or debt investors?
- Circle one: Equity   Debt

If equity investors:
- Will you offer a preferred return?
    o Circle one: Yes   No

If yes to preferred return:
- What is the preferred return (2% to 12%)?
    o Fill in the blank: the preferred return is _____%
    o For example: the preferred return is 8 %
- What is the profit split after preferred return?
    o Circle one (LP/GP): 50/50
                              60/40
                              70/30
                              80/20
                              90/10
- Will you set a hurdle? If no, leave blank. If yes, what will be the factor of the hurdle (i.e., IRR or cash-on-cash return), at what percentage, and at what new profit split?
    o Fill in the blank: once the LP receives _____% _____, the profit split is ___/___ thereafter
    o For example: once the LP receives 13 % IRR , the profit split is 50 / 50 thereafter

If no to preferred return:
- What is the profit split? Based on the team's experience and the risk of the project and your business plan.
    o Circle one (LP/GP): 50/50
                              60/40
                              70/30
                              80/20
                              90/10

- Will you set a hurdle? If yes, what will be the factor of the hurdle (i.e., IRR or cash-on-cash return), at what percentage, and at what new profit split?
  - Fill in the blank: once the LP receives ____% _____, the profit split is ___/___ thereafter
  - For example: once the LP receives <u>13</u>% <u>IRR</u>, the profit split is <u>50</u>/<u>50</u> thereafter

If debt investor:
- What interest rate will I offer?
  - Fill in the blank: ____%
  - For example: <u>12%</u>
- What will be the length of the loan? (i.e., when will I return all of the debt investor's capital?)
  - Fill in the blank: ____ years
  - For example: <u>3</u> years
- How will I return all of the debt investor's capital?
  - Circle one: refinance
    supplemental loan
    buy-out
    other:

Use the decision tree to create an LP compensation structure, remembering to keep your investors' goals in mind. Run a few scenarios so you can get the hang of this.

PART 3: THE DEAL

PART 1: THE EXPERIENCE

KNOWLEDGE — Chapters 1-4
1. What is apartment syndication?
2. How to Get Started
3. What to focus on

GOALS — Chapters 5-6
1. How do you make money?
2. Set 12-month goal and long-term vision
3. Ultimate Success Formula

BRAND BUILDING — Chapters 7-12
1. Why you need a brand
2. Select a target audience
3. How to build a brand

MARKET EVALUATION — Chapters 13-16
1. 3 Immutable Laws of Real Estate
2. Evaluate 7 markets
3. Pick 1-2 Target Markets

PART 2: THE MONEY

BUILD TEAM — Chapters 17-19
1. Find core real estate team members
2. Hire a mentor or consultant

FIND CAPITAL — Chapters 20-24
1. Why will they invest?
2. Build passive investor database
3. Create partnership structure

PART 3: THE DEAL

YOU ARE HERE

FIND DEALS — Chapters 25-28
1. Set investment criteria
2. On-market vs. off-market deals
3. How to find your first deal

UNDERWRITING — Chapters 29-31
1. Information needed to underwrite a deal
2. The 6-step underwriting process

SUBMIT OFFER — Chapter 32
1. How to submit an offer on a deal
2. Best-and-final offer
3. Purchase sales agreement

PART 4: THE EXECUTION

DUE DILIGENCE — Chapters 33-37
1. 10 due diligence reports
2. Secure financing from lender

SECURE CAPITAL — Chapters 38-42
1. Create investment summary
2. New investment offering call
3. Secure investor commitments

CLOSE — Chapters 43-44
1. Closing process
2. Notify passive investors

EXECUTE BUSINESS PLAN — Chapters 45-46
1. 10 asset management duties
2. How to sell the apartment

CHAPTER 25

A DEAL WON'T QUALIFY ITSELF

One of the final steps before setting out to find your first apartment community to purchase is to understand how to qualify a deal.

There are many different names for this qualification process, including underwriting, financial analysis, financial modeling, and running the numbers. Whenever you hear one of these terms, the same process is being referenced. Generally, it is the process of analyzing the current operations and projecting the future operations of an apartment community so you can make the necessary assumptions to determine whether an offer is warranted. If an apartment deal "passes" the underwriting process, an offer is submitted. If the offer is accepted, the apartment syndicator enters into the due diligence phase, where the underwriting assumptions are confirmed (or disproven) and private money is raised in order to close on the deal.

Similar to the analysis of fix-and-flips, smaller rental properties, or even planning a wedding, there are many different approaches to running the numbers on an apartment community. But the critical point is that you perform some sort of analysis, as opposed to going with your gut or – possibly worse

– basing your investment decisions on the underwriting provided by the listing real estate broker.

The Three-Step Financial Analysis Process

My company uses a three-step approach to conducting financial analysis, which works brilliantly for us. First, we initially qualify a deal using our specific investment criteria. For the deals that pass this first step, we then perform a full underwriting using our custom financial cash flow model. Based on the results of our financial model, if the projected returns align with the goals of both our business and – more important – our investors, we will submit an offer and perform more detailed due diligence to confirm our underwriting assumptions prior to closing.

In this chapter, you will learn how to specify your initial investment criteria, and then briefly learn about the second two steps before going into more detail in later chapters. Pay attention. This is important to your success as an apartment syndicator.

Step 1 – Setting Investment Criteria: Setting your investment criteria will save you a lot of time. The underwriting phase of financial analysis is a lengthy process. At first, it may take you an entire day to fill out a financial model. As you practice, close deals, and become an underwriting expert, you can complete that process in a few hours. Nonetheless, it would be impossible to perform the full underwriting on every deal that comes across your desk or computer screen. In order to quickly eliminate potential deals from contention, you will initially screen deals using your investment criteria.

You have already established some of your investment criteria in previous chapters, but here are all of the four factors that you will use to initially screen potential apartment deals:

1. Investment Strategy

First, what is your investment strategy? If a property doesn't align with your investment strategy, it can be immediately eliminated. For the purpose of initially qualifying a deal, your business plan will define the type of asset you will pursue.

Generally, investment strategies fall into one of three categories: value-add, distressed, or turnkey. Back in Chapter 3, I mentioned that my business follows the value-add investment strategy and briefly described how the strategy works, which is why that is the focus of this book. It is at this point that I will explain why I believe that this strategy is the superior of the three.

Highly distressed properties are non-stabilized (i.e., occupancy levels below 85% and likely much lower) due to poor operations, tenant problems, outdated interiors or amenities, mismanagement, deferred maintenance, and the list goes on. Generally, investors who follow the distressed apartment investment strategy will take over the asset, address deferred maintenance, and install a new property management company to bring the property to stabilization. Then either they will implement procedures to further increase the apartment community's occupancy levels and/or rental rates or they will sell the property to a value-add investor.

The distressed investment strategy has a lot of upside potential due to forced appreciation. Usually, the asset is purchased below market value because of the low occupancy rates and rehab requirements. Once addressed, the value of the asset is increased drastically. However, there is also the downside of more risk.

The first risk is that the asset won't make money until the issues are addressed, which – depending on how distressed the asset is – could take years to complete. That means you'll need to find passive investors who are content with not receiving a return until the asset is stabilized or until the asset is sold. Additionally, since there are many variables to take into account before purchasing a distressed asset (e.g., setting a construction budget and costs of evicting unruly tenants), there are a lot more things that could go wrong.

The turnkey investment strategy is on the opposite end of the spectrum. A turnkey investor will purchase Class A properties that require minimal to no work after acquisition. These properties are fully updated to market standard and highly stabilized (occupancy levels above 95%).

So, the turnkey investor will take over the asset and achieve their projected cash flow from day one. As a result, there is much less risk involved in this strategy. However, there is also less upside in regard to forced appreciation, as the asset is already operating at its full capacity. Therefore, the value of the asset is highly dependent on the market's cap rate. If the cap rate goes up, the value of the asset goes down, and vice versa.

Remember my ***Three Immutable Laws of Real Estate Investing?*** One of those was buy for cash flow, not appreciation. While a turnkey investor may not intentionally purchase the asset with the expectation of natural appreciation (but I am sure that some do), if a downturn were to occur, the value of the asset would take a hit. Since there isn't much of an opportunity to force appreciation, a downturn will have the highest impact on this investment strategy, specifically in regard to the amount of capital distributed to the investors at sale.

Value-add investors, as the name implies, typically purchase stabilized (85% or higher occupancy) Class B or C assets that have the opportunity to be improved by adding value. Adding value means making improvements to the operations and the physical property through exterior and interior renovations in order to increase the income and/or decrease the expenses.

Since this investment approach falls between the two extremes, it minimizes the downsides and maximizes the benefits of the distressed and turnkey strategies. The risk is reduced because the majority of the large renovations (HVAC, roofs, siding, plumbing, foundation) are up-to-date – or are at least not in complete disarray – and the asset is already stabilized. There may be the need for a few large projects, but generally speaking, the majority of the work is put into upgrading the unit interiors. Then, at the same time, the upside is higher because of the ability to force appreciation. Therefore, passive investors have the upside of both a strong return during the life of the project and a large distribution at sale.

Here is a chart that summarizes the three investment strategies:

Investment Strategy	Occupancy at Purchase	Property Condition	Returns	Risk to LP
Distressed	Non-stabilized (less than 85%)	Poor operations, tenant problems, very outdated interiors, mismanagement, deferred maintenance	Large profit at sale	High (may lose initial investment)
Turnkey	Highly stabilized (95% or higher)	Fully remodeled to market standards	Lower ongoing returns, little to no profit at sale	Low (capital preservation)
Value-Add	Stabilized (85% or higher)	Outdated units or amenities, opportunity to add value	Strong ongoing returns and upside potential at sale	Moderately low (capital preservation and cash flow)

Like most decisions in your syndication business, determining which investment strategy to use depends on the return goals set by you and your investors, your risk tolerance, and having a team that can execute the business plan.

Are your investors content with tying up their capital for a year or two with minimal to no cash flow to potentially achieve a large, lump sum return, and does your team have the experience to bring a highly distressed asset to stabilization? Then you can consider the highly distressed investment model.

Do your investors want a low-risk place to park their money, receiving a return that beats inflation and without the upside of a large distribution at sale? Then you can consider the turnkey approach.

If your investors want the positives of both approaches without the risks of the highly distressed model and the lower returns of the turnkey model, then the value-add model is the approach for you! That's why this is the investment strategy my company implements.

Therefore, for the value-add business plan, you will be searching for **B or C class apartment communities** with an **85% or higher economic occupancy rate** that you've identified as having the opportunity to **add value**.

2. Location

The second part of your investment criteria is the location. You have already determined your one or two target markets in Chapter 15, so you will also use those to initially screen deals.

Likely you've selected a market that is either in or near a large city. This is advantageous when acquiring deals because you will have access to a larger pipeline of deals. Additionally, you will have a larger buyer pool once you're ready to put the apartment back on the market.

Exercise: Fill in the blanks with your one or two target markets:

- *Market 1: _____*
- *Market 2: _____*

3. Year Built

The next step is to define the age range of the apartment communities you will pursue. Generally, this will be based on your business plan. If you follow the highly distressed approach, you will be looking at class D properties that were built 30 or more years ago; for the turnkey or newly remodeled approach, you will be looking at Class A properties that were built within the last 10 years; for the value-add approach, you will be looking at Class B or C properties that were built 10 to 30 years ago.

Properties built outside of your specified age range, plus or minus five years, can be immediately eliminated.

What is the age range of properties you will set as your investment criteria? Real estate brokers and all other information pertaining to a property will state the age as a year, so take the current year and subtract the age range to determine a range of dates:

- *Age of Apartment Community: _____ to _____*

4. Number of Units

The last part of your investment criteria is the number of units. The number of units you decide on depends on how much money you are capable of raising and the cost of acquisition per unit based on your target market and business plan.

Back in Chapter 21, you created a spreadsheet listing out your passive investors, gaining verbal interest and calculating the total potential amount of money you are capable of raising.

Using that figure, you can determine the maximum project cost you can afford. Generally, you will need to raise 35% of the all-in price of the asset, which goes toward the down payment for the loan, rehabs, financing fees, closing costs, GP fees, and the operating fund/contingency account. That means you can calculate a maximum project cost by dividing the total potential amount of money you can raise by 35%. For example, if you can potentially raise $1 million, your maximum project cost is $2.86 million.

Next, you need to determine the cost per unit of recent sales of properties that meet your investment criteria. You can easily obtain this information yourself by looking up recent sales or you can get it from your broker.

Divide your maximum project cost by the cost per unit and you will have a ballpark estimate of the number of units you can purchase. If your maximum project cost is $3.3 million and the ballpark cost per unit is $50,000, then the maximum number of units you can purchase is 66. Since this is just an estimate based on recent sales, in this example if a property has more than 90 or 100 units, it can be immediately eliminated (or you can pursue a creative financing structure strategy like seller financing, a land contract, or a master lease).

Exercise: On your own by going to the local county auditor or appraiser site or by reaching out to your real estate broker, determine the cost per unit of recent apartment sales that fit your business model. Then, using the total amount of money you can potentially raise, determine the maximum number of units you can purchase.

- *Number of units:* _____ *units*

Now that you have determined your investment criteria, you can quickly qualify any deal. If the deal doesn't meet your investment criteria, you can pass and save yourself hours or even days in wasted effort and precious time.

As I briefly described in Chapter 9, when explaining the company presentation, the general financial analysis follows a 100:30:10:1 process. For every 100 deals you look at, 30 will meet your investment criteria. That means that by defining your investment criteria, you are eliminating approximately 70 deals after a few minutes, as opposed to eliminating 70 after performing the underwriting. In other words, you will be saving at least 210 hours... or over five 40-hour work weeks... of your time!

Exercise: Fill in the blanks below for a complete picture of your investment criteria:

- *Investment Strategy:* _____
- *Occupancy Level:* _____ %
- *Property Class(es):* _____
- *Market 1:* _____
- *Market 2:* _____
- *Age of Property:* _____ *to* _____
- *Number of Units:* _____ units

These criteria will be used when you begin finding deals, which you will learn about in the next chapter.

Step 2 – Underwriting: If a deal meets your investment criteria, the next step is underwriting. For the underwriting process, you will obtain financial information from the seller, input that data into a financial model, and then determine how you will operate the property after acquisition, with the purpose of concluding whether you should submit an offer. I have dedicated an entire chapter (Chapter 31) to outlining this process in more detail.

In Chapter 4, I explained that the majority of apartment syndicators qualify a deal by focusing on the cash-on-cash (CoC) return and the internal rate of return (IRR). Both of these factors are outputs of the underwriting process. However, since you won't have the property under contract at this point, some of the inputs into your underwriting will be assumptions. Therefore, the CoC return and IRR are **projections** as opposed to **exact values**. The goal of your first iteration of underwriting is to input as much accurate information that's available, make educated assumptions for the rest, and determine whether the results warrant further investigation or, if it is a competitive situation, the submission of an offer.

Again, of the 100 deals you find, 30 might meet your initial investment criteria. Of those 30, expect that an average of 10 will meet your return goals and qualify for an offer. Let me repeat that: for every 100 deals you find, expect 10 to qualify for an offer.

<u>Step 3 – Due Diligence</u>: Once you have a property under contract, the next step prior to closing is to perform detailed due diligence. This is a topic to which I've dedicated Chapters 33 to 35. The purpose of the due diligence process is to confirm the assumptions made during underwriting so you can determine whether the deal still meets your investment goals.

Due diligence requires a variety of inspections and financial audits that you will perform. But you won't be on your own. The process involves your team and third-party contractors, as well as an intensive rent and sales comparable analysis. Once you've confirmed (or disproven and adjusted) your assumptions, the resulting return figures are still only projec- ey will just be much more accurate than the returns d during the underwriting phase.

Based on the results of your due diligence, you will either close on the deal, renegotiate the contract, or cancel the contract. Of the 10 deals that pass the underwriting phase and on which you make an offer, an average of ONE will pass this intensive analysis and close.

A typical timeline of these three steps is as follows:

1. **Investment criteria (six months to two years or more):** Setting your investment criteria involves selecting an investment strategy and a market. First, you must educate yourself on the various investment strategies, which you've initiated by reading this book. Also, you need to know how much money you are capable of raising and the return expectations of your passive investors in order to determine the size of apartments you are capable of pursuing. This part can take anywhere from a few months, if you already have a strong network of prospective investors, to more than a year if you are starting from scratch. You also need to select a target market, which can take anywhere from a few weeks, if you are investing locally, to a few months if you need to travel out-of-state. During this time, you will also begin building your brand and the rest of your team. Overall, depending on your situation, it may take anywhere from six months to a few years to get to the point where you are ready to start underwriting deals.

2. **Underwriting (a few weeks to a few months):** Before you can underwrite a deal, you need to find a deal first. It may take at least six months for your marketing campaign to begin bearing fruit, and maybe even longer to build a trusting relationship with a real estate broker. But once you find your first deal, the entire underwriting process will take you about a week or two when you

are starting out. Not only will you need to gather all of the information in order to build your financial model, but you will want to visit the property in person as well. Then you will need to submit and negotiate an offer price, which could take a day or a few weeks, depending on the deal and the seller.

3. **Due Diligence (60 to 90 days):** Once you have a property under contract, you will have the remaining time until the closing date to perform your due diligence. Generally, the closing date is 60 to 90 days from the contract date.

Now that you've set your investment criteria and have a basic understanding of the qualification process, let's start looking for deals! (I know... exciting, right?)

CHAPTER 26

Your First Time Is Always the Most Challenging

Before continuing with the content in this book, let's pause for a moment to compliment you on your progress.

So far, you've:

- Learned the apartment syndication terminology
- Set your apartment syndication one-year goal and created your long-term vision
- Launched your real estate brand to establish yourself as a credible apartment investor
- Selected one to two target apartment markets
- Surrounded yourself with an all-star real estate team
- Built a database of and had conversations with potential passive investors
- Selected your apartment syndication investment strategy

All of these accomplishments will contribute to your ability to find and ultimately close on your first deal.

In the next few chapters, you'll learn about the two main types of deals, how to find each, and how to determine which deals to underwrite and which deals to pass on.

On-Market Deals vs. Off-Market Deals

There are two main types of real estate deals: on-market and off-market. On-market deals are apartment communities that are listed by a real estate broker. Conversely, off-market deals are apartment communities whose owner is interested in selling, but – for one reason or another – isn't represented by a real estate broker.

Generally, if you want to find the best investment, focus on sourcing off-market deals. It is true that on-market deals are easier to find because they will be widely marketed by the listing real estate broker. However, you will likely have to pay more for an on-market opportunity due to the competition between multiple interested parties. Conversely, off-market deals are more difficult to find, but the benefits make the juice worth the squeeze. In fact, off-market deals are beneficial to both you as the buyer and the seller. By understanding these benefits to the owner, you put yourself in the best position to negotiate with pure intentions since both parties will benefit. The better you are able to communicate these benefits to the seller, the better chance you have of getting the property under contact. (Get good at having conversations.)

Apartment owners will benefit from doing an off-market deal in two main ways. First, they save money because they aren't paying a real estate broker's commission. Generally, commercial real estate brokers will charge a percentage of the purchase price up to a certain sales price, and then charge a flat fee for apartments above that certain sales price. On average, a real estate broker will charge 3% to 4% for apartments less than $8 million. For apartments above $8 million, they will charge a flat fee of $150,000. So, at a purchase price of $5 million, the owner will save anywhere from $150,000 to $200,000, or save $150,000 on a purchase price above $8 million.

Second, off-market deals are less hassle for the owner. There are no property tours with multiple interested parties. There are no multiple question-and-answer sessions with prospective buyers. There aren't any random people poking around their property disturbing the residents. And there are no rumors floating around about the apartment community being sold, which could negatively affect resident and/or vendor relationships.

Also, compared with on-market deals, there are three ways that you benefit by doing an off-market deal. First, you will save money. When real estate brokers list a property on-market, their main job is to find the highest-paying buyer who will close. As a result, and especially in competitive markets, you will have to submit a much higher offer price to increase your chances of being awarded a contract. However, with an off-market deal, you bypass the competitive bidding scenario. You work directly with the owner and negotiate a fair price that isn't artificially inflated.

Next, you have more opportunities for creative financing with an off-market deal. By working directly with the owner, you can identify their pain points, goals with the transaction, and what they ultimately want out of the deal. With this information, you can creatively structure your offer to meet their goals.

Finally, because off-market deals are harder to find and have less competition, they are perceived to be better deals in the eyes of your passive investors. The general partner then carries more credibility and expertise for securing an off-market opportunity.

An owner's willingness to sell their apartment building/community off-market will come down to how it will benefit them. Additionally, winning or losing a deal (both on-market and off-market) comes down to five other factors:

1. **Price**: The highest price doesn't necessarily always win, but it is a factor the seller will take into account. Keep that in mind when formulating a purchase price, especially in competitive situations.

2. **Terms**: All other things being equal, a seller may decide to go with the offer that has the best terms, like a non-refundable earnest deposit, all-cash offer, or waiving certain due diligence items.
3. **Relationships**: Having high-quality relationships with real estate brokers and local owners not only helps you find deals, but also helps you close on deals. If you have a good relationship with the owner or listing real estate broker, they are that much more likely to award you the deal.
4. **Team structure**: You can win or lose a deal based on your team structure. For example, some owners won't sell their apartment communities to syndicators who don't have an in-house management team. If you don't have an in-house management team, the seller has the perception that your company isn't as integrated as needed to initially qualify a deal. While I believe this to be bogus, especially because of the quality of the management company we work with, this is something you may come across. In fact, this happened to my company once.
5. **Underwriting**: You may lose out on a deal if you aren't able to identify value-add opportunities. If another syndicator found an opportunity to add value that you didn't, then they can purchase the apartment at a lower price while still getting the same or higher returns than you will.

If you can sufficiently convey the benefits to the owner, as well as address the five additional factors that impact your ability to win the deal, you'll succeed in creating a win-win scenario for both parties and add a new apartment to your portfolio.

Chapter 27

How to Find Your First Apartment Deal

Just as there are different benefits and drawbacks to the two types of deals, the approaches for finding on-market deals and off-market deals also differ.

One of the team members you brought on was a real estate broker. Once you are ready to start finding deals, you should send your real estate broker your investment criteria and ask them to subscribe you to their apartment lists in your target market. That way, any current or future listing that meets your investment criteria will automatically be sent to you via email.

Before and as you begin to receive deals from the real estate broker, implement the tactics outlined in Chapter 19 for how to win over the real estate broker. As a refresher, those four tactics are:

1. Offer a consulting fee
2. Drive to the real estate broker's recent sales and tell them how those apartments compare with your investment strategy
3. Provide information on the amount of money you can raise and the mortgage brokers you have spoken to
4. Frequently follow up with the real estate broker by email at the very least

On-market deals are highly marketed by a listing real estate broker. You won't be the only investor looking at the deal, so not only do you need to move quickly, but the price may be bid up to such a high degree that the return projections fall outside of the return goals of you and your investors. Additionally, since this is a passive approach, you have no control over the number of deals you're sent. It's solely based on the number of owners who decide to list their property with an agent. Some weeks you may see a lot of deals, but then you may go a month without receiving any.

To get a more predictable deal flow, you want to pursue off-market opportunities. Generally, there are two ways to find off-market deals. You either speak with an owner directly or speak with someone who knows the owner, like a wholesaler, your real estate broker, or a friend. Ideally, you speak directly with the owner every time, but that's not a reality. Sometimes, there is a middleperson who makes an introduction. These middlepeople can be very valuable, because by cultivating these relationships, you can have a quick and continuous source for off-market deals.

10 Ways to Find Off-Market Deals

Since these are the only two ways to finding off-market deals, your tactics should target owners directly or people that know the owners, and nothing else. Here are 10 ways that either I or other apartment investors have used to find and close on off-market deals:

1. Direct Mail Campaigns

A direct mail campaign is when you send out a batch of letters to apartment owners with the purpose of negotiating and putting the property under contract. When evaluating a target market in Chapters 14 and 15, you created a list of 200 properties, along with the owners' contact information. Since most of the work is already done, pull from this list the properties that meet your investment criteria and perform a direct mail campaign to the owners.

After exhausting – or in combination with – your initial list of 200 properties, here are the best practices for building a direct mail list. First and foremost, focus your direct mail campaigns on properties that meet your investment criteria, which you defined in the previous chapter.

There are many sources that you can use to build mailing lists. ListSource is a great tool for creating larger lists, as are DirectMailTools and Open Letter Marketing. My consulting clients have used these resources for automated direct mail campaigns.

Local title companies are also a good resource for obtaining a list. If you are lucky and find the right real estate broker, he/she can send out direct mail campaigns on your behalf. The point here is that regardless of the method you decide to pursue, be sure to build a list of properties that meet your investment criteria.

Additionally, to increase the chance of finding an owner interested in selling, you want to mail to properties where the owners are motivated to sell. These owners may be motivated to sell their apartment building/community because they are distressed and want out (i.e., have tenant issues, maintenance or capital expenditure issues, management issues), they are at the end of their business plan, or they implemented a different business plan (i.e., they purchased the apartment building for cash flow and didn't add value and/or only increased the rents organically). It could be that the owners want to sell because they are ready to move into another area of investing, for example big commercial deals. (You won't know their reasons until you speak with them one on one... or your real estate broker does.)

Here is a list of ways to locate motivated apartment owners:

1. **Driving for Dollars** – If your target market is local, you can drive around the market and look for apartment communities that show signs of distress. Examples would be poor landscaping, obvious deferred maintenance, signs offering rent specials, broken windows, peeling or fading paint, or an apartment that stands out from surrounding properties. Find the owner's contact information and give them a call or send them a direct mailer.
2. **Eviction Court** – Locate your local eviction court and obtain a list of apartment owners that are evicting residents. Evictions are a major headache for real estate owners in general, so they may be extremely motivated to sell. Typically, the eviction list is located on the local county's Clerk of Courts website.
3. **Building Code Violations** – Locate a list of apartment owners who recently received a building code violation from the city.
4. **Delinquent Taxes** – Locate a list of apartment owners who are delinquent on their taxes. Unless you are building a list from scratch, most of the automated direct mail list providers will allow you to set "delinquent taxes" as a criterion. If you are building a list from scratch, information on the apartments with delinquent taxes can be found on the local county's Clerk of Courts or Sheriff's Office website.
5. **Out-of-State Owners** – Owning an out-of-state apartment community won't necessarily indicate a motivated owner. However, there is a higher chance that an out-of-state owner hasn't maintained the asset or managed the property management company effectively compared with an in-state owner whose apartment community is right around the corner.

6. **View the Profile Picture on Apartments.com** – A creative way to identify motivated sellers of potential value-add apartments is by looking at the profile picture on the Apartments.com listing. If the apartment was newly renovated, the owner will show off those updates online to attract residents. If there is only one picture available, that may indicate that the interiors and/or exteriors are outdated. If there are pictures of the interiors and exteriors available, scroll through them to see whether the apartment is updated. If the interiors are old, you've identified a potential value-add deal.

Those are the six main methods, but other creative strategies include:

7. **Property Owners Whose Tax Assessments Went Way Up This Year** – Search for an apartment on the local county auditor or appraiser site and locate the annual tax data. Most auditor or appraiser sites will list the annual taxes paid each year. If the taxes paid in the most recent year are significantly higher than those for the previous year, the owner most likely had a tax assessment. Taxes are one of the largest expenses paid by the owner, so if they had a significant increase, they may be motivated to sell.

    In fact, you can go on the auditor or appraiser site to see when the local city will be performing new tax assessments on commercial real estate. Then conduct a direct mail campaign to the apartment communities that meet your investment criteria, making sure to mention the fact that the taxes were just increased.

8. **Expired Apartment Listings** – Expired apartment listings are those that were listed for sale by a real estate broker and weren't sold by the end of the period specified in

the contract between the owner and the real estate broker. The best way to locate apartment listings that have expired is on the MLS. Ask your real estate broker to send you a list of expired listing for the past 12 months.

9. **Properties That Are Likely Owned without Debt (Purchased 20 to 30 Years Ago)** – Owners who own their apartments free and clear may be willing to sell their property at a lower price, or they may be willing to accept creative financing terms, like seller financing. This can help sellers in a big way come tax time! Have a chat with your tax person about that.

   There are a few ways to locate apartments that are owned free and clear. If you are creating a list with a service like CoStar, an automated direct mail provider, or the MLS, you will have the option to apply a filter for apartments that do not have a mortgage. Another approach is to locate the property on the local auditor or appraisal site and compare the "owner name" with the "mailing name." The mailing name is usually the name of the company that holds the debt. So, if the mailing name is the same as the owner name, the property is owned free and clear. Also, you can search for properties that were purchased over 20 years to 30 years ago, because the owner will have likely paid off the debt.

10. **Health Code Violators** – The local Clerk of Courts website will have a list of all the properties in the county with health code violations.

11. **Owners Facing Foreclosure** – The list of apartment owners facing foreclosure can be found on the local Sheriff's Office website.

12. **Owners Late on Loan Payments** – The list of apartment owners who are late on their mortgage payments can be found through services like ListSource and CoStar. Some

local Clerk of Courts or auditor sites may have a list of owners who are 30, 60, or 90 days late on their mortgage.
13. **Section 8 Approved Properties** – Locate the local city's HUD website to obtain a list of section 8 approved properties. These properties are likely rented below market rates and, depending on the local regulations, can be converted to become regular apartments.
14. **Properties with Liens** – A list of apartments with liens can be found on the local Clerk of Courts website.

A word about these strategies...
Again, you might be able to use the criteria on ListSource, CoStar, or other related services to identify the characteristics of a motivated seller. But some of these strategies will require extra research – both online and in-person – on your part. And if you have trouble finding a particular list in your local market following the instructions above, conduct a quick Google search, because not all counties and cities record their property data in the same manner.

Next, you need to create a marketing piece to send out to the apartment owners from your list. There are nearly an infinite number of approaches to a direct mail campaign. Variables include the message, frequency, letter type, and color, as well as the envelope type and color.

The most successful direct mailers A/B test different mailer types to determine which is the most effective. Select a few different mailer types, send them out to owners, and record the success rates of each. Whichever performs the best, continue sending that one out. For those mailers that perform poorly, change a variable and continue to send them out. Log the success rates. As time goes on, you will find the best combination of variables that results in the highest success rate.

For starters, here are two direct mailing templates I've used:

1. Template #1

    Dear Recipient Name,
    I am the acquisition coordinator for _____. Our portfolio consists of over _____ apartment units, all acquired within the last _____ months. With one of our principals based in _____, we are looking to expand to this area. We are familiar with your apartment complex, (name complex), and we would like to discuss purchasing this property. Please reach out if you would like to discuss further. My email is _____ and my cell phone number is _____.
    Sincerely,

2. Template #2

    Dear Recipient Name,
    I am interested in purchasing your apartment community. Are you interested in selling?
    I currently hold a portfolio of apartments similar to yours and am looking to add more.
    Please contact me at your earliest convenience so we can discuss the sale of your apartment community.
    Call me directly at _____ or email me at _____.
    If you are not interested in selling at this time, please accept this inquiry as the highest compliment to your investment.
    I look forward to hearing from you.
    Sincerely,

The important point you want to get across to the owners is that you are interested in buying their property and that you are an experienced investor who is able to close. Again, if you don't currently own any properties yourself, leverage the experience of your team. For example, "my property management company manages 1,000 units in the market" or "my partner (who can be your mentor or consultant) controls 1,300 units across the country."

Additionally, you will need to create a script to use as a guide as phone calls start coming in. An example script is provided below:

> *Hi. My name is (your name). Thank you for responding to my letter. As I said, I work for a group of investors, (your company name). We were driving around your neighborhood and wanted to know whether there would be any interest in selling?*

Now, you would think that because they called you, they are interested in selling. Unfortunately, some of the callers will, politely or aggressively, tell you that they aren't interested in selling and/or ask to be removed from all future mailing campaigns.

If the caller is aggressively asking to be removed from the list, politely thank them for their time, hang up, and immediately remove them from the list.

If the caller is polite but says that they aren't interested in selling at this time, find out a little bit more information as to why they won't sell. Figure out why they aren't interested with the purpose of trying to identify a pain point or things that are holding them back. This will help you identify ways that they will benefit from selling the property. For a refresher on this topic, refer back to Chapter 15, where you learned to visit properties in person. You should have made a note of something noteworthy about the property. You want to leverage this information when chatting with the owner (e.g., the property was in distress, the property was under-rented) to identify a potential pain point.

For example, maybe you discover that they are an owner-operator who doesn't like being a property manager. Or they won't want to incur a capital gains tax by selling. Or maybe they aren't interested in selling now, but they may be interested in six months. Depending on their response, there may be a creative way to structure the deal so that you can solve their problem.

If they still aren't interested or you cannot identify any pain points, thank them for their time and hang up. However, you aren't done yet. Unless they specifically asked you to remove them from future mailing campaigns, the next step is to mail them a follow-up letter saying:

> **Thank you for your time when we spoke on (date you called). As I said, I work for (your company name). I will follow up on (date) and I look forward to speaking with you then.**

The next time you call them, you can start the conversation by referencing your previous call and the follow-up letter.

If they are interested in selling, congratulations. But you're only part way to your goal. Now you need to extract more information from them about the property.

At this point, the two main goals of the conversation are to get the owner to provide you with the trailing 12-month profit and loss statement (T-12) and the current rent roll. That is the information you will need in order to underwrite the deal and determine a fair offer price (more on how to do this and what a T-12 and rent toll are in the next chapter). Additionally, here are four other questions my company will ask during initial conversations about a potential deal:

1. What capital expenditure projects have been completed since you acquired the property?
2. When did you purchase the property?
3. Why are you selling?
4. What is your desired approximate sales price?

Regardless of whether the owner is or isn't interested (with the exception of the aggressive caller), focus on building rapport. During the course of the conversation, make sure you talk in terms of their interests in order to begin building a relationship. If they are interested, this will help you during the negotiation process. If they aren't interested at this time, they will remember you when you call back.

The key to a successful direct mail campaign is consistency. Decide with what frequency you will mail to owners – monthly, quarterly, every six months – and commit to that system. Sometimes, you may receive a hit on your first mailer, while other times it won't be until you've been mailing to the same owner for a year that you receive a sign of interest.

If you've conducted multiple direct mail campaigns (say three to four mailers) and aren't receiving enough responses, another strategy is to invite them to your Meetup group (or if they are out-of-state, invite them to your automated webinar), rather than asking to purchase their property. Tell them you will be presenting information that will add value to their business. For example, 10 ways to increase NOI on your apartment building. From there, build a relationship with them so that when they are ready to sell, you are the first person they reach out to.

My final word on both the direct mail campaign and subsequent conversations is that they are an iterative process. If you've never spoken to an owner on the phone before, don't expect to be perfect at first. Practice, specifically in regard to overcoming their objections, see what works and what doesn't, and adjust your script accordingly.

2. Cold Calling and Texting

Another way to generate apartment leads is through cold calling. Pick up the phone and call the owners of properties in your market. You can start with the owners from your

200-property spreadsheet and expand from there, calling the motivated apartment owners located using the methods above instead of or in combination with a direct mail campaign. In some markets, you can find the owner's phone number on the county auditor's site. If not, there are many paid services you can use, like ListSource or CoStar.

The approach to speaking with apartment owners when cold calling is the exact same process used to screen phone calls that come from a direct mail campaign. Refer to the process outlined in the previous section. However, you will need to tweak the opening statement script. Owners will be quite perplexed if you reference a non-existent direct mailer!

A unique twist on cold calling is cold texting. In fact, an investor I interviewed on my podcast, James K., closed on two apartment communities by sending the owner a text! His initial text message script is "Hi. I'm a prominent investor in (insert target market). I saw your property at (insert property address) and am interested in buying it. You can sell it directly to me without any broker's commission. Would you like to talk further?" Listen to episode 1273 of my podcast, Best Real Estate Investing Advice Ever, for more details on this unique cold-texting strategy.

3. Team Members

Some of your team members – real estate broker, property management company, and mentor – can be great sources for off-market deals. A main part of their job is to cultivate relationships with apartment investors, so they will be one of the first people to know if an owner or another apartment syndicator is motivated or is preparing to sell their property. Obviously, your team members will likely have relationships with other apartment investors, so it is your job to build a solid relationship with them so you are the first person they contact when they have an off-market deal.

4. Thought Leadership Platform

Your thought leadership platform not only attracts team members and private money but can be used as a source for off-market deals as well. With a podcast, blog, and/or YouTube channel, you will form relationships with your guests and build a large audience, while at the same time conveying your interest in purchasing apartment communities. With a Meetup group, you'll network face to face with attendees and speakers who are active in real estate investing. You'll be reaching both owners directly and the professional that know owners (which are the only two ways that you can find off-market deals).

Therefore, a thought leadership platform can function as a deal-generating machine.

5. "For Rent" Ads

"For rent" ads on online services like Craigslist, Zillow, or Apartments.com, or "for rent" signs scattered across your target market, are great ways to find off-market deals. Call the numbers in these ads and ask the owner whether they are interested in selling, using an iteration of the script outlined in the "Direct mail campaign" section.

If an owner is listing a unit for rent, you automatically have identified a pain point. The unit is vacant, which means they are losing money. So, you might catch them at a moment when they are motivated to sell.

6. Title Companies

A title company is closing apartment deals on a daily basis, so they can be a good source of off-market deals. Additionally, they can be a referral source for private equity because they know the groups that are currently closing on apartment communities.

7. Apartment Association Meetings

Find and join the local apartment association. You will meet the active investors in your market and learn about any current or upcoming investment opportunities. These associations usually cost a few hundred dollars a year to join, but the profits netted from one deal will more than cover any required membership fees or dues.

8. Vendors

Electricians, carpet installers, roofers, plumbers, HVAC professionals, pool repair professionals, lawn care professionals, and the like can be great resources when looking for off-market deals. Basically, anyone involved in the servicing of apartment communities. They are on the front lines and will have insider information on communities that are being neglected. First, I recommend using their services or recommending them to other apartment owners to build rapport. Then you can ask them about notifying you of potential investment opportunities.

9. BiggerPockets

Become an active member on BiggerPockets, following a similar approach to the one I outlined in Chapter 21 on finding private capital. If you are known as someone interested in investing in apartment communities, other members of the site may send you opportunities. With a Pro account, you can post about your need for apartment deals in the Marketplace.

10. Network with Local Connectors

Whom do you know who knows a lot of people and comes in contact with a lot of people regularly? Do they know what you do and what you need?

These are the local fitness trainers, residential real estate agents, insurance salespeople, restaurant owners, hair stylists, barbers, teachers, and all sorts of other feet-on-the-street peeps. Your market is full of people who make it their business to connect with others, so why not leverage their network to find deals? Speak with these local connectors and let them know that you are focused on purchasing apartment communities. Ask them to notify you if they know of anyone who owns an apartment community. In return, you can refer people to their business – perhaps residents in your building or members of you team. It's a win-win.

How to Find Deals in a Hot Market

What if the market is such that you cannot generate off-market leads from any of these ten strategies? Or the on-market leads you receive from your real estate broker relationships are overpriced? In other words, how do you find qualified leads in a hot market?

I came across this problem in the Dallas-Fort Worth submarket. However, rather pausing my investment business or changing markets, my team and I came up with a creative solution:

For every on-market deal we came across, we reached out to the owner of the surrounding properties and attempted to purchase two properties: the original property and a nearby off-market property.

More specifically, if you are facing a similar problem in your market, you should pursue off-market properties that natural complement the original deal.

In my situation, I was sent an on-market opportunity in a Dallas submarket: a 300+ unit apartment building with primarily one-bedroom units. The property's characteristics fit perfectly into our business plan. However, due to its high publicity and it being marketed by a broker, the building price inched higher and higher. We were not confident in our ability to manage the project in a way that would achieve our investor's goals.

We found that there was another complex directly across the street from this on-market deal: a 200+ unit building with primarily two-and-three bedroom unit. Our broker contacted the owner of this off-market building, and after a brief negotiation, we secured a contract to purchase the property at a significantly discounted price. We were concurrently in negotiations to purchase the original deal and felt secure in offering a higher bid than we otherwise would have if it weren't for the complementary off-market property across the street. As a result, we were awarded the on-market deal.

Aside from finding a deal in a hot market, here are three more advantages of this strategy:

1. **Economies of scale:** One major advantage to this approach is the cost savings that result from economies of scale. For example, a major apartment building's expense is the cost of a lead maintenance supervisor. Therefore, rather than paying an on-site maintenance function to manage one property for $50,000 a year, we can split that cost across both properties. Additionally, these economies of scale can apply to many other fixed and variable expenses, including advertising and marketing, salaries and commissions for leasing office personnel and property management teams.
2. **Referral source:** Another advantage – and the reason why I advise you to pursue complementary properties – is having a natural referral source. This applied to my particular case because the original property was primarily comprised of one-bedroom units and the off-market property of two-and-three bedroom units. If a potential resident is interested in a one-bedroom unit, we are covered. If they decide instead that they want

more bedrooms, rather than turning them away, we send them to our property across the street.
3. **Flexible underwriting:** Finally, the most obvious advantage I see is the ability to be flexible with the underwriting to create a competitive offer. Essentially, you are able to tap into the discount you are receiving on the off-market property – in combination with the previous two advantages – to offset the premium paid for the original opportunity.

So, the advice I offer to those who are having difficulties with finding deals that are compatible with their financial goals is to create your own opportunities. Don't just look at the original listings. Instead, search for properties in immediate areas surrounding the original deal, reach out to the owners and work toward packaging two deals into one.

Ultimately, because of our willingness to create our own opportunities in this competitive market, we were able to add two cash flowing assets to our portfolio. By following this approach on the next deal you come across, you can too.

For additional strategies on finding incredible deals, even in a competitive market, I recommend reading *The Book on Rental Property Investing* by Brandon Turner.

I recommend selecting two methods from this list, as well as use my secret to finding deals in a hot market, and focusing on generating leads from those for at least six months. We live in an instant-gratification culture where people expect quick or immediate results. In general, when it comes to apartment syndication that isn't the case, and it's especially true when you're dealing with multimillion-dollar properties.

It takes time to generate apartment leads; it requires constant action and, moreover, constant tracking and consistent improvement. Speaking of tracking...

CHAPTER 28

DEAL-FINDING TRACKER

During your six-month trial period (and thereafter), track the results of each of your marketing methods. This will include both your off-market and on-market strategies. To track the results, you will need the Excel spreadsheet that I call the "Deal-Finding Tracker."

The reasons for tracking your results are fairly obvious. If you don't know your results, you don't know whether you have the best marketing strategy in the world or whether you are just wasting your time and money. If you have the best market strategy that's ever existed, fantastic! But if you don't, and you aren't tracking your results, you will never even know, which means you will never have the opportunity to improve. You will continue spinning your wheels until either you are burnt out or the world ends.

At the end of each month during the six-month period, or as you receive deals (whichever you prefer), log your results in your "Deal-Finding Tracker" spreadsheet.

The "Deal-Finding Tracker" spreadsheet will have a separate tab for each of your lead-generation strategies, in addition to a tab to record notes from conversations with the owners. The five tabs are: (1) real estate brokers, (2) off-market strategy #1, (3) off-market strategy #2, (4) thought leadership platforms and (5) owner conversation notes. Email info@joefairless.com for your free "Deal-Finding Tracker" or follow the instructions below to create your own spreadsheet from scratch.

"Real Estate Brokers" Tab

Brokers are a great source for on-market opportunities (which, as a reminder, are apartments represented by a real estate broker) and – after establishing a relationship – off-market deals (which are apartments not represented by a real estate broker). The purpose of the "Real Estate Brokers" tab is not only to keep track of these on-market and off-market opportunities, but also to determine which brokers are sending you the most high-quality leads. When structuring this tab in Excel, the first four columns will be dedicated to the actual real estate brokers. At the top of the columns, insert the following headers:

- Real Estate Broker Name
- Real Estate Broker Phone Number
- Real Estate Broker Email
- Number of Deals Sent

Since you've already interviewed and brought on a real estate broker, you can include their name and contact information here. Then, as you build relationships with other real estate brokers, you can input their contact information as well.

You also want to dedicate another portion of this tab to tracking the deals that you received from a real estate broker. The column headers you want to input to track this information are:

- Date Received
- Apartment Address
- On-Market or Off-Market?
- Number of Units
- Year Built
- Market
- Current Occupancy
- Value-Add?

- Link (if applicable)
- Sent From (the name of the real estate broker)
- If On-Market, Did You Reach the Best and Final Round?
- Contract?
- Closed?

Each time you receive a deal from a real estate broker, input the information into your tracker. After the six-month trial period, you will know exactly how many deals you received from each real estate broker, the quality of the lead (i.e., was it stabilized with value-add opportunities?), and whether you closed. From there you can determine which real estate broker/brokers add the most or least value to your business and should warrant more or less of your attention.

However, since the number of deals you receive from a specific real estate broker is based on the relationship you have with them (which takes time), don't make any rash decisions just because a real estate broker hasn't sent you many deals. Continue cultivating that relationship. If you haven't seen results after a few years, then by all means discontinue or throttle back the relationship.

"OFF-MARKET STRATEGIES #1 AND #2" TABS

On these tabs, you will track the results of the two off-market lead-generation strategies you selected in the last chapter.

For each strategy, create a separate tab. The data points you want to track are:

- Date – What was the date of your marketing campaign?
- Number of Marketing Efforts – What is the total number of marketing pieces, calls, drives, and searches you will execute?

- Number of Conversations with Owners – How many conversations resulted from the marketing campaign?
- Number of Interested Owners – Of those conversations, how many owners showed an interest in selling?
- Number of Uninterested Owners – Of those conversations, how many owners showed zero interest in selling?
- Number of Follow-ups – How many uninterested owners did you follow-up with? (Hint: this number should be equal to the number of uninterested owners.)
- Number of Best and Final Rounds – The best and final round is when the owner has investors with the most competitive offers provide a "best and final" offer, which may also involve a phone interview with the seller. If the owner had a best and final round, how many were you invited to?
- Number of Contracts – How many leads from this marketing campaign did you put under contract?
- Number of Closes – How many leads from this market campaign did you close on?

After creating these tabs, input the dates that you commit to performing a marketing campaign, whether that's monthly, bi-monthly, or quarterly. As you fulfill those commitments, track the results.

At the end of the six-month period, you will not only know whether you stuck to your commitments, but you will also know the results of your two off-market lead-generation strategies. It is at this point that you can determine whether you will continue with, tweak, or replace one or both strategies. If you decide to alter a strategy or select a new strategy, start the entire process over again with a new six-month trial period. And even if you decide to continue, keep tracking the results on an ongoing basis, because what works today isn't guaranteed to work in the future.

"Thought Leadership Platforms" Tab

With this tab, you will track the leads you receive from your thought leadership platform(s). In this case, you technically aren't directly reaching out to a specific apartment owner. Therefore, the information you want to track here is quite simple:

- Lead Date
- Lead Source – What thought leadership platform did the lead come from?
- Owner Name
- Owner Phone Number
- Owner Email
- Did the Deal Meet My Investment Criteria?
- Contract?
- Close?

Since your thought leadership platform has more utility than just finding off-market deals, don't stop if you discover that you aren't receiving any apartment leads. Instead, be resourceful and brainstorm ideas for attracting more leads. For example, you can (and probably should) create a landing page on your website and include a link to it in your newsletter once a month. Then, if your followers have a potential deal or know someone with a potential deal, they have an easy way to notify you. Also, invite on more apartment owners, property managers, and real estate brokers as interviewees for thought leadership platform. Tell them what you do and ask them to send you any apartment deals they come across, offering them a finder's fee.

"Owner Conversation Notes" Tab

The final tab in your tracker is a place to record any notes from conversations you have with owners. As I mentioned in an earlier part of this book, whenever I speak with owners, I open up a blank Word document to take notes. Then I transfer the relevant information to the tracker.

Relevant information to include on the tracker are:

- Date
- Deal Source
- Owner Name
- Owner Phone Number
- Owner Email Address
- Apartment Address
- On-Market or Off-Market?
- Number of Units
- Year Built
- Market
- Current Occupancy
- Value-add Opportunities?
- Other
- Contract?
- Close?

Overall, you need to find a tactic that aligns with what you're uniquely good at, what you're interested in, and what is conducive to the market. So, it will take some trial and error.

Your goal isn't to have 10 lead sources. It's about finding one or two that you are incredibly good at and that are generating (on average) at least one new lead per week.

PART 1: THE EXPERIENCE

KNOWLEDGE — Chapters 1-4
1. What is apartment syndication?
2. How to Get Started
3. What to focus on

GOALS — Chapters 5-6
1. How do you make money?
2. Set 12-month goal and long-term vision
3. Ultimate Success Formula

BRAND BUILDING — Chapters 7-12
1. Why you need a brand
2. Select a target audience
3. How to build a brand

MARKET EVALUATION — Chapters 13-16
1. 3 Immutable Laws of Real Estate
2. Evaluate 7 markets
3. Pick 1-2 Target Markets

PART 2: THE MONEY

BUILD TEAM — Chapters 17-19
1. Find core real estate team members
2. Hire a mentor or consultant

FIND CAPITAL — Chapters 20-24
1. Why will they invest?
2. Build passive investor database
3. Create partnership structure

PART 3: THE DEAL

FIND DEALS — Chapters 25-28
1. Set investment criteria
2. On-market vs. off-market deals
3. How to find your first deal

YOU ARE HERE
UNDERWRITING — Chapters 29-31
1. Information needed to underwrite a deal
2. The 6-step underwriting process

SUBMIT OFFER — Chapter 32
1. How to submit an offer on a deal
2. Best-and-final offer
3. Purchase sales agreement

PART 4: THE EXECUTION

DUE DILIGENCE — Chapters 33-37
1. 10 due diligence reports
2. Secure financing from lender

SECURE CAPITAL — Chapters 38-42
1. Create investment summary
2. New investment offering call
3. Secure investor commitments

CLOSE — Chapters 43-44
1. Closing process
2. Notify passive investors

EXECUTE BUSINESS PLAN — Chapters 45-46
1. 10 asset management duties
2. How to sell the apartment

CHAPTER 29

TIME TO NERD OUT ON MATH

Congratulations!

Your prospecting efforts have paid off. You've found your first deal – either an on-market deal represented by a real estate broker or an off-market deal that isn't represented by a broker – that meets your investment criteria.

Woo hoo!

The next step in the syndication process is to calculate an offer price and terms that will meet both your and your investors' goals. Time to put your nerd hat on, because the calculation is accomplished through underwriting.

Broadly stated, the underwriting process involves inputting the historical and current revenue and expense data, along with the assumptions for how you will operate the property once you've taken it over, into a financial model to calculate the projected returns over the life of the business plan.

Every single apartment syndicator or investor has his or her own unique way of underwriting a deal. Some keep things very simple while others address every detail imaginable.

In the next three chapters, I outline the process we use in my company when analyzing deals to give you an understanding of what information is required, the calculations involved, and how to interpret the results.

Oh, boy. Here comes the math part. So grab a Fannie Pack and your favorite pair of suspenders, because it's time to nerd out...

CHAPTER 30

GATHER YOUR INTEL

Before you can underwrite a deal properly, at a minimum you need to acquire two pieces of information: (1) the current rent roll and (2) the trailing 12-month profit and loss statement (T-12). If it is an on-market deal, you should also get your hands on the offering memorandum (OM).

Before moving on to the financial model, you need to understand what the rent roll, T-12, and OM are.

1. WHAT IS A RENT ROLL

A rent roll contains detailed information on each of the units at the apartment community, along with a summary of the different unit types or floor plans.

For example, here is a portion of a rent roll of a 216-unit apartment community my company purchased:

Unit	Unit Type	Soft	Resident	Status	Market Rent	Amount	Move In	Lease Start	Lease End	Deposit	Balance
001	A2	806.00		Occupied	646.00	629.00	08/20/2012	8/20/12	08/31/2016	300.00	$0
002	A2F	806.00		Occupied	711.00	697.00	01/30/2015	1/30/15	02/28/2017	338.00	($7)
003	A2	806.00		Occupied	646.00	667.00	08/26/2015	8/26/15	09/30/2017	500.00	$0
004	A2	806.00		Occupied	631.00	654.00	04/03/2013	4/3/13	05/31/2017	0.00	$0
005	A2F	806.00		Occupied	726.00	705.00	06/27/2015	6/27/15	08/31/2017	500.00	$0
006	A2	806.00		Occupied	631.00	564.00	10/01/2013	10/1/13	09/30/2016	200.00	($27)
007	A2F	806.00		Occupied	726.00	747.00	06/22/2015	6/22/15	08/31/2017	350.00	$0
008	A2	806.00		Occupied	631.00	652.00	07/31/2006	7/31/06	08/30/2017	100.00	$0
009	A1	741.00		Occupied	586.00	679.00	08/06/2016	8/6/16	08/31/2017	500.00	($117)
010	A1	741.00		Occupied	571.00	530.00	08/20/2013	8/20/13	02/28/2017	350.00	$0
011	A1	741.00		Occupied	586.00	555.00	07/27/2010	7/27/10	05/31/2017	0.00	$0
012	A1P	741.00		Occupied	616.00	715.00	11/09/2013	11/9/13	05/31/2017	300.00	$0
013	A1	741.00		Occupied	586.00	642.00	06/02/2016	6/2/16	07/01/2017	100.00	$0
014	A1	741.00		Occupied	571.00	527.00	07/02/2012	7/2/12	06/30/2016	0.00	($10)
015	A1	741.00		Occupied	586.00	618.00	07/02/2012	7/2/12	07/31/2017	0.00	$0
016	A1	741.00		Occupied	571.00	653.00	06/03/2015	6/3/15	07/30/2017	500.00	$0
017	A1	741.00		Occupied	586.00	593.00	08/29/2014	8/29/14	09/30/2016	200.00	$0
018	A1	741.00		Occupied	581.00	630.00	02/16/2016	2/16/16	03/15/2017	500.00	$0
019	A1	741.00		Occupied	596.00	599.00	10/04/2014	10/4/14	10/31/2017	200.00	$172
020	A1	741.00		Vacant	571.00						

255

The majority of the rent roll document will provide information for each unit. The format of rent rolls can vary greatly, but generally the information provided is:

- **Unit**: The number assigned to the unit. Typically, it includes the building number and the room number (e.g., unit number 1001 is room number 1 in building 1).
- **Unit type**: A number and/or letter assigned to the unit denoting the type of unit (e.g., number of beds/baths), floor plan type (if there are multiple floor plans for the same number of beds and baths), and condition (e.g., renovated vs. non-renovated, premium location).
- **Square footage (SqFt)**: Simply the size of the unit.
- **Resident**: Name of the individual(s) that occupy the unit.
- **Status**: Letter, number, or word denoting the occupancy status of the unit. The types of status will vary from rent roll to rent roll. But the main status types are "occupied" and "vacant." Other status types are "vacant-leased," "occupied with a notice to vacate," and "occupied with notice to vacate and leased."
- **Market rent**: The current market rental rate of the unit. The market rent is the rent amount a willing landlord might reasonably expect to receive, and a willing resident might reasonably expect to pay for tenancy, which is based on the rent charged at similar apartment communities in the area.
- **Amount**: Current dollar amount collected or credited for the unit, including rent and any other monthly fees or concessions (e.g., month-to-month charges, monthly pet fees, renter's insurance, parking, subsidized rent, employee unit rent credit).

- **Move in**: The date the current resident moved into the unit.
- **Lease start**: The start date of the current lease.
- **Lease end**: The end date of the current lease.
- **Deposits**: The total amount of deposits paid by the current resident.
- **Balance**: Dollar amount owed by or to the current resident.

Some rent rolls will include all of the above factors, while others will include only some of the above factors. The more detailed the rent roll, the better. But at the very least, in order to effectively underwrite a deal, which is the subject of the next chapter, the rent roll must include the following five factors:

- **Unit type**: You need to know the number of different unit types and the number of each unit type. This will help you determine the overall interior renovation budget and the rental premiums for each unit type.
- **Square footage:** You need to know the square footage of the different unit types. This will help you calculate a rent per square foot, which you will need to calculate the market rent of a renovated unit during the rental comparable analysis.
- **Status**: You need to know the occupancy status for each of the unit types. This will help you determine the current vacancy rate of the apartment community.
- **Market rent**: You need to know the current market rent for each of the unit types. This will help you, in combination with the current rent, to calculate the loss-to-lease factor, as well as the gross potential rent.
- **Current rent**: You need to know the actual rent collected for each of the unit types. This will help you, in combination with the market rent, to calculate the

loss-to-lease factor, as well as the net operating income and, ultimately, the cash flow.

2. WHAT IS A T-12?

The trailing 12-month profit and loss statement (T-12) contains detailed monthly information about the income and expenses of the apartment over the last 12 months. The T-12 will include the summarized information from the rent roll (market rent, current rent, loss-to-lease, and vacancy). Additionally, it will include any other source of income, as well as the detailed expense information.

For example, here is a portion of a T-12 for the 216-unit apartment community my company purchased:

As with the rent roll, the T-12 will vary greatly depending on how organized and/or forthcoming the seller is. That said, the income and expense data are generally summarized into categories. Other times, you will be provided with the raw data and will have to categorize each line item yourself manually.

- Income-related categories
  - **Market rent (or Gross Potential Rent):** Total revenue if all units were rented at the current market rates.
  - **Loss-to-lease:** Total revenue lost due to units currently rented at below market rent.
  - **Concessions:** Total credits given to residents, usually to persuade them to sign the lease.
  - **Vacancy:** Total revenue lost due to unoccupied units.
  - **Units (employee, model, admin):** Total revenue lost due to employee units, model units, and administration units.
  - **Bad debt:** Total revenue lost due to uncollected debts. Generally, bad debt is money owed by a resident that isn't covered by their security deposit after they moved out due to uncollected rent, fees, or damages.
  - **Other income:** Total revenue from sources other than rent, like coin-operated laundry machines, late fees, and/or application fees.
  - **Ratio Utility Billing System (RUBS):** Total revenue from utility reimbursements (i.e., water/sewer, trash, gas, and/or electricity reimbursements).
- Expense-related categories
  - **Payroll:** Total costs associated with payroll (e.g., maintenance and administrative salaries, bonuses, temp employee salaries, health insurance, workers compensation).
  - **Maintenance and Repairs:** Total costs of supplies and labor to perform ongoing maintenance.
  - **Contract Services:** Total costs associated with contractors (e.g., landscaping, security, alarm monitoring, pest control, pool service).

- **Turn/Make Ready:** Total costs for preparing a unit to be re-leased (e.g., unit paint, unit clean). Sometimes, an owner will lump this cost into the maintenance and repairs expense.
- **Advertising or Marketing:** Total costs for marketing to attract new residents or retain current residents (e.g., resident parties, locator fees, referral fees, promotional fees, internet ads).
- **Admin:** Total costs for administration duties (e.g., professional fees, office supplies, bank service charges, telephones, evictions).
- **Utilities:** Total costs for water, electric, gas, and sewer.
- **Management:** Total costs paid to the property management company.
- **Taxes:** Total costs for real estate taxes.
- **Insurance:** Total costs for property insurance.

3. WHAT IS AN OFFERING MEMORANDUM?

If it is an on-market deal, the listing broker will have prepared an offering memorandum (OM), which is a sales package that highlights the ins and outs of the investment.

The key word here is "sales" package. It is important to never take the information in the OM as absolute truth. It will likely be biased, but there will be some information that is helpful for the underwriting process.

Every broker has his/her own approach and structure for the OM. That said, the OM will typically include the following five sections:

1. Executive Summary
The executive summary section highlights the most important information about the deal. The information will be

summarized in paragraph form and then reiterated in more detail in the next few pages. Essentially, this summary allows interested investors to quickly review the investment to determine whether it meets their initial investment criteria without having to read the entire document.

If there are opportunities to add value to the apartment, that information will be provided in this section. Any upgrades previously implemented will be outlined, along with the associated costs and rental premiums achieved.

Then they will provide highlights of the market, including demographic trends, employment drivers, and other attractive information about the surrounding areas.

2. Property Description

The property description section will provide details on the asset itself.

This part offers a description of the property (location, year built, number of units, size, and construction information) and outlines other relevant information, like the property personnel, fee structures, tax information, and who pays for which utilities.

The property description section also highlights the selling points of the unit interiors and lists out the community amenities. Additionally, this section provides the floor plans for the different unit types, a site plan, and a map of the area surrounding the apartment community, which includes nearby retail stores, schools, hospitals, grocery stores, and other attractions.

3. Location Analysis

The location analysis is where investors find detailed information about the selling points of the market in which the apartment community is located.

Most of this information will be redundant since you've already evaluated the market, but there may be information included in this section that you missed in other sections. Generally, this section will include data about:

- The larger metropolitan area in which the apartment is situated, as well as the submarket and even the neighborhood.
- Infrastructure or transportation, like nearby airports, highways, and public transportation.
- Demographic data and trends, like population, age, educational attainment, and income.
- Economic analysis, including industry/job type breakdown and growth, GDP growth, top companies, and business.
- Labor breakdown, like the number of workers, new jobs, and overall labor growth.
- Apartment market overview, including total number of units, new construction, average rent, rent growth, and average occupancy.

4. Rental Comparables

The rental comparables, or rent comps, is an analysis of similar apartment communities in the submarket, comparing them with the subject property.

The comparison is made across multiple variables. Generally, it includes the year the apartments were built, the total number of units, average square footage, occupancy levels, unit upgrades, property-wide amenities offered, and market and current rental rates. This comparison is made on the overall property level (i.e., average rent of the subject property to that of the rental comps), as well as the unit type level (i.e., the average rent for each unit type of the subject property to the same unit types of the rental comps).

5. Financial Analysis

The financial analysis section provides results of the real estate broker's underwriting, with the output typically being a 1-year pro forma and 5- to 10-year projections.

The real estate broker's pro forma will calculate the income and expense factors, which is an extrapolation based on both the rent roll and the T-12, as well as their assumptions for how the property will be operated after purchase.

As I stated earlier, do not base your investment decision on the real estate broker's pro forma. Instead, you will use the raw rent roll and T-12 to build a financial model and create your own pro forma for how YOU will operate the asset.

Once you've gathered the proper intel (rent roll, T-12, and OM), it's time to get to the meat of the underwriting process – filling out your financial model.

CHAPTER 31

THE UNDERWRITING PROCESS

Once you've obtained the required documentation (the T-12 and rent roll if it is an off-market deal not represented by a real estate broker, or the T-12, rent roll, and OM if it is an on-market deal represented by a real estate broker) from the listing real estate broker or owner, you are ready to underwrite the deal.

As I previously mentioned, every apartment syndicator and investor has his/her own preferred underwriting methodology and financial model. Some syndicators create their own model from scratch; some might purchase a model from an apartment syndicator consultant or educator; rookies might simply base their investment decision on the underwriting provided in the OM. If you know someone who follows this last strategy, tell that person to read this book before they go bankrupt.

Regarding which method to use, I recommend creating your own financial model from scratch and adjusting it as you gain more experience rather than purchasing an already completed model from someone else. As the saying goes, it's better to teach someone to fish than to catch the fish for them.

You will be setting yourself up for greater success by actually building out your own model and inputting all the formulas yourself than you would by purchasing an already created model. However, if you want a starting point or a guide, I have created a simplified financial model that you can use. Email info@joefairless.com with the subject line "Simplified Financial Model."

In the following sections, you get a detailed picture of the process we use when filling out our custom financial model, including visual representations of the data tables included in the model. Use this as a guide for creating your own model from scratch (or adding to your free Simplified Financial Model).

Not to sound like a broken record, but I will reiterate it one more time: **NEVER trust the real estate broker's pro forma provided in the offering memorandum**. It is their goal, as well as his/her job, to sell the asset for the highest price possible to a party that can close. Because the results of the pro forma rely heavily on the underwriter's assumptions for how the property will be operated after acquisition, do you think the real estate broker's pro forma is going to be conservative or based on the best-case scenario?

Since we are dealing with other people's money, we can't leave this to chance. Therefore, it is important to perform your own underwriting, using your own assumptions for how you will operate the property.

For the purposes of this chapter, I am outlining the exact process of how my company underwrites a new deal, using the same 216-unit apartment community my company purchased for $12,200,000 as the example. As such, all market averages discussed below are based on apartment communities in the 200-or-more-unit range in or near large U.S. cities. If you are looking at smaller deals or deals in a smaller market, some of the revenue and expense assumptions will be different. When I explain these assumptions below, take note that I mention when they only apply to these larger deals.

Our process is:

1. Reading through the OM (if it is an on-market deal represented by a real estate broker)
2. Inputting the rent roll and T-12
3. Setting assumptions for how we will operate the property
4. Calculating an offer price
5. Performing our own rental comparable analysis
6. Visiting the asset to perform additional due diligence

While underwriting, whenever something is unclear or we find a discrepancy, we make a note and create a list of questions to ask the listing real estate broker or owner. As I explain the underwriting process below, I will let you know when you should stop, analyze, and, if necessary, add a question to your list of real estate broker/owner questions. That said, let's dive right in.

1. Reading Through the Offering Memorandum (OM)

If it is an on-market deal represented by a real estate broker, our first action is to read through the OM. This takes anywhere from 15 to 30 minutes. The purpose of reviewing the OM is to familiarize ourselves with the investment, jotting down very high-level bullet points.

Notes that we take include, but are not limited to:

- What is the unit count?
- What is the year of construction?
- Is it a value-add deal? Highly distressed? Turnkey?
  - If value-add, will it be through renovations or something else?

- Have they performed renovations on any units?
  - If so, how many and what rental premium are they demanding?
- What type of financing is on the property now?
  - Is there a pre-payment penalty?
  - Is it assumable? If assumable, how much is owed, what is the interest rate, amortization, and mortgage payment?
- Location notes
  - Is it a good submarket?
  - Blue-collar or white-collar demographic?
  - What is the breakdown of the job industries?

Once we reach the financial analysis or pro forma section, we stop reading and start underwriting. We don't want our assumptions to be skewed or influenced by the real estate broker's assumptions. However, we will come back to their pro forma later on in the process.

2. Inputting the Rent Roll and T-12

After we've reviewed the OM, the next steps are to fill out our financial model. For context, this step of the underwriting process takes between 2 and 3 hours for an experienced underwriter. As a beginner, this process takes anywhere from 3 hours to a full day.

This process starts by determining the income and expense figures of the property, which are calculated through a combination of the property financials – T-12 and rent roll – and assumptions for how we will operate the property. From the property's rent roll, we will have the rental breakdown for each of the unit types. Typically, we obtain the rent roll in its raw form, meaning that each individual unit is listed on its own line.

Unit	Unit Type	SqFt	Status	Name	Move-in Date	Market Rent	Rent
040	A1	741	Occupied	John Doe	9/30/16	$601	$684
149	B1	1,014	Occupied	Jane Doe	9/29/16	$831	$850
130	B1F	1,014	Occupied	James Smith	9/27/16	$906	$931
031	A1	741	Occupied	Janet Smith	9/26/16	$586	$683
096	A1P	741	Occupied	Joe Doe	9/26/16	$616	$711
167	B1	1,014	Occupied	Jean Carter	9/10/16	$831	$887

On this particular property, some of the units were partially or fully renovated, which is denoted by a "P" or "F" in the unit type.

Sometimes, a summarized rent roll is provided in the OM. Regardless, since we never take the OM at face value, we will still create our own summary based on the actual current rent roll provided. An example of a converted rent roll will look like this:

Unit Type	Type	SqFt	Units	Vacant	Market Rent	Current Rent	LtL	Market Premium	Effective Premium
A1	1x1	741	29	2	$581	$612	-$31		
A1P	1x1	741	12	1	$627	$667	-$40	$46	$55
A1F	1x1	741	7	1	$662	$661	$0	$81	$50
A2	1x1	806	56	5	$639	$635	$4		
A2P	1x1	806	19	1	$686	$673	$14	$47	$37
A2F	1x1	806	21	2	$721	$710	$11	$82	$74
B1	2x2	1,014	40	1	$828	$798	$30		
B1P	2x2	1,014	15	1	$886	$830	$56	$57	$32
B1F	2x2	1,014	17	1	$915	$875	$39	$87	$77
		861	216	6.9%	$154,946	$152,889	1.3%		

Market premium is the difference between the market rate of the upgraded unit and the market rate of the non-upgraded unit. **Effective premium** is the difference in rent between the current rate of an upgraded unit and the current rent of the non-upgraded unit. These figures will become relevant when determining the rent premium assumption later on in the underwriting process.

Once we have the summarized rent information, we take note of anything that stands out. Examples of things to look for are:

- Is the vacancy rate unusually high or low for the market?
  - The current vacancy rate of 6.9% is in line with the market vacancy rate of approximately 7% (which we obtain from our real estate broker and/or property management company).
- Loss-to-lease (LtL) varies on a case-by-case basis, but the standard is 3% to 5%, so does the property's LtL fall outside this range?
  - The LtL of 1.3% is below the standard range due to the 1-bed unit types being rented above market rates.
- Does the number of renovated units mentioned in the OM equal the number of renovated units from the rent roll?
  - Yes. 46 units are partially renovated and 45 units are fully renovated.
- If the current owners have performed renovations and stated a rental premium figure in the OM, does that number align with the rent roll?
  - Yes. In the OM, they stated that they are achieving a rental premium of $50 to $75 on fully renovated units. If you look back at the summarized rent roll above, the market rental premiums are between $45 and $90.

Based on these notes, you will create a list of questions to ask the real estate broker when appropriate.

The income data from the rent roll only covers the most recent month, making it a T-1. We need to know how the property has operated for an entire year to make our assumptions on how we will operate the asset.

From the property's T-12, we will have the income and expense breakdown for the last 12 months, which we use to make assumptions for how we will operate the property – whether that means assuming the same figure as the current operators or using a figure that is higher or lower.

Similar to the rent roll, the T-12 is usually provided in its raw form. With that in mind, we need to organize each line item into its respective income- or expense-related category. Here is the fully organized T-12 for the 216-unit apartment community:

T-12	Total
Gross Potential Rent	$1,836,889
LTL	-$60,049 (3.3%)
Gross Rent	$1,776,840
Concessions	-$29,462 (1.6%)
Vacancy	-$155,661 (8.5%)
Employee Units	$0
Model Units	$0
Admin Units	$0
Bad Debt	-$44,751 (2.4%)
Rental Income	$1,546,966
Other Income	$105,371 (5.7%)
RUBS	$64,464 (3.5%)
Total Other Income	$169,834 (9.2%)
Total Income	$1,716,801
Payroll	$261,665
Maintenance	$70,458
Contract Services	$88,558

Turn/Make Ready	$80,627
Advertising	$34,282
Admin	$30,378
Utilities	$184,594
Mgmt. Fee	$60,062
Taxes - Real Estate	$179,269
Insurance	$36,881
Total Expenses	**$1,026,774**
Net Operating Income	**$690,027**

Again, we will review the T-12 and make a note of any red flags:

- When looking at the T-12 broken out by month, is the income trending negatively?
  - When looking at monthly breakdown of the T-12, the revenue has gradually increased.
- Is bad debt higher than 1.5%?
  - Yes.
- Is vacancy above the market rates?
  - Yes. 8.5% is above the 7% market vacancy rate.
- Are the concessions greater than 3%?
  - No. 1.6%, so concessions are within the standard range.
- Are there any one-time charges in the expenses that look high? If so, what are they?
  - No.

If applicable, we add any red flags to our list of real estate broker questions.

3. Setting Assumptions for How We Will Operate the Property

Once we've accounted for the property's financial data, our next step in underwriting is to set acquisition and post-acquisition assumptions. This step of the underwriting process is the most important. However, we will never have 100% of the required information on which to base our assumptions, especially when we only have access to the property's financials and an OM.

If we aimed for near-perfect assumptions, the underwriting process would take days, or even weeks. Therefore, if we have difficulty with a certain assumption, we will make the best assumption possible, make a note to ask the real estate broker, as well as our property management company, mortgage broker, or vendor/contractor (depending on the assumption), for clarification, and then move on. Moreover, when we perform our due diligence after putting the property under contract, we will go back through and confirm each assumption. I've dedicated Chapters 33 to 35 to outlining the due diligence process.

The first set of assumptions we make serve the purpose of calculating the equity required to close the deal, which is based on the following five factors:

1. Acquisition fee
2. Closing costs
3. Financing fee
4. Operating account fund
5. Down payment

The first three factors are relatively simple to calculate.

Our standard acquisition fee is usually 2% of the gross transaction amount (which means an amount equal to the sum of all capital contributions, the initial principal balance of the loan, and any other sums required to acquire, own, renovate, operate, maintain, or manage the property), but yours might be higher or lower (see Chapter 5 for the GP fees).

Closing costs are based on the purchase price, and are obtained from the lender. A good ballpark assumption is 1% of the purchase price.

Financing fees are all other costs associated with the lender or mortgage broker. Typically, 1.75% of the purchase price is a good assumption, but you need to confirm this with your lender.

My company always has an operating account fund for times when our capital expenditure projects go over budget, as well as to cover shortfalls – like dips in occupancy, unexpected maintenance issues, or paying for insurance or taxes in one lump sum upfront. This figure will depend on your comfort level and renovation plan, but as a good rule of thumb, my company adds in around 1% to 5% of the purchase price to create the operating account fund.

The down payment for financing is also simple to calculate but contains multiple factors. The first portion of the down payment is based on the loan-to-value ratio offered by the lender, which is typically between 70% and 80%. That means the lender will finance 70% to 80% of the property value, while we will finance the remaining 20% to 30%. Unlike single-family or smaller multifamily properties, a sales price may not always be listed on the OM. Regardless of whether a sales price is listed or not, you will calculate an offer price using an iterative process.

After setting all of your income and expense assumptions, you will change the purchase price in your model until you've achieved your desired return on investment, IRR, or whichever return factor you and your investors use. It doesn't matter what the seller wants as a sales price. Your purchase price will always be based on your underwriting assumptions and your desired returns.

Additionally, renovation costs – depending on financing type – will be included in the loan or paid "out of pocket" (by the equity you raised for the deal). So, the first step is to determine what percentage of the renovation costs will be included in the loan. Our business model for this 216-unit deal had 100% of renovations covered by financing. This allows us to increase the returns during the renovation period, because we have less equity in the deal but this is a riskier strategy. The other option is to obtain a Fannie Mae or Freddie Mac long-term (3-, 5-, 7-, 10-, 12- or more year) loan with a fixed interest rate and interest-only payments for the first one or two years while paying for 100% of the renovations with investor capital.

The next step is to calculate a renovation budget, which includes interior upgrades, exterior upgrades, and contingencies.

Generally, assuming a value-add asset, as opposed to turnkey or highly distressed, the standard range for interior upgrade costs is between $4,000 and $7,500 per unit. Again, our goal here is to set a safe assumption before calculating the exact interior renovation costs during the due diligence phase. The process for setting the initial interior renovation assumption is to first outline the interior renovation program.

What improvements will be made to the interiors? Examples of value-add upgrades are flooring, cabinets and vanities, door/cabinet/bathroom hardware, appliance upgrades, light fixtures, and washers and dryers. In some cases, this will be outlined for you already in the OM, because the current operators will have performed full or partial renovations on a percentage of the units.

Here are the four pieces of information required to determine the interior renovation budget:

1. What is the cost associated with the interior renovation plan?
2. What percentage of units are already upgraded and to what extent?
3. What period of time were the units renovated over and what were the premiums achieved? (This helps

you determine the demand for renovated units in the market.)
4. What is the rental premium achieved from the renovation plan?

Any questions that the OM doesn't answer in regard to the interior conditions or improvement plan should be directed to the real estate broker. With this information, you can determine whether you should replicate their business plan or do something different.

For the 216-unit apartment community, the previous owners had already fully renovated 45 units and partially renovated another 46 units. The upgrades for the fully renovated units included new kitchen appliances and vinyl flooring, while the partially renovated units only had vinyl flooring already installed.

Our business plan was to fully renovate the remaining 125 units and 46 partially renovated units. However, we looked at the rental comps and determined that if we performed a higher level of updates, we could achieve a higher rental premium. So, in addition to completing the previous owner's renovation strategy, we decided to also replace the kitchen cabinet doors and hardware, modernize the fireplace, install granite countertops, and add washers and dryers to all 216 units.

Here was the cost breakdown for the upgrades for each unit type:

Unit Type	Type	SqFt	Units	Rehab Costs Per Unit
A1	1x1	741	29	$6,500
A1P	1x1	741	12	$4,925
A1F	1x1	741	7	$2,150
A2	1x1	806	56	$6,500
A2P	1x1	806	19	$4,925

A2F	1x1	806	21	$2,150
B1	2x2	1,014	40	$6,500
B1P	2x2	1,014	15	$4,925
B1F	2x2	1,014	17	$2,150
Total		**861**	**216**	**$1,076,700**

In terms of the rental premiums associated with an interior upgrade plan, they are calculated using one of two approaches:

1. **If the current owner has initiated an interior renovation plan,** premiums are based on the proven rental premiums, which should be confirmed on the rent roll and by reviewing rental comparables in the area. If the proven rental premiums are higher than the rental comparables, use the rental comparables. If the proven rental premiums are lower than the rental comparables, use the proven rental premiums. Basically, be conservative, remembering that both of these approaches are conservative projections.
2. **If the current owner hasn't initiated an interior renovation plan or you are performing additional or different renovations,** you will need obtain the rental premiums during the rental comparables step of the underwriting process.

For the 216-unit, the previous owners already initiated an interior renovation plan with proven rental premiums, which we confirmed by reviewing the rent roll. For the 45 fully renovated units, they were achieving rental premiums between $50 and $75 per month compared with non-renovated units. However, since we planned on performing additional renovations on all units, including the fully renovated units, we relied on the results of the rental comps to determine the rent premium assumptions.

I will go over the rental comparables in more detail later in this chapter, but the short story here is that we concluded that we would be able to conservatively **achieve a $75 rental premium above the market rental rates of the fully renovated units.**

Unit Type	Type	SqFt	Units	Market Rent	Renovated Rent	Reno. Rent/SqFt
A1	1x1	741	29	$581	$737	$0.99
A1P	1x1	741	12	$627	$737	$0.99
A1F	1x1	741	7	$662	$737	$0.99
A2	1x1	806	56	$639	$796	$0.99
A2P	1x1	806	19	$686	$796	$0.99
A2F	1x1	806	21	$721	$796	$0.99
B1	2x2	1,014	40	$828	$990	$0.98
B1P	2x2	1,014	15	$886	$990	$0.98
B1F	2x2	1,014	17	$915	$990	$0.98
Total		861	216	$154,946	$183,072	

The next part of the renovation budget involves the exterior upgrade costs. This expense includes the costs to address deferred maintenance on your big-ticket items and any amenity upgrades. To calculate this expense, we gather as much information from the OM and real estate broker as possible.

- What is the roof type?
  - Flat roofs are less expensive to install, but they won't last as long as the other common roof type, which is the pitched roof.
- When was the roofing last replaced?
  - The average life of a flat roof is 15 years and the average life of a pitched roof is 25 years. So, if the roof is approaching the end of the life cycle, you will need to find out the costs to replace it.

- When was the siding last replaced?
  - Vinyl siding lasts around 60 years and aluminum siding lasts 25 to 40 years. If the siding is approaching the end of the life cycle, you will need to find out the replacement costs.
- When was the last time the property was painted?
  - On average, you need to paint every 5 to 10 years. Unless the property was freshly painted, you will need to find out how much a new paint job will cost.
- When was the clubhouse last renovated?
  - If the clubhouse is outdated, you may need to update it in order to demand your projected rental premiums. See how the clubhouse compares with those in other apartment communities in your rental comparables.
- What is the condition of the pool?
  - If the pool is outdated or has maintenance issues, how much will it cost to repair?
- When was the last time the property was landscaped?
  - If the landscaping hasn't been maintained throughout the years, you will need to find out how much it will cost to update, as well as the ongoing costs to maintain
- What are the ages of the boilers/HVAC systems?
  - Most HVAC systems last 15 to 20 years, and most boiler systems last 10 to 15 years, depending on how well they are maintained. If the HVAC or boiler system is approaching the end of its life, you will need to find out the costs to replace it.
- Does each unit have an individual water heater and when were those replaced?
  - If there is one central water heating system, you're paying the bills. Consider the costs to install individual water heaters.

- The average life of most water heaters is about 15 years. So, if it is approaching the end of its life, you need to find out the costs to replace it.

Based on this information-gathering phase, we determine an exterior renovation budget. You won't be anywhere near certain of this expense until you've performed the inspections during due diligence, so a best practice is to budget more than you think you might need. Likely, you will revise this assumption (hopefully down) after inspections.

For our 216-unit, the previous owners had recently painted the exteriors and replaced the roof, and the landscaping was well maintained. However, due to the age and condition of the boiler and HVAC systems, we had to replace those items. On top of that, we constructed 12 carports, which we leased to residents at a monthly rate. We extended some of the patios, which allowed us to charge more rent for those units. Due to the market penetration rate, which is a measure of the number of washers and dryers used in our market, we installed washers and dryers in 35% of the units. We decided to rebrand the property to get a fresh start and step away from the previous brand, which required new signage throughout the community. We purchased a golf cart for our management team and treated the units for bedbugs. (Those things are nasty!)

The total cost for these exterior renovations was $534,800.

Total Renovation Budget: $1,611,500

- Interior renovations: $1,076,700
- Exterior renovations: $534,800

I've outlined all five of the equity factors (acquisition fee, financing fee, operating account fund, closing costs, and down payment), but we can't calculate the total amount of equity required to purchase the property until we input the rest of our assumptions and set an offer price. We will revisit this topic later.

So, what's next?

The next set of assumptions are those that are associated with how we will operate the property once we've taken over and stabilized the asset.

First, we need to set growth assumptions. What do we assume will be the rate of growth – expressed as a percentage – for the income and the expenses on an annual basis? As I am sure you're catching on, these growth assumptions vary from syndicator to syndicator. However, my company always underwrites conservative growth assumptions, which are 3% for rent growth and 2% for expense growth. Even if the historical market data shows a 5% rent growth over the past five years, we still stick to our conservative numbers, because we assume the periods of larger rent growth or smaller expense growth will be averaged out by dips in the market.

Next are the project assumptions. That is to say, what is your renovation timeline and how long do you plan on holding the asset? The renovation timeline assumption is important because the asset will operate differently during renovations than it does post renovations, from a rent, occupancy, and loss-to-lease perspective.

Your gross rent will steadily increase over the course of the renovation timeline as you rehab units and lease them to new residents at the projected rental premium. Then, understanding how long you will hold the asset will be used when calculating the proceeds at sale, which will affect the overall internal rate of return (IRR). When my company underwrites a deal, we typically assume a 12- to 24-month renovation timeline and a five-year overall hold. This held true for our 216-unit apartment community as well. We projected an 18-month renovation timeline and a five-year hold. Ultimately, due to the market conditions, we ended up selling this asset after 20 months. We purchased the asset for $12,200,000, put in $1,611,500 in renovations – an all-in cost of $13,811,500 – and sold it for $18,250,000. After paying closing costs and returning the LP's equity investment, the total profit (26 months of cash flow plus sales proceeds) was $3,777,219. Since we did a 70/30 profit split on this deal, our investors made $2,644,053 and we as the GP made $1,133,166 in profit. When we add in the upfront acquisition fee, ongoing asset management fees, and disposition fee, we achieved a total gain of over $1.6 million in less than two years. Cha ching! Yeah, Baby!

The next two sets of assumptions are the meat of underwriting. Here I'm talking about the stabilized income and stabilized expenses assumptions. We've already pulled the income and expense data from the current T-12 and rent roll, and now we will use those as a guide to calculate our stabilized assumptions.

Below are the best practices for setting the stabilized income and expense assumptions.

- Stabilized income assumptions
  - **Loss-to-Lease (LtL)**: This assumption may differ during renovations and after renovations are completed. Always set the year 1 LtL to what you calculated on either the rent roll or T-12, unless your property manager tells you otherwise. If the LtL is high and you think you will be able to operate at a lower percentage, you can set the LtL accordingly for year 2 and beyond. This is an income loss.
  - **Concessions**: Assume the same percentage of gross potential rent that is listed on the T-12 or rent roll, whichever you think is the most accurate representation of future operations. This is an income loss.
  - **Vacancy**: We are always conservative with our vacancy assumption. We assume *at least* an 8% vacancy

rate during renovations and 5% to 6% post renovations (depending on how the current operators have been doing). We use these assumptions even if we take over an asset with a current vacancy rate of less than 5%. This is an income loss. However, if the market vacancy rate is higher, like 10% for example, then our renovation and post-renovation vacancy rate assumptions will be higher
- **Employee/Admin Units:** Assume the same percentage of gross potential rent that is listed on the T-12. This is an income loss. The exception would be if you plan on doing something differently. If you are going to eliminate all of the employee and admin units, then you should assume a $0 loss. If you are going to create additional employee/admin units, then you need to increase this value.
- **Model Units:** Assume the same percentage of gross potential rent that is listed on the T-12. This is an income loss. The exception would be if you are going to add or eliminate a model unit, in which case you need to determine the market rent for the model unit and account for that income loss or gain.
- **Bad Debt:** Assume the same percentage of gross potential rent that is listed on the T-12. This is an income loss. The exception would be if the bad debt figure is ridiculously high (greater than 3%). If that is the case, make a note and ask the real estate broker why the bad debt is so high.
- **Other Income:** Assume the same percentage of gross potential rent that is listed on the T-12, unless you are doing something that will increase this income (like a RUBS program, adding carports, adding coin-operated washers and dryers).

Following our 216-unit example, here are the stabilized income assumptions:

	T-12	Assumption	Notes
Loss-to-Lease Year 1	3.3%	3%	Based on property mgmt. conversation
Loss-to-Lease Thereafter		3%	Based on property mgmt. conversation
Concessions	1.6%	1.6%	Same as T-12
Vacancy (During Reno.)	8.5%	8%	Conservative assumption
Vacancy Thereafter		7%	Conservative assumption
Employee/Admin Units	0%	0%	Same as T-12
Model Units	0%	0%	Same as T-12
Bad Debt	2.4%	2.4%	Same as T-12
Other Income	9.2%	9.0%	Conservative assumption

When it comes to the stabilized expenses, we base our assumptions either on the T-12 or on the standard market range, which is usually expressed as a dollar value per unit per year. Here is how you set your expense assumptions and, as a reminder, all of the market ranges are based on apartment communities over 200 units:

- **Payroll:** $1,000 to $1,200 per unit per year is the standard market range. If the T-12 payroll expense is within this range, assume you will operate at the same expense. If the T-12 payroll expense is above this range, set at $1,200; if it is below this range, set at $1,000.
- **Maintenance:** $250 to $350 per unit per year is the standard market range for all property sizes. Assume you will operate at the same expense listed in the T-12, no matter what.

- **Contract Services:** $200 to $400 per unit per year is the standard market range. Use the same logic with this assumption as you do with the maintenance expense.
- **Turn/Make Ready:** $150 to $300 per unit per year is the standard market range. Use the same logic with this assumption as you do with the payroll expense.
- **Advertising:** $100 to $200 per unit per year is the standard market range. Use the same logic with this assumption as you do with the maintenance expense.
- **Admin:** $150 to $250 per unit per year is the standard market range. Use the same logic with this assumption as you do with the maintenance expense.
- **Utilities:** $750 to $900 per unit per year is the standard market range. Use the same logic with this assumption as you do with the maintenance expense.
- **Management Fee:** Ask your property manager what they will charge to manage the asset. This is typically a percentage of the total income.
- **Taxes:** Property taxes always adjust after a sale and are based on the appraised value of the property. For this assumption, locate the asset on the county assessor or appraisal office website to determine the tax rate. If the county in which the asset is located doesn't have a website, call the county assessor or appraisal office and ask how a sale might or might not change the assessed value and property taxes.
- **Insurance:** Assume the same insurance expense that is listed on the T-12 until you obtain a quote from your insurance vendor. Expect to pay a minimum of $225 per unit per year for insurance.
- **Lender Reserves:** This expense will vary based on the asset class. If it is a Class B product, for example, assume $250 per unit per year for lender reserves.
- **Asset Management Fee:** If you are charging an asset management fee, which is a percentage of the total

income make sure you take that into account. My company usually charges a 2% asset management fee (see GP fees in Chapter 5).

For all these assumptions, if the T-12 number falls outside of the market range, make a note to ask the real estate broker why the expense is above or below the market range. Also, if you are underwriting a property with fewer than 200 units, have a conversation with your property management company to get the market range for each expense for that property size.

Depending on how small the apartment is, you might eliminate certain expenses all together. For example, a 20-unit apartment probably won't have a payroll expense, but the property management fee will be higher.

Following our 216-unit example, here are the annual stabilized expense assumptions:

Expense	T-12	Assumption	Notes
Payroll	$261,665	$237,600	Based on market averages
Maintenance	$70,458	$64,800	Based on T-12
Contract Services	$88,558	$82,000	Based on T-12 (eliminating security patrol)
Turn/Make Ready	$80,637	$43,200	Based on market averages
Advertising	$34,282	$32,400	Based on market averages
Admin	$30,378	$32,400	Based on T-12
Utilities	$184,594	$189,000	Based on T-12
Mgmt. Fee	$60,062	$66,053	3.5% management fee
Taxes	$179,269	$278,260	Tax rate times 80% of purchase price
Insurance	$36,881	$48,600	Based on market averages
Reserves	$0	$54,000	$250/unit per year
Asset Mgmt. Fee	$0	$37,745	2%

The last set of data required before calculating a purchase price are the debt terms. Based on the terms of your loan, you will calculate the monthly mortgage payment. Earlier, I stated that the loan-to-value ratio is used to calculate our loan down payment. Additional information required to calculate a monthly payment are the interest rate, number of interest-only years (if applicable), amortization schedule, and loan terms. You will obtain all of this information from your lender. For our 216-unit, we secured an initial two-year interest-only bridge loan at 77% loan to value, covering 100% of the renovation costs, at a 5.28% interest rate amortized over 30 years. Since a purchase price wasn't listed for this apartment community, we will input these assumptions into our financial model and come back to calculate a monthly mortgage payment after setting an offer price.

4. Calculating an Offer Price

Now that you've set all of your assumptions, it is time to determine an offer price, which you will calculate using an iterative process. But first you need to define a desired return on investment for both you and your investors. Then you will change the purchase price in your model until you've achieved that desired factor. At that point, any income or expense figure that is a percentage of the purchase price and the down payment will be automatically populated, assuming all of your formulas are correct.

For my company and my investors, the aim is a cash-on-cash return during the hold period to the LP of at least 8% or higher (not including the profit from the sale), and a 14% or higher LP IRR, unless the hold period is longer than five years (in which case the IRR will be lower). At this point, we will start to input purchase prices into our financial model until we achieve our desired return. In the

216-unit example we've been following, based on our assumptions, we will achieve a year 1 cash-on-cash return of 8.6% for our investors and a 5-year average cash-on-cash return of 10.6% and an LP IRR of 18.1% at a $12,200,000 purchase price.

Now that we've set an offer price, we can calculate the total amount of money we need to raise in order to close the deal. Going back to our five equity factors:

- Acquisition fee: $244,000
  - 2% of the purchase price
- Closing costs: $143,003
  - Our actual closing costs were 1.2% of the purchase price, or $143,003
- Financing fee: $214,700
  - Our actual financing fee came out to 1.75% of the purchase price, or $214,700
- Operating account fund: $435,567
  - Our operating account was 3.6% of the purchase price, or $435,567
- Down payment: $2,806,000
  - A $12,200,000 purchase price at 77% LTV requires a down payment of $2,806,000. The loan is covering 100% of the renovation costs, so no additional equity down is required
- **Total: $3,843,270**

Additionally, it's not difficult to calculate the monthly mortgage payments. As long as you input the correct formula for mortgage payments into the financial model, the mortgage payment should automatically calculate when you input the debt assumptions and an offer price. With a loan amount of $11,005,500 (77% of the purchase price plus 100% of the renovations), amortized over 30 years at an interest rate of 5.28% with two years of I/O payments, the monthly debt service is $48,424, or $581,088 annually.

Another return factor that will be relevant to your investors is the IRR, which is a popular metric used to estimate the profitability of a potential investment. To calculate the project's IRR, you need to set disposition assumptions, also known as the sales assumptions. The IRR is calculated using the equity put into the deal and the dollars returned over the lifetime of the project, including the sales proceeds. The equity put into the deal and the projected cash returned each year excluding the sales proceeds should already be calculated in your model.

To calculate the sales proceeds, you need to set an exit cap rate. For my company, we always assume the market is **worse** at sale than when we purchased the property. So, we set our exit cap rate assumption to 20 to 50 basis points (or 0.2% to 0.5%) higher than the cap rate at which we purchase the property. Using the exit cap rate and the exit net operating income, we can calculate a sales price. The majority of that sales price will be used to pay the lender back the remaining debt, as well as to cover closing costs. The money that remains is the sales proceeds.

For our 216-unit example, our projected exit NOI is $1,134,723. The cap rate when we purchased the asset was 5.7% (based on the purchase price and the in-place net operating income), so we assume the exit cap rate is 5.9%, giving us a sales price of $18,853,002 after five years. (Note: as I mentioned already, we sold the property for $18,250,000 after just 20 months!)

Generally, all the closing costs will be approximately 1% of the sales price. Depending on how you structured the partnership, you may charge a disposition fee. If you do, make sure you are accounting for that in your disposition assumptions. For this deal, we projected the closing costs and disposition fee to be a total of 2% of the sales price, which equates to $377,060.

The remaining debt after paying down the principal is $10,711,909, which leaves us with $7,764,033 in sales proceeds.

In addition to receiving the remainder of their equity balance (which we projected as $2,198,439), based on our 70/30 partnership structure, the LP would receive an additional $3,803,677, which is a total of $6,002,116.

Based on the initial down payment, cash flow for five years, and sales proceeds, the project has a projected 18.1% five-year IRR to the limited partners.

Remember when I said that out of every 100 deals, 30 will meet your initial investment criteria and 10 will pass the underwriting phase? Well, we've just reached that fork in the road. If you are unable to project the desired returns of your investors at this point in the process, after inputting your conservative assumptions and setting an offer price, you may want to pass before performing the rental comparable analysis. Go back over your assumptions to make sure you didn't make any input errors.

Have your mentor and property manager review the underwriting to see whether you made any mistakes or whether any of your assumptions were too conservative. If the deal still doesn't pencil in, congratulate yourself for underwriting your first deal, be happy that you got the practice, and move on to the next one.

If the underwriting projections meet, exceed, or are on the cusp of meeting your investors' desired returns, then you can move on to the next section and perform the rental comparable analysis.

5. Performing Our Own Rental Comparable Analysis

As I mentioned earlier in this chapter, the rental comparable analysis is an evaluation in which the subject property is compared with a list of similar properties in the immediate area across a variety of different factors in order to determine the fair market rents of the subject property post-renovation. As value-add investors, our goal is to perform renovations on the property in order to increase the rents, and the purpose of the rental comparable analysis is to accurately calculate the resulting rental premiums.

Similar to the underwriting process, apartment syndicators have different approaches to conducting rental comps. For example, a syndicator may rely solely on the rental comps provided in the offering memorandum (mistake!). Or they may wait until they have the property under contract and have their property management company perform the analysis during the due diligence phase (nope, not right either!). I've found that both of these approaches are problematic. For the first approach, you are entrusting the success of your deal to the broker, whose main motivation is to sell the deal. In the second approach, you'll have already invested time and capital into the deal without fully understanding the potential upside.

Therefore, I recommend that you always perform a rental comp analysis during the underwriting process and then again during the due diligence phase. In fact, we actually perform two separate rental comp analyses – a detailed online research analysis and secret shopping on the phone or in-person analysis. The first approach will give us enough information to calculate accurate rental premiums. The second approach not only allows us to confirm the results of our online research (since some of the online information may be inaccurate or missing), but also lets us obtain property information that can only be obtained by talking to an actual person who works at the asset.

To perform the online portion of the rental comparable analysis, the first step is to build a list of similar properties. Here are the criteria to keep in mind when searching for similar properties:

- **Year built**: The comparable properties should have been built around the same year as the subject property. Properties built much earlier or later are too dissimilar to use as a comparison, due to things like deferred maintenance, unit layout, and amenities.
- **Distance**: Depending on the market size and density of apartment communities, the comparable properties should be within a certain distance. The more apartment communities, the closer the comparable properties should be.
- **Number of units:** The comparable properties should have a similar unit count to the subject property.
- **Unit type and size**: The comparable properties should have similar unit types and square footage. For example, if the subject property consists of all 1-bed, 1-bath units, an apartment community with all 2-bed, 2-bath units is a poor choice. For the square footage, these don't need to be exactly the same, because we will be calculating a rent per square foot during the analysis.
- **Interior renovations**: The quality of interior renovations at the comparable property should be similar to the quality of interior renovations you're planning to perform on the subject property.
- **Amenities**: The quality and type of amenities offered at the comparable property should be similar to the quality and type of amenities at the subject property once it is fully updated.

A really good tool for finding comparable properties is an amenities checklist. It will let you quickly see the current amenities at the subject apartment community compared with both the amenities of the updated version of the subject property and the amenities offered at the rental comparable assets.

Creating the checklist is simple.

First, in Excel, create an exhaustive list of all the interior and/or exterior upgrades that will be offered at the updated subject apartment. Then create columns for the subject property in its current form and its rehabbed form, and for all the rental comps selected (which I will outline how to do later on in this section). Then, for each apartment column, put a checkmark if the asset has the amenity and leave it blank if it doesn't have the amenity. For example, here is an amenities checklist we created for the 216-unit apartment community:

Unit Features	216-unit Pre-Reno	216-unit Post-Reno	Comp A Post-Reno	Comp B Post-Reno	Comp C Post-Reno
New cabinet doors		x		x	x
Granite counters		x	x	x	x
Black appliances	x	x	x	x	x
Microwave	x	x	x	x	x
Vinyl flooring	x	x	x	x	x
Modernized fireplace		x		x	x
New paint	x	x	x	x	x
Tile backsplash		x		x	x
Washer and dryer in unit		x		x	x
New light fixtures		x	x	x	x
New plumbing fixtures		x	x	x	x
2" blinds	x	x	x	x	x
Carport		x			
Patio	x	x	x	x	x

The unit amenities listed in this example are the interior updates and renovations my company has found to demand the highest rental premiums in our target market and are based on our value-add investment strategy. Have a conversation with your property management company prior to creating your checklist to come up with the desired amenities that add the most value.

Additionally, to determine what is an acceptable year built, distance, and number of units of a rental comp, I recommend asking your experienced property management company.

Remember when I said we would revisit the real estate broker's pro forma? A good starting place for finding rental comps is the OM. But, there are three main things to look out for when reviewing the comps that the real estate broker used to create their pro forma.

First, see how far the comps are from the subject property. I was looking at a property and the rent comps were in a completely different neighborhood. I was local, so I knew that the comp was located in a neighborhood of college graduates while the subject property was not. The comps need to be close enough to the subject property to be in the same or a very similar neighborhood.

The second thing to look out for is the year the property was renovated. I was looking at another property that had proven rental premiums but the renovations had been performed over two years to only 25 units. Our renovation timeline moves faster than that, so that is not a good comparison, because the renovations were too slow.

Last, look at the operations of the property to see whether they match up with the subject property. For example, I was reviewing an OM that had a mixture of rental comps where the owner paid for all of the utilities and rental comps where the owner paid for some of the utilities. If the subject property has the owner pay for all of the utilities, all of the rental comps need to be the same, because this impacts the rental rates.

If the list of properties in the OM pass the smell test, you can use them for your rental comp analysis. But, instead of using the rental data provided, we will do our own research. If the rental comps in the OM are off-base, create a list of more similar rental comps using Apartments.com, making sure they align across the criteria outlined above.

Once you have your list of rental comps, create an Excel document and list out the property name and property address. Here are the comparables we used for our 216-unit apartment community:

Property Name	Property Address	Year Built	No. of Units
Comp A	Comp A Address	1983	422
Comp B	Comp B Address	1983	798
Comp C	Comp C Address	1984	1216
Comp D	Comp D Address	1980	152
Comp E	Comp E Address	1982	469
Comp F	Comp F Address	1983	326
216-unit Apartment	216-unit Apartment Address	1981	216

Next, you will do research to find the relevant information about the apartment communities. The best resource I've found that includes most of the information required for the rental comps analysis is Apartments.com. Here's a list of the data you'll pull from the Apartments.com listing:

BEST EVER APARTMENT SYNDICATION BOOK

- Year built
- Number of units
- One-bedroom unit types, square footage, and rents
- Two-bedroom unit types, square footage, and rents
- Three-bedroom unit types, square footage, and rents
- Other bedroom (four, five, or more) unit types, square footage, and rents

Create an Excel document similar to the one shown below for inputting this data, which includes data following our 216-unit example:

1-bedroom rent comparables

Property Name	Unit Type	SqFt	Rent per Unit	Rent PSF
Comp A	1x1 - Renovated	718	$854	$1.19
Comp A	1x1 - Renovated	775	$841	$1.09
Comp A	1x1 - Renovated	777	$910	$1.17
Comp B	1x1 - Renovated	770	$745	$0.97
Comp B	1x1 - Renovated	732	$725	$0.99
Comp C	1x1 - Renovated	722	$714	$0.99
Comp E	1x1 - Renovated	664	$659	$0.99
Comp E	1x1 - Renovated	756	$699	$0.92
Comp F	1x1 - Renovated	732	$899	$1.23
Comp F	1x1 - Renovated	759	$899	$1.18
Comp F	1x1 - Renovated	760	$909	$1.20
Comp F	1x1 - Renovated	768	$937	$1.22
Average		**723**	**$795**	**$1.10**
216-unit Apartment	A1 - Renovated	741	$661	$0.89
216-unit Apartment	A2 - Renovated	806	$710	$0.88

2-bedroom rent comparables

Property Name	Unit Type	SqFt	Rent per Unit	Rent PSF
Comp A	2x2 - Renovated	911	$993	$1.09
Comp A	2x2 - Renovated	1,115	$1,338	$1.20
Comp B	2x2 - Renovated	886	$830	$0.94
Comp D	2x2 - Renovated	1,004	$890	$0.89
Comp D	2x2 - Renovated	1,024	$915	$0.89
Comp E	2x2 - Renovated	892	$868	$0.97
Comp F	2x2 - Renovated	1,038	$1,075	$1.04
Average		**981**	**$987**	**$1.01**
216-unit Apartment	B1 - Renovated	1,014	$875	$0.86

Once we've compiled the rental data, we calculate an average rent per square foot for each of the unit types, which are the current market rental rates. If you look back at our example, when we calculated the rental premiums, I stated that we would achieve a $75 premium based on the rental comps. That is, once we've performed the premium upgrades on all rental units, we project that we will achieve the same rental rates per square footage as the comparable properties. If we were to discover a different rent premium, we would need to update the rent premium in our financial model. If the updated return projections fall below our target, we will also need to update our offer price.

As you see in the data table below, the renovated rent per square foot is in alignment with the average rent per square foot calculated in our rental comp above.

Unit Type	Type	SqFt	Renovated Rent	Rent/SqFt
A1	1x1	741	$737	$0.99
A2	1x1	806	$796	$0.99
B1	2x2	1,014	$990	$0.98

In fact, based on the rental comps, we could achieve $1.10 per square foot for the 1x1 units and $1.01 per square foot for the 2x2 units. However, to remain conservative, we will keep the assumption of just under $1 per square foot.

Now, not every rental comp you've selected will have unit and rental information readily available online. If that is the case, you will have to perform the secret shopping rental comp approach prior to the detailed approach outlined above.

Get ready for your Broadway performance, because you will now play the role of a resident who is interested in renting a unit. Or, if you want something a little bit easier, you can say that you are calling on behalf of a family member or friend. The goal is to confirm the information you gathered during your online investigation.

To start, create a new Excel document, listing out the same property name and addresses used in the detailed analysis above. Additionally, you will need to obtain the phone number of the leasing office.

Prior to your acting debut, fill out the rest of the Excel document by labeling the columns as follows:

1. 1-bedroom rents
2. 2-bedroom rents
3. 3-bedroom rents (when applicable)
4. Rent specials
5. Amenities package
6. Unit upgrades
7. Parking

8. Points of interest
9. Demand
10. Notes on customer service

Upon completing the secret shopping call or in-person visit, you should have acquired enough information to input data for each of the 10 factors above.

Since you will likely be nervous, especially on your first few phone calls or in-person visits, I recommend having a list of questions prepared prior to the call or visit. The list of questions below (in quotation marks) should get you all the information you need to fill out the Excel document.

- **Rental data and demand**
    - "I am relocating to the area in the next couple of months. Do you have any available units or is there a waiting list?"
    - If the apartment has one- and two-bedroom units:
        - "I am interested in renting a 2-bedroom unit. How much do those rent for?"
        - Once they respond with a rental rate: "Oh. $800 may be slightly outside of my price range. I was hoping for an extra bedroom, but how much are the 1-bedroom rents?"
    - If the apartment has 1-, 2-, and 3-bedroom units:
        - Use the same approach as above, and call back a few days later to ask about the three-bedroom rents.
- **Rent specials**
    - "Do you currently offer any rent or move-in specials?"
    - Example: Security deposit specials, rental discount if you sign a longer lease, concessions, move-in specials, referral programs, military/law enforcement/first responder discounts.

- **Amenities package**
  - "Something that will heavily weigh into my decision is the amenities package offered. What are the individual unit and property amenities?"
  - Individual amenity examples: pet friendly, wood flooring, washer and dryer in unit, updated kitchens, storage, fenced-in yards, balcony, patio.
  - Property amenity examples: fitness center, pool, online rent payment, online maintenance requests, parking, common areas.
  - Follow-up questions: "Are there additional monthly fees for any of the amenities you listed or are they included in the rent?"
- **Upgrades**
  - "Have you done any unit upgrades recently, specifically in the kitchens or bathrooms?"
  - "What about property-wide upgrades?"
- **Parking**
  - "What is the parking situation?"
  - "Will I have a free spot near my unit?"
- **Points of interest**
  - "What are popular attractions or points of interest that are within a few miles of the property?"
  - "Is there anything worth noting that is within walking distance?"

You should do a few practice calls or visits to non-rental comp apartment communities so that you get comfortable with the flow of the conversation. Also, this is by no means a step-by-step guide that you should robotically follow in the exact order above. It should be used as more of a guide for what questions to ask in order to get the information you need to confirm your online investigations and to give you a better understanding of the market.

At the conclusion of the conversation or once you get back to your car, take a few minutes to make notes on the quality of customer service you received. If you haven't already, fill out the Excel document with the answers you received. Then compare that information with the data you uncovered through your online investigations. Do the amenities, unit upgrades, and rents match up? If they don't, you will need to adjust your detailed rental comp spreadsheet and, if necessary, select a new rental comp. Finally, repeat this same process for the remaining rental comp communities.

6. Visiting the Asset to Perform Additional Due Diligence

While visiting the asset in person may be a headache, especially if the subject property is out of state, I strongly recommend that you suck it up and make the trip. The only true way to get a clear picture of the property's current condition and the surrounding market is to see it in person with your own eyes. Usually, for these 200-unit or larger deals, you'll have plenty of time to schedule a trip to see the property in person before the best and final offer call.

Ideally, you'll perform the in-person visit with a representative from your project management company. They will have experience managing and touring properties, so they will catch things that you may miss. As I will outline in the Chapters 34 and 35, you and your property management company will perform detailed due diligence on the property once you've secured a contract. However, if a major, disqualifying issue is found at the property, they can catch it before you spend an unnecessary amount of time and money going through the offer and due diligence process.

Plan on spending an entire day going through the in-person evaluation of the property and surrounding market. The first portion of the day will be spent at the subject property. Then you will assess the surrounding area. Finally, you will visit a handful of comps to further confirm your rental premium assumptions. Make sure you bring a notepad and your smartphone. You'll be taking a lot of notes and pictures during the evaluation. Since you will be visiting a few apartment communities, unless you are a savant, don't expect to remember everything you will hear and see. These notes and pictures will be your external memory bank.

Make sure that when you are visiting this property, you dress the part. You are going in as a prospective resident, so you need to look like one. So, get out your favorite pair of jeans and a T-shirt with the logo of your favorite college. (If it's a college town situation.)

When you first arrive at the property, drive or walk around the community and take notes on and pictures of the big-ticket items. These include:

- Roofs
- Parking lots
- Landscaping
- Exterior conditions (e.g., siding, exterior paint, clubhouse, amenities)
- Signage

Confirm that the condition of these big-ticket items aligns with your underwriting assumptions. Make a note to adjust your renovation budget if necessary.

Next, visit the clubhouse and find the property manager. Before touring the clubhouse or units, ask them a list of prepared questions about the property's operations. These include:

- How long have you been at the property?
- What is today's occupancy?

- How has the property operated over the past year?
- What's the lowest occupancy has been since you've been here?
- How many people are calling in each week to rent an apartment?
- Do the amenities get a lot of traffic from residents?
- What are the demographics of the residents? (e.g., students, young professionals, blue-collar workers, senior citizens, families)
- When was the last time you repaired the roofs? Parking lots? HVAC?
- Does this property have any deferred maintenance? Bad debt?
- How is the crime at the property?
- Who is your biggest competitor?
- Why do people rent here instead of at the competition?
- What types of units are in demand in the area?
- You've done a great job here. If I gave you $150,000, besides making sure you were compensated for your work, how would you spend it to fix or improve the community?
- What did I forget to ask you? What else is there to know about the property?

After going through your list of questions, ask for a tour of the clubhouse. Take notes and pictures along the way. Do the clubhouse conditions, amenities, and level of updates align with your underwriting assumptions, or will it require renovations?

Next, ask to tour a few units. While touring the units, make notes on and take pictures of the interior conditions. These include:

- How does the condition of the units compare with that of the unit type the property manager said was in demand?
- Are there large walk-in closets?
- Is there an open floorplan?
- What is the level of renovations and does that align with your underwriting assumptions?
- What is the main highlight/selling point of the units?

After the unit tours, the evaluation of the apartment community is completed. Thank the property manager for his/her time and prepare for the next step of the evaluation. Get in your car and drive two miles in each direction from the property. Ideally, you will have mapped out your driving route prior to the trip. Make notes on and take pictures of the following, keeping in mind to avoid doing so while the vehicle is in motion:

- What is the distance between the community and the closest retail center? Is it new or old? What's the demographic of people and does that align with the demographic of the apartment community?
- Find the closest Chipotle, McDonalds, Walmart, and Starbucks. How far are they from the community? Are they new or old? What is the demographic of people and does that align with the demographic of the apartment community?

Last, visit the list of apartment communities from your rental comps. The approach is similar to the secret shopping process you already conducted over the phone. Drive around the community, making notes on and taking pictures of the exterior conditions. Meet with the property manager, asking them the same list of questions that you asked on the phone. Tour the clubhouse, making notes on and taking pictures of the condition and amenities. Finally, tour two or three different unit types by mentioning that you are unsure whether you want a 1-bedroom or 2-bedroom unit, getting the rents for each layout, as well as what is included in the rent.

Once you've returned home from your trip, go through your notes and compare them with the assumptions you made in your underwriting model, making any final, pre-offer adjustments, if necessary.

I have done all of the things I'm telling you to do in the long list above, but not for every single deal. Sometimes, you might not have the time to visit all of the comps before submitting an offer. The main objective is to visit the subject property; the other steps are helpful but not necessary or even possible every single time.

PART 1: THE EXPERIENCE

KNOWLEDGE — Chapters 1-4
1. What is apartment syndication?
2. How to Get Started
3. What to focus on

GOALS — Chapters 5-6
1. How do you make money?
2. Set 12-month goal and long-term vision
3. Ultimate Success Formula

BRAND BUILDING — Chapters 7-12
1. Why you need a brand
2. Select a target audience
3. How to build a brand

MARKET EVALUATION — Chapters 13-16
1. 3 Immutable Laws of Real Estate
2. Evaluate 7 markets
3. Pick 1-2 Target Markets

PART 2: THE MONEY

BUILD TEAM — Chapters 17-19
1. Find core real estate team members
2. Hire a mentor or consultant

FIND CAPITAL — Chapters 20-24
1. Why will they invest?
2. Build passive investor database
3. Create partnership structure

PART 3: THE DEAL

FIND DEALS — Chapters 25-28
1. Set investment criteria
2. On-market vs. off-market deals
3. How to find your first deal

UNDERWRITING — Chapters 29-31
1. Information needed to underwrite a deal
2. The 6-step underwriting process

SUBMIT OFFER — Chapter 32 *(YOU ARE HERE)*
1. How to submit an offer on a deal
2. Best-and-final offer
3. Purchase sales agreement

PART 4: THE EXECUTION

DUE DILIGENCE — Chapters 33-37
1. 10 due diligence reports
2. Secure financing from lender

SECURE CAPITAL — Chapters 38-42
1. Create investment summary
2. New investment offering call
3. Secure investor commitments

CLOSE — Chapters 43-44
1. Closing process
2. Notify passive investors

EXECUTE BUSINESS PLAN — Chapters 45-46
1. 10 asset management duties
2. How to sell the apartment

CHAPTER 32

WHAT DO YOU HAVE TO OFFER?

Once you've completed the entire six-step underwriting process, you've arrived at the point where you need to determine whether you will submit your offer. Unfortunately, there are no black-and-white, universal "this is a good deal" and "this is a bad deal" criteria. I cannot tell you whether a deal is good or bad. It is a subjective decision that is based on the goals of you and your investors. I wish there was a line in the sand where on one side the deal is great and on the other the deal is horrible. That is why it's important to discuss return goals with your investors.

As an example, my company's investors want at least 14% internal rate of return on a five-year exit (but if we end up holding onto the deal for more than five years, the IRR will be lower), as well as at least 8% cash-on-cash (CoC) return during the hold period. Therefore, if our final underwriting model results in an IRR and CoC to the limited partners at or above 14% and 8% respectively, we will submit an offer. If the deal falls below these returns at any of the steps in the underwriting process, we will pass.

Just to give you a better idea of what I just said, a project with an IRR to the limited partners of 14% would equate to a project IRR of 16% or more, assuming the limited partners brought most of the equity and the distribution structure was an 8% preferred return with a 70/30 split thereafter. The average annual CoC return, excluding the profit at sale, for the overall project would be around 10% or more.

Don't underwrite a deal if it doesn't meet your initial investment criteria, which you defined in Chapter 25. For my company, those criteria are properties that are either in a major city or within a commutable distance of a major city, have value-add opportunities, and built in 1980 or later.

So… again, what do you have to offer?

How to Submit a Letter of Intent

If the results of your final underwriting model meet or exceed the desired return goals of your investors, congratulations! You've located a potential deal and are now ready to submit an offer. The offer process will vary from deal to deal. But, generally, you start off by submitting a letter of intent (LOI). If it is an on-market deal represented by a real estate broker, you may be invited to the best and final round. Finally, if you have the best offer, terms, and team, you will be awarded the deal.

The LOI is a non-binding letter (meaning you are not legally bound to the terms you propose) that represents your intent to purchase the property and defines the primary terms of your offer. It is best to work with an experienced real estate attorney to prepare the first couple of LOIs that you submit. After the first couple, you will know what should be in there and probably don't need to consult an attorney before submitting.

You might be wondering why consult an attorney if it is a non-binding letter? The reason is that you're setting the ground rules with the seller on what terms you will and won't accept. Therefore, it is good to have an attorney review your terms in the LOI to see whether there is anything you might want to include.

Terms and conditions that will be included in the LOI are at the very least:

- Purchase price
- Financing structure
- Earnest money amount and deposit schedule (e.g., $100,000 earnest deposit within three days of executing the purchase and sale agreement)
- Length of due diligence period (e.g., 30 days to perform due diligence after executing the purchase and sale agreement)
- Closing schedule (e.g., 60 days after executing the purchase and sale agreement)
- Purchase and sale agreement schedule (e.g., will submit formal purchase and sale agreement five days after executing the LOI)

My recommendation for the terms of the initial LOI is to come in with a strong offer that you'd be able to close. Don't overoffer, don't provide your highest and best offer, and don't submit an offer that you know will be rejected. Also, don't get emotionally attached to the deal and sacrifice your underwriting when submitting an offer.

Your offer should be competitive so that it is a win-win scenario for you and the seller. If you know the market really well and are confident that you will be able to make a lot of money on the deal, a more aggressive offer is to include a non-refundable earnest money deposit. Just be prepared to lose your money if you don't do your due diligence. I don't recommend this approach until you are experienced and/or have experienced team members on your side who have reviewed the deal.

Once you've submitted your LOI, one of four things will happen:

1. Your LOI will be accepted
2. Your LOI will be rejected
3. Your LOI will be countered
4. In an on-market deal represented by a real estate broker, you will be invited to the best and final offer round

If your offer is accepted, congratulations! The next step will be to submit a purchase and sale agreement, which is the binding contract to purchase the apartment at the terms and conditions defined in the LOI.

If your offer is rejected outright, without a counter, you can either resubmit a stronger offer or walk away. Don't get discouraged if your offer is rejected. I have seen plenty of examples of syndicators' offers being rejected just to be awarded the deal because the original buyer fell through or to be awarded a different deal from the same or different seller.

If your LOI is countered, you will have to update your financial model to reflect the new purchase price to determine whether the deal still meets your return criteria. Remember, you didn't initially give them your best offer, so it's likely that you will have some wiggle room on terms or pricing or both. If it does still meet your criteria, you can accept the counter. If it doesn't, you can either counter their counter offer or walk away from the deal. A really good book you should read to hone your negotiating skills is *The Book on Negotiating Real Estate* by J. Scott and Mark Ferguson.

Finally, on most on-market, mid-sized to larger apartment deals, the seller will invite the individual or individuals who submitted the most attractive offer(s) to a best and final offer round. If you are invited to the best and final offer round, you will need to resubmit your highest and best offer. Based on your conversations with either the listing real estate broker (if it is an on-market deal) or the owner (if it is an off-market deal), you won't know the exact price and terms that will result in you being awarded the deal.

However, you will have a pretty good understanding of what price and/or terms will and won't appeal to the seller's goal. Therefore, based on those conversations, you will either create and submit a final offer or walk away from the deal.

After submitting your best and final offer, one of three things will happen:

1. You will be awarded the deal
2. You will be notified that you were not awarded the deal
3. You will be invited to a best and final call with the seller

If you are awarded or not awarded the deal, the next steps are straightforward. However, if you are invited to a best and final seller call, you have some preparations to make.

THE BEST AND FINAL SELLER CALL

The purpose of the best and final seller call is for the seller to vet the buyer, which is you. The last thing the seller wants is to have their property tied up with a buyer who is unable to close the deal, because that's a waste of their time and money. That means you will need to sell the owner on the experience of you and your team and your plan for the property once you've taken over operations.

The more you come prepared to the best and final call with the seller, the more confident the seller will be in your ability to close on the deal. Here is a list of questions that you should be prepared to answer:

- Background questions
  - What is your prior experience in real estate?

- Can you explain the prior transactions that you have completed?
  - Location?
  - Financials?
  - Partnership type?
  - Outcome?
- What is your future deal outlook?
- Who else is a part of your team?
• Business plan questions
  - What is your overall business plan for the subject property?
    - Are you conducting rehabs? If so, what is the plan?
    - What is your capital budget breakdown?
    - Interior budget and plan?
    - Exterior budget and plan?
    - Contingency?
  - How will you be securing debt?
    - Who will you be using?
    - What are the terms?
    - Have you worked with your debt source in the past?
  - Where will the equity be coming from?
    - How many investors?
    - What is your relationship with the investors?
    - Are they investing their personal funds or investing institutional funds?
    - What is your backup plan if your primary investment source doesn't follow through?
  - Who is your property management company?
    - Are they partners in the deal or a third party?
    - Have you worked with them in the past?
    - Have they reviewed and signed off on the underwriting?

- Miscellaneous questions
  - Have you toured the deal?
  - Are you currently pursuing other deals?
  - Are you familiar with an XXX (e.g., REO or Fannie Mae) contract?
  - <u>If off-market</u>: Why would I sell to you directly and not take my chances putting it on market (see Chapter 26 to refresh yourself on the benefits of selling off-market)?
  - How can you sweeten the offer?

At the end of the call, remember to ask this question:

"Is there any reason why we would not be awarded the deal?"

Once you've completed the best and final call, your fate is in the seller's hands. If you aren't awarded the deal, dust yourself off, find a new deal, and restart the underwriting process. If you are awarded the deal, the seller will send you an official purchase and sale agreement. You've already agreed to a purchase price, so the purpose of the purchase and sale agreement, aside from officially putting the property under contract, is to define the terms of the contract.

The contract includes things like the earnest money deposit (collateral so the seller knows that you are serious about closing), the seller deliverables (what the seller is committing to provide to you during the due diligence period), and a due diligence timeline. Typically, there will be a few negotiations back and forth on the terms, which are ideally reflective of the terms outline in the LOI.

Once you've signed on the dotted line, don't celebrate just yet, because the work is just getting started!

PART 4: THE EXECUTION

PART 1: THE EXPERIENCE

KNOWLEDGE — Chapters 1 - 4
1. What is apartment syndication?
2. How to Get Started
3. What to focus on

GOALS — Chapters 5 - 6
1. How do you make money?
2. Set 12-month goal and long-term vision
3. Ultimate Success Formula

BRAND BUILDING — Chapters 7 - 12
1. Why you need a brand
2. Select a target audience
3. How to build a brand

MARKET EVALUATION — Chapters 13 - 16
1. 3 Immutable Laws of Real Estate
2. Evaluate 7 markets
3. Pick 1-2 Target Markets

PART 2: THE MONEY

BUILD TEAM — Chapters 17 - 19
1. Find core real estate team members
2. Hire a mentor or consultant

FIND CAPITAL — Chapters 20 - 24
1. Why will they invest?
2. Build passive investor database
3. Create partnership structure

PART 3: THE DEAL

FIND DEALS — Chapters 25 - 28
1. Set investment criteria
2. On-market vs. off-market deals
3. How to find your first deal

UNDERWRITING — Chapters 29 - 31
1. Information needed to underwrite a deal
2. The 6-step underwriting process

SUBMIT OFFER — Chapters 32
1. How to submit an offer on a deal
2. Best-and-final offer
3. Purchase sales agreement

PART 4: THE EXECUTION

YOU ARE HERE

DUE DILIGENCE — Chapters 33 - 37
1. 10 due diligence reports
2. Secure financing from lender

SECURE CAPITAL — Chapters 38 - 42
1. Create investment summary
2. New investment offering call
3. Secure investor commitments

CLOSE — Chapters 43 - 44
1. Closing process
2. Notify passive investors

EXECUTE BUSINESS PLAN — Chapters 45 - 46
1. 10 asset management duties
2. How to sell the apartment

CHAPTER 33

SO YOU'RE SAYING THERE'S A CHANCE?

Upon executing the purchase and sale agreement, officially putting the apartment community under contract, you enter the final phase of the syndication process before closing – due diligence.

When underwriting the deal, you made a lot of assumptions. Granted, you didn't pull them out of thin air, but many of the assumptions were highly based on faithfully trusting the information provided by the owner and the listing broker. Now that you have the property under contract, you'll have access to all the information you need to confirm the accuracy of this information and renegotiate or cancel the contract if necessary.

In your purchase and sale agreement, the seller and you agreed on a due diligence timeline. During this period, you must obtain the due diligence reports, compare the results with your underwriting assumptions, update your financial model, and negotiate new terms with the owner if necessary. Strive to stay on schedule or, even better, stay ahead of schedule.

You should start the due diligence process on day one on every deal. You don't want to miss a deadline, because the seller could technically cancel the contract if you do. Additionally, prior to closing, you will need to secure financing from a lender AND funding from your passive investors (which I will go over starting in Chapter 37), so that's why you'll have no time to celebrate securing your first contract. (Okay, maybe you can celebrate a little.)

Like most aspects of the apartment syndication process, there are nuances to the due diligence process. But, generally, the process is:

- Obtain the due diligence reports (Chapter 34)
- Review the reports with your property management company, comparing the results with the assumptions you made in your financial model (Chapter 35)
- Either move forward with your original offer, negotiate a new purchase price with the seller, or cancel the contract (Chapter 36)
- Secure financing from your lender (Chapter 37)

CHAPTER 34

THE DUE DILIGENCE REPORT CARDS

There are 10 major reports you need to obtain during the due diligence process. The majority of these reports are required by the lender before providing financing for the deal, but all of them will be used to confirm your underwriting and business plan assumptions. For each of the 10 reports, I now outline the contents and how to obtain the reports, and I give you an approximate cost for each.

THE 10 DUE DILIGENCE REPORTS

1. Financial document audit

The financial document audit is the analysis of the apartment's historical operations compared with your budgeted income and expense figures.

For this audit, a consultant will collect detailed historical financial reports and leases from the sellers, including the last three years of income and expense data, bank statements, and rent rolls. The output of the analysis is a detailed spreadsheet of the asset's historical income, operating expenses, non-operating expenses, and net cash flow compared with the budgeted figures you provided, as well as the raw data used to create the audit summary.

The summary will take a form that is similar to a pro forma, with the income and expenses broken down into individual line items for an easy comparison on your end. The consultant will also provide you with an executive summary document, which will outline how to interpret the audit, what data was used to create the audit spreadsheet, and an explanation of any figures that deviate from your budget.

To obtain this document, you will need to hire a commercial real estate consulting firm that specializes in creating financial document audits. An approximate cost for this report is $6,000. Your property management company might be able to perform this audit as well. We used to hire an outside group but now we use our property management company, which saves us $6,000.

2. Internal property condition assessment
The internal property condition assessment (PCA) is a detailed inspection report on the overall condition of the apartment community.

A licensed contractor will inspect the property from top to bottom. Based on the inspection, the contractor will prepare a report with recommendations, preliminary costs, and priorities for immediate repairs, recommended repairs, and continued replacements, along with accompanying pictures of the interiors, exteriors, and the items needing repair.

Being an internal report, you will be responsible for hiring a licensed commercial contractor to perform the assessment. An approximate cost for this assessment is $2,500.

3. Market survey report
The market survey is a more formal and comprehensive rental comparison analysis than the one you performed during the underwriting phase.

Your property manager will locate direct competitors of the apartment community. Then they will compare your apartment community with each of the direct competitors over various factors to determine the market rents on an overall and a unit type basis.

4. Lease audit report
The lease audit is the process of examining the individual leases at the apartment community. Your property manager will collect all of the leases of the current residents at the apartment community and perform an audit. They will analyze each lease, recording the rents, security deposits, concessions, and terms. Then they compare the information gathered from the leases with the rent roll provided by the owner, recording any discrepancies.

5. Unit walk report
The unit walk is the inspection of each individual unit at the apartment community. During the unit walk, your property manager will inspect each individual unit. The purpose of the unit walk is to determine the current condition of each unit. While conducting the unit walk, they will take notes on things like the condition of the rooms, the type and condition of appliances, the presence or absence of washer/dryer hookups, the conditions of the light fixtures, missing GFCI outlets, and anything else that stands out as a potential maintenance or resident issue.

Most likely, your property manager will perform the market survey, lease audit, and unit walk report, and they will usually do it for free if you close. They may charge you for their work if you don't close on the deal. If you have to hire a third party to create these three reports, the cost is approximately $4,000 for all three.

6. Site survey
The site survey is a map of the apartment community that indicates the boundaries of the community and lot size. Included in this report is a written description of the community.

The site survey will be performed by a third-party vendor that specializes in site surveys. You need to get multiple bids for your project. The approximate cost is $6,000.

7. Property condition assessment
This is the same assessment as the internal PCA, but this one is performed by a third-party vendor selected by your lender. Compare and contrast the results of this PCA with those from your internal PCA. Maybe the lender caught something that your inspector didn't, or vice versa.

The cost is approximately $2,000.

8. Environmental site assessment
The environmental site assessment is an inspection that identifies potential or existing environmental contamination liabilities. It addresses the underlying land, as well as any physical improvements to the property, and will offer conclusions or recommendations for further investigations if an issue is found.

The environmental site assessment is also performed by a third-party vendor selected by your lender. The approximate cost is $2,500.

9. Appraisal
The appraisal determines the as-is value of the apartment community.

An appraiser will inspect the property, and then calculate the as-is value of the apartment community. The three appraisal methods that will be used to determine the property value are the sales comparison approach (comparing the subject property to similar properties that were recently sold), the income capitalization approach (using the net operating income and the market capitalization rate), and cost approach (the cost to replace/rebuild the property).

The appraisal report is created by an appraiser selected by your lender. The cost is approximately $5,000.

10. Green report
The green report is an optional assessment that evaluates potential energy and water conservation measures for the apartment community. The report will include a list of all measures found, along with the associated cost savings, and initial investment.

The report is created by a third-party vendor selected by your lender. The approximate cost is $3,500.

If you are going to implement a RUBS program, which evaluates the usage of utilities and reports the amount you can bill back to the residents, you will need to consult with a RUBS company in your local market to obtain a few quotes.

As the reports begin to trickle in, you will review the results to determine the accuracy of your financial model.

In the next chapter, you will learn how to interpret the results of each report and how the information will impact your financial model. All of the pricing figures are based on an apartment community that is in the 100- to 300-unit range. If your apartment deal falls outside of that range, consult with the various vendors to get the approximate costs.

CHAPTER 35

YOUR FINAL EXAM

Up until this point, your assumptions about a property that you want to purchase have been based on the data provided by the seller (the rent roll and the T-12) and your own research, as well as your knowledge of the market. While this is enough information to initially qualify a deal and submit an offer, it is not enough information to risk millions of dollars on. That's why you will spend 60 to 90 days (and thousands of dollars) to perform detailed due diligence before close.

REVIEWING THE 10 DUE DILIGENCE REPORTS

The results of each due diligence report will allow you to confirm one or more assumptions from your underwriting and business plan. However, a few of the reports, depending on your findings, may disqualify the deal entirely.

Here are the best practices for interpreting the results of the 10 due diligence reports.

1. Financial document audit

Use the results of the financial document audit to confirm your income and expense assumptions. During underwriting, these assumptions were based on the T-12 and rent roll provided by the sellers and on the market cost per unit per year rates for the expenses.

Open your financial model and go through each stabilized income and expense line item, seeing how they compare with the results of the financial audit. Or, most likely, the consultant that performed the audit will have already compared the results with your budget, made adjustments based on their expertise and any inputs you provided, and commented on any discrepancies.

If there are adjustments made or discrepancies found, discuss them with your property management company to see whether you need to change any income or expense figures in your financial model. Depending on the number and size of adjustments or discrepancies, they may change your projected returns to the point that the deal no longer meets or exceeds your investor expectations.

2. Internal property condition assessment

The internal property condition assessment will provide you with the priority levels of immediate replacement, which indicates things that need to be addressed immediately after closing or sometimes even before; recommended replacement, which indicates maintenance issues identified that aren't required to be replaced; and continued replacement, which indicates things that don't need to be replaced now but will need to be replaced at some point during the business plan.

It will also list the preliminary costs of interior and exterior items that require repair. During the underwriting process, you created a renovation/upgrade plan for the interior and exterior of the apartment community, including the estimated costs.

Once you receive the internal PCA, compare the results with your business plan assumptions. For the exteriors, how do the contractor's findings compare with your budgeted exterior renovations figure? Did they find any issues that require either immediate repair or repair in the near future that weren't accounted for in your budgeted costs? Similarly, how do the contractor's findings on the interiors of the units compare with your budgeted costs?

These are preliminary costs, not exact. However, they will be more accurate than the assumptions you made during the underwriting process. Therefore, if there are discrepancies between the contractor's estimated repairs costs and your budgeted costs, change the renovation figures on your financial model to reflect the results of the PCA. Hopefully, your assumptions were fairly accurate. Ideally, since you should have made very conservative renovation assumptions, you discover that the estimated repairs are less than your assumptions. However, if unaccounted-for expenses arise, they may push your return projections outside of the range of your investors' goals.

3. Market survey report

The market survey report will compare the subject apartment community with direct competitors' communities across a variety of factors. Ultimately, it will provide you with the market rents you will achieve once you've completed your value-add business plan.

To determine the accuracy of your rental premium assumptions, compare the average market rents for each unit type with the stabilized rent assumptions in your financial model. Since this report was likely created by your property management company, you can trust that these are the rental premiums with which they are most comfortable. Therefore, if there are discrepancies between these results and the assumption on the financial model, make the necessary adjustments and review the projected returns to see whether they still align with your investors' goals.

4. Lease audit report

The lease audit report compares the data obtained from the actual leases with the information provided in the rent roll.

Any discrepancies will be highlighted by your property management company, including the causes of the discrepancies and whether the causes have been addressed. Unless the current property managers are extremely incompetent, the discrepancies should be minor, if there are any at all, and should not affect your financial model.

5. Unit walk report

The unit walk report will summarize the current interior conditions of each unit. It will outline the exact number of units that require upgrades, including details on the type of upgrade and any maintenance or replacement of certain items that needs to be addressed. Additionally, it will highlight any resident issues discovered.

Once you receive the unit walk report, compare the data with your interior renovation assumptions to determine the accuracy of your interior business plan.

Does the number of units that require interior upgrades match your business plan? Is there unexpected deferred maintenance that wasn't accounted for in your budget? Are there a high number of residents who will need to be evicted once you've taken over the operations?

Using that data, you can create a more detailed, unit-by-unit interior renovation plan and calculate a more accurate budget. Make any adjustments to your interior renovation assumption on your financial model and review the projected returns, making sure they still align with your investors' expectations.

6. Site survey

The site survey report will list any boundary, easement, utility, and zoning issues for the apartment community. Generally, if a problem is found during the site survey, the bank will not provide a loan on the property. If something does come up, your options are limited and should be addressed on a case-by-case basis. If the problem can't be resolved, you will have to cancel the contract.

7. Property condition assessment
This PCA is performed by a third-party lender selected by the owner. Analyze this report using the same approach used when evaluating the internal PCA.

8. Environmental site assessment
The environmental assessment report will list potential or existing environmental issues with the apartment community. Similar to the site survey, if the contractor identifies an environmental problem, the lender will not provide a loan for the property. Again, these issues should be addressed on a case-by-case basis.

9. Appraisal report
The appraisal report will provide an as-is value of the apartment community. Once you receive the appraisal, you should compare the appraised value with the contract purchase price.

There are a few different ways to appraise the property value. First, the value will be calculated using the income approach, which is dividing the net operating income by the market cap rate. Second, the value will be calculated using the sales comparison approach, which compares the subject property with comparable properties that sold within the last 12 months. Last, the value will be calculated by determining the replacement cost of the property.

The lender will base the financing on the appraised value, not the contract price. Therefore, if the appraisal comes back at a value higher than the contract price, fantastic! That's essentially free equity. However, if the appraised value is lower than the contract price, you will likely have to either make up the difference by raising additional capital or renegotiate the purchase price with the seller.

If you are implementing a value-add business plan, if the appraisal comes back a little low, the lender may not re-trade you, which means they may not change the loan to reflect the lower appraisal value.

10. Green report

The green report, which is the only document that won't disqualify a deal, outlines all of the potential energy and water conservation opportunities. It will list all of the opportunities that were identified, the estimated initial investment to implement, the associated cost savings, and the return on investment. Deciding which opportunities to move forward with should be based on the payback period and the projected hold period of the property.

For example, the following energy-efficient opportunities were identified at the 216-unit apartment community we had assessed:

- Dual-pane windows
- Wall insulation and leakage sealing
- Roof insulation
- Programmable thermostats
- Low-flow showerheads and toilets
- Interior and exterior LED lighting
- Energy Star-rated refrigerators and dishwashers

After analyzing the investment amount and cost savings, the opportunities we implemented and the associated savings and payback periods were:

- Low-flow showerheads: 1-year payback, $16,827 annual savings
- Exterior LED lighting: 14.4-year payback, $3,236 annual savings
- Pool cover: 1.5-year payback, $409 annual savings

The reasoning behind implementing the low-flow showerheads and pool cover was that we planned on holding the property for five years, so once we paid back the initial investment amount, it was pure profit. We ended up losing money on the exterior LED lighting project. We installed these lights to increase resident safety anyway.

You will find that the green report will list ALL opportunities, even if the payback period is absurdly long. If we implemented all the opportunities identified in the example above, the overall payback period would have been 91.9 years, with the longest payback period being 165 years for the Energy Star-rated dishwashers. Unless we have decided to hold onto a building until we die or until they've discovered an immortality serum, we will stick to the opportunities that either result in a payback period lower than our projected hold time or address a resident safety concern.

Once the results of these due diligence reports have been reviewed and your underwriting assumptions have been confirmed/updated, it is time to make a decision… to invest or not to invest?

CHAPTER 36

YAY OR NAY?

After reviewing the results of the 10 due diligence reports as I just explained, you will likely have to go back to your financial model and update the assumptions. Once you've updated the assumptions in the financial model, your projected returns will have changed. Ideally, they've gone up or stayed the same. If that is the case, once you've secured financing and private money from your investors, you're ready to close the deal (more on this in the following chapters).

If an issue comes up during the site survey or the environmental site assessment, which is rare, it will need to be resolved prior to closing. If the seller is unwilling or unable to address these issues, the lender will likely not provide a loan on the property, which means you will have to cancel the contract.

If the updated projections fall below your investors' returns goals, you will have to renegotiate the contract with the seller. Adjust the purchase price in your financial model until the projected returns meet your investors' goals. Then explain to your broker that you want to renegotiate the purchase price and state the reasons for doing so. If the seller will not accept the new contract terms, don't be afraid to walk away from the deal.

Why?

At the end of the day, it is your job to preserve your investors' capital first and foremost, and then to grow it.

CHAPTER 37

YOU CAN TAKE IT TO THE BANK

Before putting the property under contract, you should have already had a conversation with a lender or mortgage broker, who will have provided you with the projected loan terms that you input into your financial model. Once the property is under contract, and while you are in the process of obtaining the 10 due diligence documents, you should begin the process of securing financing.

HOW TO SECURE FINANCING FROM A LENDER

If it is your first time securing financing for an apartment community, you will need to make a strong case to the lender regarding why they should provide you with financing for the apartment community (refer back to Chapter 23 on how to create alignment of interest with your team members to increase your credibility). When meeting with the lender for the first time, come prepared with the following documentation:

Biography – Create a short biography of your company's experience in the commercial real estate industry. You should already have this information included on the company presentation you created in Chapter 9. Just summarize it in a one-page Word document, print it out, and bring it to your meeting with your lender.

Financial statements – Bring the financial statements for the past three years of the subject apartment community. Obtaining financial statements for the last three years may be difficult, so acquire the trailing 12-month financials at the very least. You need to bring a copy of a current rent roll, too.

Budget and business plan – Your business plan is what you plan on doing after taking over the asset. As a value-add investor, your business plan is to perform renovations in order to increase the revenue and/or improve the operations in order to reduce the expenses. Therefore, you need to bring a copy of your pro forma, which states the projected stabilized revenue and expense line items.

The lender will want to see a copy of your capital expenditure budget for the interior and exterior of the apartment as well as a list of property details (i.e., property photos, address, description, unit-mix, property age, and construction type).

Personal financial statements for each loan guarantor – When you are obtaining a loan for your apartment deal, the lender will require a guarantee from the individual or entity that is borrowing the funds. This individual or entity is referred to as the "loan guarantor," who personally guarantees the loan if it is a recourse type. If it is a non-recourse loan they still require someone that meets the liquidity, net worth, and experience requirements.

According to the IRS, a recourse debt holds the borrower personally liable, while all other debt is considered non-recourse. In general, recourse debt allows lenders to collect what is owed for the debt even after they've taken collateral (i.e., the property). Lenders have the right to garnish wages or levy accounts to collect what is owed.

On the other hand, non-recourse debt does not allow the lender to pursue anything other than the collateral. But there are a few exceptions. If a recourse carve-out is triggered, the non-recourse loan is treated as a recourse loan, and the lender can pursue what is owed even after they've taken the collateral. The two most common bad-boy carve-outs are gross negligence (i.e., if the borrower forsakes the property) and fraud (i.e., if the borrower does something illegal).

If you are starting out, you will likely not meet the lender requirements to be the only loan guarantor on paper, because you don't have either the liquidity, experience, or net worth. Therefore, you will need to find a high net worth individual and an experienced apartment syndicator or investor to become the loan guarantor in order to qualify for the loan.

Ideally, the loan guarantor meets the liquidity and net worth requirements, and has real estate experience in the apartment real estate niche. However, if the high net worth individual does not meet the experience requirements, you will need to bring on a seasoned investor who has owned a similar property for at least 12 months (i.e., a value-add apartment deal of a similar size and in a similar market) to sign on the loan.

The liquidity and net worth requirements will vary depending on the size of the deal and the lender. However, for a general understanding, when looking for a loan guarantor this individual must meet the following requirements:

- Be a U.S. citizen
- Have a minimum net worth equal to the mortgage amount
- Have minimum liquidity equal to nine months of debt service or 10% of the loan amount post-closing

- Have a FICO score of 650 or better with at least two of the national credit bureaus, or an average FICO score of 650 or better with all three national credit bureaus

Don't expect someone who meets these qualifications to guarantee the loan for free. There are risks involved in being a loan guarantor. To offset these risks, offer them compensation. The compensation structure for a loan guarantor will depend on the type of loan they are signing. Since a recourse loan is riskier than a non-recourse loan, you'll likely have to compensate the loan guarantor more if obtaining a recourse loan.

The two main ways to compensate a loan guarantor are:

1. **Paying an upfront fee:** If it is a non-recourse loan, the typical one-time fee is 0.5% to 2% of the principal balance of the mortgage loan paid at close (3.5% to 5% for recourse loans). If the loan balance is $10 million, for example, the fee would be $25,000 to $100,000 for a nonrecourse loan, or $350,000 to $500,000 for a recourse loan.
2. **Equity stake in the deal:** In addition to or instead of a one-time fee, you can offer an equity stake in the deal. Depending on how you negotiate, the projected returns, and how many other options you have to guarantee the loan, the percentage can be 5% to 30% of the general partnership with the percentage offered on nonrecourse debt being lower than what is offered on recourse debt.

All of these fees and percentages are rules of thumb. They can fluctuate based on variables like your team, your relationship with the loan guarantor, and the business plan.

It is a very good deal for high net worth investors or individuals to do a loan guarantee, especially if it is a non-recourse loan and they know the sponsor well. (That's you.) They are essentially getting free equity and free cash, because they aren't investing any money into the deal. They are just providing their balance sheet with minimum risk.

At the same time, there is risk involved, as with any investment opportunity. For example, if your business partner commits fraud without your knowledge, as a result the bank can call the note. That would mean the payment in full would be due immediately. That could put the property into foreclosure and then the loan guarantor could be at risk for the entire amount that is owed to the bank. That is a big problem. (This is a good reason to get to know people before doing business with them. Building trust is a must.)

When approaching potential loan guarantors, you have to look at it from both perspectives (yours and theirs). Sure, a fraudulent business partner isn't a likely scenario, but be aware of how they may perceive things. It's not a complete slam-dunk for them. There is risk involved.

Once you've located your loan guarantor(s), you need to obtain a personal financial statement and a resume for each guarantor.

THE TWO MAIN TYPES OF DEBT FINANCING

There are two main types of financing: a permanent agency loan and a bridge loan. What follows is a high-level overview of the general characteristics of each loan type and the situations where each loan type is ideal:

1. Permanent agency loan

A permanent agency loan is secured from Fannie Mae or Freddie Mac and is longer term in nature. Typical loan term lengths are 5, 7, 10, or 12 years and amortized over 20 to 30 years. Amortization refers to the process of paying down the principal of a loan over the life of the loan. Each loan payment is the same amount, but a different portion is allocated to principal and interest. The first loan payment is mostly interest, with more and more of the loan payment going toward paying down the principal with each subsequent loan payment. The longer the amortization period, the smaller the overall payments but the higher total interest costs over the lifespan of the loan.

Generally, you can secure a permanent agency loan at a LTV (loan-to-value) ratio of 70% to 80% (i.e., with a 20% to 30% down payment).

Depending on the lender, there may or may not be restrictions on prepayment. If there is a prepayment clause, if you pay off the loan in its entirety by selling or refinancing the property early, you will be charged a prepayment fee, yield maintenance (allows the lender to get the same yield as if you made all scheduled mortgage payments until the end of the loan term), and/or defeasance (a substitution of collateral for the loan).

For a permanent agency loan, you will have the potential to secure a non-recourse loan and have the potential for interest-only payments for one to five years, depending on the strength of the borrower (i.e., the loan guarantor).

Overall, a permanent agency loan is a "set it and forget it" loan. This can work well, assuming you adhere to all your loan covenants. You won't have to check back in with the lender to receive additional funds or worry about having to refinance in the middle of your business plan (assuming the loan term is longer than your projected hold period).

An example of a permanent agency loan is a five-year, 80% LTV loan amortized over 25 years with an interest rate of 5.25%. If the purchase price is $10,000,000 for example, the down payment would be $2,000,000, the loan would be $8,000,000, and the monthly payment (principal + interest) would be $47,939.82. At the end of five years, you must make a balloon payment, refinance into a new loan, or sell the property. If the first two years are interest-only, that means the monthly mortgage payment during those two years would be $35,000.

2. Bridge loan

A bridge loan is defined as a short-term loan that is used until a person or company secures long-term financing or sells the property.

A bridge loan ranges from six months to three years. Additionally, many bridge loan lenders will grant the option to extend the term for another six months to two years for a fee.

Generally, a bridge loan has interest-only payments for the term of the loan.

Compared with permanent financing, bridge loans have faster closings but higher interest rates. A typical interest rate is the six-month LIBOR (London Inter-Bank Offered Rate, which is the average of interest rates estimated by each of the leading banks) plus a spread of 4.5% to 5.5% or higher.

Because of the short-term nature of a bridge loan, most will not have a prepayment penalty.

Typically, a bridge loan is used when an investor needs to complete a certain task. The most common reason to obtain a bridge loan is to improve an underperforming property. Other reasons for a bridge loan include covering costs of finding new tenants and/or doing something about an unsatisfactory occupancy rate, because you are selling the property, or when the borrower cannot qualify for a permanent loan.

Most bridge loans are available for up to 80% LTC (loan-to-cost) as opposed to LTV, because the construction/renovation costs are included in the loan. For example, a property with a value of $10,000,000 and a renovation budget of $2,500,000 has a total project cost of $12,500,000. For an 80% LTV loan, the lender would loan 80% of the property value, or $8,000,000. But for an 80% LTC loan, the lender would loan 80% of the project cost, or $10,000,000.

The standard minimum bridge loan is $1 million. Similar to the permanent agency loan, there is the opportunity for non-recourse with a financially strong borrower.

Here is an example of a bridge loan: An investor purchases a 20-unit building for $1 million that is in poor condition and has 50% occupancy. After $1 million in renovations and achieving a 90% occupancy rate (which a lender will consider stabilized), the net operating income is $175,000 per year. The market capitalization rate is 7%, so the building is valued at $2.5 million.

The total project cost is $2 million ($1 million purchase price + $1 million in renovations). The lender offers a 1-year bridge loan at 80% LTC, which is $1.6 million. The remaining $400,000 will come from the investor.

Once the renovations are completed and the occupancy is stabilized, the $2.5 million property is refinanced into a long-term permanent loan.

Here is a chart that summarizes the characteristics of the two loan types:

	Permanent Agency Loan	**Bridge Loan**
Term Length	3, 5, 7, 10, or 12+ years	Six months to three years (with an option to extend six months to two years)
Amortization	Up to 30 years	Generally interest-only
Interest Rate	Fixed or floating	~1% higher than agency interest rate
Size	$1 million to $100 million	$1 million or more
LTV	70% to 80% LTV	75% to 80% LTC
Recourse	Non-recourse with recourse carve-outs and a financially strong borrower	Usually non-recourse with recourse carve-outs

Ideally, you want to obtain a permanent agency loan, because it is longer term in nature and has a lower interest rate. However, if the deal is under-rented or non-stabilized and/or requires significant renovations, it may not qualify for agency debt. Also, you may not qualify for agency debt if you don't have enough apartment experience or if you have never received agency debt before. If this is the case, you will need to find a better loan guarantor or you may need to obtain a bridge loan and refinance into a permanent loan at a later date.

Finally, you may not be able to get the leverage you need with an agency loan. For example, you may only qualify for a 70% LTV loan, and the resulting increase in the down payment may mean that you will not get the desired returns.

Once a lender is confident in your team's ability to execute the deal, they will provide financing on the project and move forward with their own underwriting process to qualify the deal.

As the lender is doing their thing, and after you've confirmed your assumptions and return projections, it is time to start securing private money from your investors to fund the deal.

PART 1: THE EXPERIENCE

KNOWLEDGE — Chapters 1-4
1. What is apartment syndication?
2. How to Get Started
3. What to focus on

GOALS — Chapters 5-6
1. How do you make money?
2. Set 12-month goal and long-term vision
3. Ultimate Success Formula

BRAND BUILDING — Chapters 7-12
1. Why you need a brand
2. Select a target audience
3. How to build a brand

MARKET EVALUATION — Chapters 13-16
1. 3 Immutable Laws of Real Estate
2. Evaluate 7 markets
3. Pick 1-2 Target Markets

PART 2: THE MONEY

BUILD TEAM — Chapters 17-19
1. Find core real estate team members
2. Hire a mentor or consultant

FIND CAPITAL — Chapters 20-24
1. Why will they invest?
2. Build passive investor database
3. Create partnership structure

PART 3: THE DEAL

FIND DEALS — Chapters 25-28
1. Set investment criteria
2. On-market vs. off-market deals
3. How to find your first deal

UNDERWRITING — Chapters 29-31
1. Information needed to underwrite a deal
2. The 6-step underwriting process

SUBMIT OFFER — Chapter 32
1. How to submit an offer on a deal
2. Best-and-final offer
3. Purchase sales agreement

PART 4: THE EXECUTION

DUE DILIGENCE — Chapters 33-37
1. 10 due diligence reports
2. Secure financing from lender

SECURE CAPITAL — Chapters 38-42 **(YOU ARE HERE)**
1. Create investment summary
2. New investment offering call
3. Secure investor commitments

CLOSE — Chapters 43-44
1. Closing process
2. Notify passive investors

EXECUTE BUSINESS PLAN — Chapters 45-46
1. 10 asset management duties
2. How to sell the apartment

CHAPTER 38

TIME TO COMMIT

Following the execution of the purchase and sale agreement (where you officially place the apartment community under contract) you immediately enter the funding phase. During this phase, and concurrent with the due diligence phase, you have to start generating interest and securing commitments from your passive investors. Throughout the due diligence process, you'll be waiting around for inspections to be completed and reports to be produced. Conversely, securing commitments from your investors is a more hands-on process that spans the entirety of the post-contract, pre-closing period.

You shouldn't be scrambling to find passive investors after putting the deal under contract. You shouldn't even start looking for a deal before getting enough verbal interest to close on a potential deal. By this point you should have already taken action on the advice provided in this book. Talking to investors is an ongoing process. It's something that you will do all the time, because once you have a deal you'll be calling on these interested parties.

If you are taking the advice found in the pages of this book, you've already compiled a list of people who have verbally committed to investing in a deal with you (as long as the projected returns aligned with their goals). It is now time to convert these potential investors into investors that are officially committed to putting capital into your deal.

When you've successfully completed a few deals with your investors, proving that you can follow through with the projected returns by distributing the preferred returns (hopefully more), the process of securing commitments is much easier. In fact, the investors will more than likely come to you. That said, if it is your first deal, you won't have a proven track record with your investors, so the process of securing commitments will require more proactive effort on your part. Either way, the overall outline remains the same. You will:

- Create an investment summary.
- Email your investor database, notifying them of the new investment opportunity, and the time and date of the new investment offering conference call.
- After you've conducted the conference call, send the recording of the conference call to your investor database.
- If you aren't an experienced syndicator who has investors coming to them, you will follow up with each of your investors to secure their capital commitments.
- Send the committed investors the proper documentation to formalize their investment in the deal.

Before I take you into the process of securing commitments in more detail, let's go over how much money you actually need to raise for the deal. Once you've notified your lender of a new deal and you've submitted the required documentation outlined in previous chapters, the lender will provide you with a breakdown of the cash required to close the loan. This figure should be very close to the total equity requirement you calculated when underwriting the deal.

That said, as I mentioned in the intensive underwriting chapter, you will also want to raise additional money for your operating budget to cover shortfalls – periods of occupancy dips, paying insurance in one lump sum, and taxes. That means you will want to raise an additional 1% to 5% of the purchase price.

After securing enough investor commitments to close the loan and cover shortfalls, don't turn away other interested investors. Let them know that you've raised enough money for this deal, but that you will add them to a waiting list. Unexpected events will come up for you throughout the entire syndication process. Similarly, unexpected events will come up for the investors who have committed capital to your deals. When that happens, you don't want that to be the reason you cannot close on the deal. Nor do you want to be a bundle of nerves, scrambling to find replacement capital.

On one of my early deals, I learned the hard way that I would always need a waiting list of investors. A few weeks leading up to close on the deal, a handful of my investors backed out. Since I was just starting out, I didn't have passive investors on a waiting list. Fortunately, another passive investor ended up investing more than his initial commitment, which covered the deficit.

On future deals, I always make sure that I have passive investors on a waiting list, just in case, to the tune of 50% of the total money raise. Now if an investor has to back out of a deal, I just fill their spot with one or more investors on my waiting list.

After you've calculated how much money you need to raise to close your apartment deal, cover shortfall, and have as a backup in case of last-minute emergencies, the real fun begins!

CHAPTER 39

PAINTING THE FULL PICTURE

Before introducing the new deal to your investors, you need to create an investment summary that outlines the business plan for the apartment community. The purpose of the summary is to get the main investment highlights across to your investors in a simple way that allows the investors to know exactly how they will benefit from investing in the deal and so they can feel confident in the abilities of you and your team to deliver on your projections.

The majority of the information included in the investment summary will come from the information you gathered while underwriting the deal. Simply summarize the investment highlights and business plan in a nicely designed and concise format.

If you are just starting out, you likely will not have many professional passive investors. In fact, the majority of your investors may have never invested in an apartment building before. They will not have the same level of comprehension and understanding of the apartment niche as you do. Therefore, keep your audience in mind when preparing your investment summary.

After you build a proven track record, because you have gained the trust of your investors, you will just send them an email with the high-level investment highlights. That typically will be enough information for them to make the decision on whether to invest or not. However, you will always have investors who want an outline of the business plan, whether they are repeat investors or new investors. That's why is it always best to create a detailed investment summary.

The summary should be broken into the following seven sections:

1. Executive Summary
2. Investment Highlights
3. Property Overview
4. Financial Analysis
5. Market Overview
6. Portfolio and Case Studies
7. Appendix

Each section will outline information about the deal that is required by the passive investor to make an educated investment decision. The following sections can be used as a guide in the creation of your own detailed investment summary for a value-add apartment deal.

How to Create the Investment Summary
1. Executive Summary

The first slide (as in PowerPoint... though the summary can be created as a PDF) after the cover page and a table of contents is the executive summary. This one summary slide should communicate all of the major investment highlights of the deal. The rest of the investment summary will unpack these highlights in more detail. Following is a list of information to include:

- A paragraph explaining the opportunity, including the property name, built date, number of units, whether the

deal was acquired on-market or off-market, the business plan (i.e., your value-add strategy), and the details of the business plan (e.g., continuing the upgrades of the interiors, securing long-term debt, optimizing operations)
- A data table with the offering summary that includes the cap rate and the expense ratio based on the T-12, the debt service coverage ratio (DSCR), the purchase price, the projected hold period, the equity required to close, the equity multiple to the limited partners, the average annual return, and the internal rate of return (IRR)
- A summary of the top two or three investment highlights of the deal that explains why you are investing in the deal
- The partnership structure, including how the cash flow and the profit at sale is distributed
- A data table that shows the projected yearly returns to the limited partner for a sample investment of $100,000

2. Investment Highlights

The investment highlights section is essentially a written explanation of the information outlined on the executive summary slide/page. This section is four slides in length and is broken into four subsections: (1) the business plan, (2) the interior renovations, (3) the capital improvement budget, and (4) the debt summary.

Examples of things to highlight for each subsection are:

- **Business Plan**
  - <u>Interior Renovations</u>: What percentage of units are already upgraded and what percentage of units will you be upgrading? What types of upgrades will you

be implementing? How much will the renovations cost for each unit and what is the renovation timeline? What rental premiums will you achieve for upgraded units?
- Operational Improvements: How will you improve the operations of the apartment? Will you rebrand the apartment? Who will take over the operations, what is their experience level, and which strategies will they implement to improve the operations?
- Financing: Is there a prepayment penalty or will you be allowed to refinance in order to return a sizable amount of equity to your investors? Is the interest rate fixed or floating? If floating, did you purchase a cap on the interest rate?
- Exit Strategy: When do you plan on selling the asset? Do you plan on refinancing the asset and, if so, when? And is the refinance included in your return projections? What is the projected IRR and equity multiple at sale?

- **Interior Renovations**
  - Include a picture of a non-renovated and a renovated unit so the investors can visually see the types of upgrades you will be implementing.
  - If the current owner has already started a renovation program, the renovated picture will be of an actual unit. If the current owner has not started a renovation program, ask your property management company to provide you with a picture of a unit from an apartment community they currently manage that has similar upgrades.
  - Also include a description of the non-renovated unit and the renovated unit, listing out the main amenities for each.

- **Capital Improvement Budget**
  - Provide a data table that outlines the interior and exterior capital improvement costs.
- **Debt Summary**
  - Outline the debt structure, including the loan balance, future funding for renovations, the interest rate, the number of interest-only months, loan term, amortization period, and prepayment penalty.

3. Property Overview

The property overview section will provide an overall description of the apartment community. Examples of information to include are:

- **Portfolio Amenities**
  - What are the main amenities offered at the apartment community? (Pool, fitness center, in-unit laundry, clubhouse, large closets)
  - Create a gallery of pictures of the main amenities.
- **Property Overview**
  - <u>Property information</u>: Data table with a description of the asset, including the purchase price, number of buildings, number of units, rentable square footage, year built, land size, who pays which utilities (electric, water, sewer, gas), and the construction type.
  - <u>Unit features</u>: What are the standard features for each unit? (Fireplace, stainless steel appliances, patio/balcony, hardwood floors)
  - <u>Community amenities</u>: What amenities are offered by the community? Try not to repeat the same amenities here that are included in the "portfolio amenities" subsection.

- **Unit Mix**
  - Include a snapshot of the unit-mix information, including the unit types and the number of bedrooms and bathrooms, square footage, number of units, market rent, and current rent for each unit type.
  - For each bedroom/bathroom unit type combination, dedicate a slide/page to providing a snapshot of the floorplans for each unit type. For example, if there are four different floorplans with one bedroom, include a picture of all four floorplans on one slide/page.
- **Site Plan**
  - Include a picture of the overall site plan of the apartment community, which you should be able to obtain from the OM, the listing real estate broker (if on-market), or directly from the owner (if off-market).

4. Financial Analysis

The financial analysis section will show your investors the most current results from your underwriting. Examples of information to highlight are:

- **Offering summary**: This is a repeat of the offering summary you provided in the executive summary. Insert a data table with the offering summary, which includes the cap rate and the expense ratio based on the T-12, the debt service coverage ratio (DSCR), the purchase price, the projected hold period, the equity required to close, the equity multiple to the limited partners, the average annual return, and the internal rate of return.
- **Debt summary**: This is a summary of the debt terms, which is a repeat of the data you provided in the debt

summary table in the investment highlights section. Outline the debt structure, including the loan balance, future funding for renovations, the interest rate, number of interest-only months, loan term, amortization period, and prepayment penalty.
- **Sample investment returns**: This is a data table that shows the projected yearly returns to the limited partner for a sample investment of $100,000.
- **Pro forma**: Include your five-year (can be shorter or longer, depending on your projected hold period) pro forma, which outlines the revenue and expense line items from your underwriting.

5. Market Overview

The first part of the market overview section will highlight the selling points of the local market in which the apartment community is located. The information in this slide/page will vary based on the strengths of your target market. During the market evaluation and selection phase you learned about in Chapter 15, you listed out market insights for each market factor analyzed. Use those findings to determine the selling points to highlight.

Examples of things to highlight are:

- Does the market appear on any "Top City in the Nation" lists?
- What is the status of the current business climate?
- Is the apartment community situated near any major highways or transportation hubs?
- What are nearby employment centers? Retail centers?
- Is there construction (retail, commercial) currently underway or coming in the near future?
- Have any new businesses recently moved to the area?

- What is the market's job growth? Population growth? Unemployment reduction? How does it compare with other markets in the country?
- Is the market's GDP growing?

Select two of the major insights and include data tables, charts, and/or graphs for a visual reinforcement of the market's selling points.

Additionally, include information about the rental and sales comparables. To support your rental premium projections, include the detailed rental comp analysis data tables you created during the underwriting phase.

6. Portfolio and Case Studies

Here you show off your apartment experience. If you haven't completed a deal yet, you won't be able to include any of your own deals in this section in your investment summary. However, what you can do is include case studies of deals that are managed by your property management company or, better yet, the deals from your experienced loan guarantor or mentor.

NOTE: If you follow this approach, make sure you are transparent about your role, if any, in those deals. Do not misrepresent yourself or your business partners to your investors.

For this section, create an investment summary slide/page for each deal, highlighting the property details, the business plan implemented, and the results to the investors.

7. Appendix

The appendix section is where you include your team members' biographies and the definitions of real estate terms used in the investment summary.

The section for the team managing the project will include biographies of the companies and individuals that will be managing the asset and interacting with the investors in some form. First and foremost, that includes your company. Create a biography highlighting your experience and the experience/expertise of each member of your company that will be communicating with your investors once you have taken over the asset. Limit each member's biography to a paragraph. Include information that will inform your investors about your real estate background, employment background, and relevant extracurricular activities in which you are currently involved.

You will also want to dedicate a slide that introduces your property management company. You should have partnered up with an experienced, professional management company, and they should already have a biography for their company available on their website or upon request.

If you are partnering with another syndication firm to complete the deal, dedicate a slide/page that introduces them, as well.

Additionally, if you are just starting out, the individuals who will be investing in the deal may have little to no experience with apartments, syndications, or real estate in general. Therefore, just like you had to learn the apartment syndication lingo, you will want to include a slide that defines the apartment syndication terms that are scattered throughout the investment summary presentation package.

Important terms to define are accredited and sophisticated investor, capitalization rate (cap rate), cash flow, cash-on-cash return (CoC), debt service coverage ratio (DSCR), internal rate of return (IRR), and equity multiple, all of which are defined in the glossary section in the back of this book. (You're welcome.)

As new information comes back from the due diligence documents, make sure you update your investors. My company notifies our investors of any changes or updates via email rather than updating and sending out a new investment summary.

You should create the investment summary as quickly as possible – while you are working on the purchase and sale agreement – because it will be referenced or included in your initial email introducing the new deal to your investors.

CHAPTER 40

It's My Honor to Introduce You to...

Once you have created your investment summary, the next step is to notify your investors about your new deal.

When I first started out, I would send an individual email to each investor on my list. Over time, the process evolved to sending out a mass email using the email service Mail Chimp. If you want to spend an entire day writing a whole bunch of emails, more power to you. But you can save yourself a lot of time and increase the professionalism of your initial investor outreach by using an automated email system as I do. It's not the only one available to you. I'm just saying that this is the one I like to use.

Why an automated email system and why not just use your Gmail or other personal account? The answer is simple. You will be sending out a lot of emails. You have four goals with the first email:

- To notify investors that you have an apartment building/community under contract
- To provide investors with your summary of investment highlights
- To offer to send them an investment summary (or include a link to download the investment summary in the email)
- To invite them to a conference call

To achieve your first goal, create a short subject line stating the fact that you have a new deal under contract. It is really good to include a quick investment highlight in the subject line to grab their attention. For example, "Off-Market Opportunity Under Contract at 25% Below Recent Sales."

Next, you want to include the main highlights of the deal, which are outlined in section two of your investment summary. Select two to three main investment highlights and include them in the email. For example, you could include the projected cash-on-cash return and IRR to the limited partners, details about the value-add investment strategy, and the type of debt you will secure. It would be good to include information about the minimum and maximum investment amount available for investors (19% of the total equity raise is the typical maximum, because anything higher and the investor will be underwritten by the lender), the funding schedule (i.e., when you will officially begin accepting commitments), and the closing date.

Rather than including a link to download or attaching the investment summary, you can ask your investors to reply to the email if they are interested in receiving it. With this approach, you will know who requested the investment summary, so you know who is interested and who to follow up with. This was my approach for my first few years, but now I include a link to download the investment summary in the email.

Last, you want to provide the details for the new investment conference call. For all my deals, I set up a conference call on FreeConferenceCall.com, which allows me to host and record a call. You can use another system, too, like ZOOM.com. There are a variety of conference-call portals available to you that allow you to record the calls. Plus, most are free. You will send the link to the call and any directions they need. Include the date, time, and dial-in information.

The system should also send an automated email for you, but it comes across as far more personal if you include that information in your email.

As long as you get these four points across in your email, you can design it however you want.

So let's review...

Give your investment summary a good looking over to make sure everything is correct, prepare and send an email to your investors, and begin the process of preparing for the conference call.

CHAPTER 41

YOU HAVE THE RIGHT TO ONE PHONE CALL

As mentioned in the previous chapter, in the email template you invited your investors to a private conference call and included information for how to join that call. In the previous chapter, you learned that this is something I do for all my deals; I host a conference call where I provide an overview of the opportunity and answer any questions my investors may have.

Further, you learned that I use FreeConferenceCall.com. It's free and, more important, it records the conference call, which will come in handy in the next step in the process. But you also learned that there are other such call-conferencing providers, and you need to choose the one that is right for you.

Before hitting send on your initial new deal email, set up a conference call, and be sure to include the phone number and passcode in your email.

It is always best to schedule the conference call two weeks after sending the initial email, at least when you are starting out as an apartment syndicator.

Once you have a few deals under your belt, you can schedule the conference call a few days after sending the initial email. And once you have had the deal under contract for two weeks, you should already be well into the due diligence process. You will have already confirmed some, if not the majority, of your assumptions and will know whether there are any deal disqualifiers. Also, presenting a deal to investors can be a stressful experience, especially if it is your first time, so give yourself some time to prepare for the call. This should mitigate some of your anxiety.

NINE-STEP PROCESS TO A SUCCESSFUL NEW INVESTMENT OFFERING CONFERENCE CALL

Here is the outline I prepare before the conference call. I use it as a guide during the conference call. I've created it based on my experiences presenting many deals to thousands of passive investors. Feel free to use it as a guide when presenting deals to your investors.

1. Get Your Mind Right

First, get into the right frame of mind. That means answering the question, "Why am I presenting this opportunity to investors?" I write the answer to this question at the top of the Word document outline. In bold letters, it reads, **"I am here to serve. I am here to help my investors preserve their capital and then grow it. When they get the returns we're projecting, then they're going to be able to spend their time the way they want to spend it. And the world will be a better place because of it."**

That's what I say to myself. You get to pick your own reasons. Ultimately, I think it's best to have a purpose much larger than yourself when thinking about your business. That gets "you" out of the way and puts the focus on "them," which is where it needs to be. Again, this is something I say to myself. I don't read it to investors! That would be a little wacko.

If I accomplish the goal of this statement, it is a win-win for both my business and my investors. As I mentioned in Chapter 2, a personal belief I hold is that when people spend their time how they want to spend it, they will naturally gravitate toward doing more altruistic things. Therefore, I'm not just helping my investors make money, but I am also helping them have the financial freedom to do what they want with their time, which in turn will result in more contribution and philanthropy in the world.

Starting out with the right mindset, as well as coming from the heart and knowing that you're there to serve the investors, is the foundation for a successful conference call.

2. What Is Your Main Focus?

In addition to getting myself in the "service" mindset, I also remind myself what my main point of focus is – capital preservation.

This became my main point of focus in part due to an interesting psychological concept called "loss aversion." Loss aversion refers to people's preference toward avoiding losses relative to acquiring an equivalent gain. In other words, people's negative reaction to losing $5 is greater than the positive reaction to gaining $5. Through my personal investment experience and after interviewing more than 1,000 real estate professionals on my podcast, I've seen this concept play out in real estate, too.

Oh, and if we lose money, it's a lot harder to reach our financial goals than if we keep it then grow it. That's a pretty good reason to focus on capital preservation!

3. Welcome

At the start of the call, I welcome and thank the investors for taking the time to attend the call. Unless you are a neurotic mess, you won't need to prepare for this one-sentence opening statement.

4. Summary of the Call

Next, I outline the flow of the conversation and what I am going to be talking about. Then, I explain that there will be time for a Q&A session at the conclusion of the presentation.

A quick tip for an efficient Q&A session: Provide the investors with your email address. Tell them that they can email you with their questions as they come up during the conversation. In doing so, they won't forget their questions and they won't have to interrupt the conversation to ask a question. I usually mute everyone on the call but myself. This cuts down on confusion during the call. Simultaneously hearing the background noise of tens or even hundreds of investors at one time isn't fun. It isn't productive. You want this call to be productive and informative, because you are having it to raise capital for your deal. You want to be in control.

5. Introduce Yourself
After summarizing what to expect on the call, I provide a brief bio about me that includes my background, what I do, my strengths as they relate to the deal, and my overall investment goals. Then, my business partner does the same. (He's on the call, too.)

6. Why Is This a Good Deal? High Level...
I recommend structuring the conference call around three categories: the deal, the market, and the team. I start out by explaining that I have a good deal in a good market that will be managed by a good team.

Then I explain the reasons this is true by presenting the answers to the following list of questions:

- The Deal
    - Why is it a conservative deal?
    - What stands out about the deal?
    - Has the business model we plan to implement been proven?
    - What is the upside potential?

- Will we put in new upgrades? If so, how will that affect the bottom line?
- The Market
  - How well do we know the market?
  - How does the submarket compare with other submarkets in the same area?
  - What makes this submarket a good location to invest?
  - What is the demographic that will live in the property? Where do they work, go to school, and shop? How close are these to the property?
  - Do we own any other properties in the area?
- The Team
  - Who is part of the team?
  - Are they invested in the deal?
  - What is their track record with apartments?
  - Have I worked with them in the past?

Starting out with this overview is important, because I'm getting across the main reasons I like the deal right away. For the rest of the call I can focus on reinforcing these reasons with real data. This part of the call should take approximately 15 minutes.

7. The Detailed Business Plan

Next it's time for me to provide more details on the business plan. (More recently, my partner has been presenting this part on the calls.) We always remember to tie everything back to the three main selling points: good deal, good market, and good team.

- Overall Plan
  - What is our overall plan? (For example, you will add value through renovations to increase rents.)
  - How does this specific deal fit into this strategy?

- What are our target markets and submarkets?
- Why do we target those specific markets?
* The Market
  - Economy, jobs, rent projections, and vacancy projections.
  - Do we own additional properties in the area? If so, how is that advantageous for this deal?
  - Other location advantages? Include information like accessibility to highways and distance in minutes from downtown.
  - What is the competition in the area?
  - What is the demographic?
  - What are the rentals comps?
* Exterior and Interior
  - What is the current condition of the property?
  - What, if any, are recent upgrades? (Be specific. For example, what types of upgrades and how much will they cost?)
  - What do we plan to upgrade, fix, and/or replace on the exterior? How will that have a positive effect on income or expenses?
  - What do we plan to upgrade, fix, and/or replace on the interior? How will that have a positive effect on income or expenses?
  - Any other projects? (Exercise room, pool, repaving the parking lot, water conservation.) Will that have a positive effect on income or expenses?
* Other
  - What aspects of the exterior and interior plan make us attracted to the property?
  - How will we mitigate risk?
  - What are the underwriting projections? Rent growth, vacancy, and cap rate?

- What is the debt situation? Loan type, terms and conditions, interest rate, or refinancing?
- What is our exit strategy?

This part of the call should take approximately 20 minutes to present.

8. Q&A

We spend the remaining time answering questions submitted by our investors.

Because I've given many new investment offering presentations, I've compiled a list of the 30 most common questions I've received. Make sure you know how to answer all of these questions prior to the conference call.

You won't likely be asked every single question on this list, but the more prepared you are, the better, and the fewer "I will have to look that up and get back to you" responses you'll be forced to provide.

The questions are broken down into two categories: frequently asked questions and property-dependent questions. Frequently asked questions are general questions that will most likely be asked on every investment offering call you host. Property-dependent questions are those questions unique to the deal itself.

Below is a list of questions I've received that fall into each category and the approach to formulating an answer. Some of these are repeat questions from the section on investor objections in Chapter 23. However, it is worth your time to review them again and then go over your investment summary to brainstorm a list of potential questions you think investors may ask. These can be questions about the deal itself or even about current events, like a new presidency, the raising of interest rates, or a natural disaster.

NOTE: *The PPM (private placement memorandum) and OM (operating agreement) referenced in some of the questions and answers below will be defined in the next chapter.*

Frequently asked questions: These are general questions that will most likely be asked on every investment offering call that you host.

1. What damage is covered by property insurance?
   a. Have a conversation with your insurance provider to understand what is covered under your plan.
   b. Is there business interruption insurance? That is, if the building goes down, will the insurance cover the loss of income?
   c. Does the plan include wind, hail, and storm insurance?
   d. What is and isn't covered?
2. Is there any concern with this property from an environmental perspective?
   a. If environmental inspection is completed, what are the results of the inspection and are there any concerns?
   b. If inspection hasn't occurred yet, mention that you are getting one done and that if any issue comes up you will adjust the business plan accordingly, and then notify the investors of any changes via email.
3. What is the flood history of the property?
   a. There will likely be a flood history if you are investing near a coastal city or a large body of water like a river or a lake.
   b. Has there been any past flooding that has affected the property or area?

4. When was the property built?
    a. Tell the investors on the call when the property was built and refer them to the investment summary or PPM for similar information about the property.
5. What is the compensation structure for how you (the syndicator) get paid? Is it incentive based?
    a. Outline how you get paid on the call and/or point them to where they can find that information (PPM and/or operating agreement).
6. How much did the previous owner pay for the property?
    a. Tell them what the previous owner paid for the property. However, you don't really care how much the owner paid. You look at the NOI, the market cap rate, and the value-add business plan to determine an offer price.
7. Why are the current owners selling?
    a. If you know why they are selling, tell the investors. The sellers could be distressed, have reached the end of their business plan, or be looking to purchase another property and need equity.
    b. If applicable, provide an example of why you or someone on your team has sold in the past.
8. What is the liability insurance policy? Who is liable?
    a. Again, have a conversation with your insurance provider to ensure that you can answer all insurance-related questions. Also, you should talk to your real estate lawyer to confirm that your investors don't have any personal liability.
    b. Do you have an umbrella policy?
    c. What are you and your team doing to mitigate the chances of and protect your investors from a negligence suit from a resident? (For example, what are

you doing to eliminate trip hazards, make sure everything is up to code, address maintenance issues in a timely manner, maintain the overall property, and put the property into an LLC?)
9. What happens if the property is wiped out completely down to the foundation?
    a. Does the property have replacement coverage?
    b. Will you sell the land or will you rebuild the property?
10. Can you provide details on the upgrades and repairs?
    a. Provide an overview of any upgrades and repairs (paint, roof, fitness center, clubhouse, cost per unit, interior upgrades).
    b. Direct the investors to the investment summary and PPM for more details on the capital improvement projects and budget.
11. What other offerings do you have in the pipeline in the next year?
    a. Your primary goal is to focus on your existing portfolio and the current deal, but if you are in negotiations on another deal, you can mention that fact to your investors.
12. Is this non-recourse debt?
    a. Provide a yes or no answer, but explain that the limited partners have no debt liability or legal liability either way.
13. What are the terms of the loan? Will they change through the course of the project?
    a. What are the terms of the loan? Is it an agency or bridge loan, fixed or floating interest rate, interest only?
    b. Will there be any changes to the loan throughout the course of the business plan? Do you intend to refinance or use a floating interest rate?

14. What are the pros and cons of the market, specifically in terms of industry and jobs?
    a. Provide an overview of the market. (What are the main industries and how stable are they?)
15. What is the minimum investment? What is the typical investment?
    a. Explain the minimum and maximum investment requirements.
    b. If you have done a deal in the past, tell them the average investment size. If you haven't, tell them the average verbal commitment you've received.
    c. "Our minimum investment is _____."
16. What improvements/repairs/upgrades have already been done to the property?
    a. Outline the improvements (exterior and interior) made by the current owner over the past year or two, as well as the rental premium received for upgrading the unit interiors.
17. What is the overall project strategy/timeline? Exit strategy?
    a. How long do you plan on holding onto the property?
    b. Do you plan on refinancing? If so, when? You don't need to include the projected refinance proceeds in your return projections to investors. It could set the bar too high for you if you end up having to delay the refinance. Instead, have your projections show just the cash-on-cash return plus sales proceeds. Tell investors that you plan on refinancing or taking out a supplemental loan (depending on the financing you initially secure), but that you aren't including it in the projections. So, if/when the refinance or supplemental loan takes place, it will be returning their capital faster than what you have projected.

      c. Will you consider selling the asset early? As you will learn in Chapter 45, you should consistently evaluate the market to see whether it makes sense to sell early.
18. What is your ideal investor's investment strategy?
      a. As a value-add investor, your ideal investor wants a monthly cash flow with potential for additional profits at the sale of the property.
19. Do I (the investor) have to stay in the deal the entire time or can I (the investor) sell my interest?
      a. Usually, the limited partners can sell their interest in the deal after the first year, with the consent of the general partner. But the investment is not liquid like the stock market.
      b. If you don't want to allow your investors to sell their interests, make sure that is included in the PPM.
20. What is the funding schedule?
      a. Generally, there is a set date range in which you can officially accept funds, which you will specify in the initial email.
      b. I like to be 100% funded 30 days before closing. But this likely won't be the case for your first few deals. Technically, you have until the closing date to secure all of the commitments from investors.
21. How will I be able to stay updated on the project after closing?
      a. General partners send out email updates or host conference calls throughout the year. These can be monthly, quarterly, or yearly. Information that you can provide are operational updates (e.g., the occupancy rate, number of new leases or lease renewals), capital improvement updates, relevant market information (e.g., a new company is moving to the area), and financial statements.

22. When will distributions begin?
    a. Tell the investors on the call if they will be receiving monthly, quarterly, or annual distributions, depending on what you've decided.
    b. Consult with your property management company and look at your financial projections to determine when you can send the first distribution.
23. Can you review a projected return scenario?
    a. Refer them to the investment summary page of the PPM, where the return scenario is explained.
    b. Outline what a $100,000 investment is projected to return on an annual basis.
24. How do you do renovations with people currently living there?
    a. Likely, your property management company will oversee the renovations. Have a conversation with them on how they approach renovations.
    b. If someone is living in the unit, you can do the renovations while they are at work or put them in another unit for free but, again, confirm with your property management team on how it will happen for your deal.
25. Can you please discuss the tax benefits for the deal?
    a. Usually, people are attracted to real estate because of the depreciation. Most likely, the depreciation will be such that the investors will not pay taxes until they receive their proceeds at sale. That said, since you are not a CPA, tell them to have a discussion with their accountant for more details on how they will benefit from a tax perspective.

Property-dependent questions: You will have to find out the answers to these questions on a deal-by-deal basis.

26. What is the most likely risk with the property?
    a. Remember the three risks points of an apartment syndication: the deal, the market, and the team. Genuinely assess which of those three areas poses the greatest risk and why, and communicate that to your investors.
27. What is the current vacancy rate?
    a. The current vacancy rate is listed on the rent roll. Also explain what your vacancy rate assumptions are during renovations and once the property is stabilized, and why you set those assumptions.
28. How does this deal – in terms of projected returns, risk, and purchase price – compare with your past deals?
    a. If you've completed deals in the past, they should be included in the case studies section of your investment summary. Explain how the returns for this deal compare with those from previous deals and direct them to the case studies section in the investment summary for more information.
29. Who will be the buyer you're aiming for at the end of the business plan?
    a. This depends on your business plan and exit strategy. If you are a value-add investor, you will have a different buyer if you update the entire property (you'd be selling to a turnkey investor) than you would if you only updated a portion of the property (you'd be selling to another value-add investor).
30. Are you and your partners putting money in the deal?
    a. It is strongly recommended that you put your own capital in the deal, because this brings an extra alignment of interest to the table. If your investors lose money, you lose money, which means you are exposed

to the same level of risk. Also, this signals that you are confident in the deal and in the projected returns.

9. Conclusion

Once you've answered all the questions submitted to you by your investors, conclude the call. Thank all the participants for joining the call. Let them know that they can email you any other questions they have, that you will be sending out a recording of the conference call within the next few days, and what the next steps are for those interested in investing.

POST-CONFERENCE CALL EMAIL

As soon after the call as possible, prepare an email to send to your investor list that includes a link to the investor recording. Due to scheduling issues, not every single investor who is interested will be able to attend the call. Also, investors who weren't interested at the time may become interested later. Therefore, send the email out to your entire investor list and not just those who attended.

I would recap those two to three investment highlights in the email as well, and include any new updates you received between the initial email and this email. For example, you can tell your investors that a due diligence report came back clean.

Finally, you want to outline the process for funding the deal. I ask the investors who are ready to commit to send me an email with their commitment amount. Then I explain that I will reserve a space for them in the deal pending their review and signing of the PPM.

After you've closed on a few deals, meeting or exceeding your investors' return expectations, your email may well be flooded with investor commitments once you've notified them of a new deal. However, without a proven track record, you will have to be more proactive when securing investor money for a deal.

A few weeks after sending out the new investment offering conference call, send out another email to non-committed investors. Provide them with a new piece of information from your deal that reinforces your confidence in the deal – the appraisal came back above the contract price, market rents are higher than your projections, occupancy is up at the property, income was higher, or expenses were lower than you projected. Also, mention how much capital you've secured to date (e.g., we are currently 60% full). Repeat this process as needed until you've raised all the money required to close.

CHAPTER 42

THE FIVE INVESTOR FORMS YOUR INVESTORS WILL SIGN

After your flawless conference call, the investor commitments are pouring in and/or you are following up with investors to secure commitments. Once an investor has committed to investing in the deal, there are five documents they're required to sign to make the partnership official. Each of these documents should be created by your securities or real estate attorney. A great book that covers the basics that you need to grasp on the US Securities and Exchange Commission (SEC) regulations governing apartment syndications is *It's a Whole New Business* by Gene Trowbridge and Jillian Sidoti.

1. Private Placement Memorandum (PPM)
The PPM is a legal document that highlights all the legal disclaimers for how the investor could lose their money in the deal. The PPM protects you and your personal assets from your investors in the event of them losing a portion or all of their capital invested. It also gives investors all the potential risk factors in the deal (whether or not each is likely to happen). Generally, a PPM will include two major components. One is the introduction, which includes a summary of the offering, description of the asset being purchased, the minimum and maximum investment amounts, key risks involved in the

offering, and a disclosure on how the sponsor (that's you) are paid. The other section covers basic disclosures, which includes sponsor information, offering description, and a list of all the risks associated with the offering.

Your first PPM should be prepared by both your securities attorney and real estate attorney. All future PPMs can likely be created by your real estate attorney and then reviewed by your securities attorney. Usually, you can just have your original PPM as the template. Then your attorney will track the changes from one to the next so that you don't have to start from scratch each time.

2. Operating Agreement

For each apartment deal, my company forms a new limited liability company (LLC). My company is a general partner (GP). Our investors will purchase shares in that LLC and become a limited partner (LP). The operating agreement outlines the responsibilities and ownership percentages for the GP and LP. Like the PPM, the operating agreement should be prepared by your real estate attorney for each apartment deal. Further, it is a best practice to have your securities attorney review it.

3. Subscription Agreement

Simply put, the subscription agreement is a promise by your LLC to sell a specified number of shares to your investors at a specified price, and a promise by your investors to pay that price. For example, an investor that is investing $50,000 would purchase 50,000 shares of your LLC at $1 per share. Like the PPM and operating agreement, the subscription agreement should be prepared by your real estate attorney for each deal. It is a best practice to have your securities attorney review the operating agreement.

4. Accredited Investor Qualifier Form

The accredited investor form required is based on whether the offering is 506(b) or 506(c). There are other offerings but we'll stick to two here because they are the most common. Most likely, you are selling private securities to your limited partners under either Rule 506(b) or Rule 506(c). One key difference is that 506(c) allows for general solicitation or advertising of your deal to the public, while 506(b) offerings do not, which means you must rely on family and friends. The other difference is the type of person who can invest in each offering type. For the 506(b), you can have up to 35 sophisticated (not accredited) investors, while 506(c) is strictly for accredited investors. That said, you want to have a conversation with your securities attorney to see which offering is the best fit for you.

If you are doing a 506(c) offering, you must have a third-party service verify the accredited investor status of each investor, which requires the review of tax returns or bank statements, verification of net worth, or written confirmation from a broker, attorney, or certified account. The accredited investor qualifications are an individual (1) with a net worth exceeding $1,000,000, excluding a personal residence, (2) with an individual annual income exceeding $200,000 in the last two years, or (3) who has a joint income with a spouse exceeding $300,000.

If you are doing a 506(b), a third-party service is not required to verify the accredited investors' status – they can self-verify that they are accredited or sophisticated. In addition, for the 506(b) offering, to prove that you didn't solicit the offering, you must be able to demonstrate that you've had a relationship with the investor before their knowledge of the investment opportunity, which is determined by the duration and extent of the relationship.

This form should also be prepared by your securities attorney, but you will not need to create a new form for each deal (unless the accredited investor qualifications change).

5. ACH Application

Last is the ACH application. This document is optional but recommended. It will allow the investor to receive their distributions via direct deposit into a bank of their choice.

Again, once an investor has committed to investing in your deal, send them these five documents to make the partnership official.

When you've secured enough investor commitments to cover the costs to close, as well as the additionally 50% in backup commitments, closing is right around the corner!

PART 1: THE EXPERIENCE

KNOWLEDGE — Chapters 1-4
1. What is apartment syndication?
2. How to Get Started
3. What to focus on

GOALS — Chapters 5-6
1. How do you make money?
2. Set 12-month goal and long-term vision
3. Ultimate Success Formula

BRAND BUILDING — Chapters 7-12
1. Why you need a brand
2. Select a target audience
3. How to build a brand

MARKET EVALUATION — Chapters 13-16
1. 3 Immutable Laws of Real Estate
2. Evaluate 7 markets
3. Pick 1-2 Target Markets

PART 2: THE MONEY

BUILD TEAM — Chapters 17-19
1. Find core real estate team members
2. Hire a mentor or consultant

FIND CAPITAL — Chapters 20-24
1. Why will they invest?
2. Build passive investor database
3. Create partnership structure

PART 3: THE DEAL

FIND DEALS — Chapters 25-28
1. Set investment criteria
2. On-market vs. off-market deals
3. How to find your first deal

UNDERWRITING — Chapters 29-31
1. Information needed to underwrite a deal
2. The 6-step underwriting process

SUBMIT OFFER — Chapter 32
1. How to submit an offer on a deal
2. Best-and-final offer
3. Purchase sales agreement

PART 4: THE EXECUTION

DUE DILIGENCE — Chapters 33-37
1. 10 due diligence reports
2. Secure financing from lender

SECURE CAPITAL — Chapters 38-42
1. Create investment summary
2. New investment offering call
3. Secure investor commitments

CLOSE — Chapters 43-44 *(YOU ARE HERE)*
1. Closing process
2. Notify passive investors

EXECUTE BUSINESS PLAN — Chapters 45-46
1. 10 asset management duties
2. How to sell the apartment

Chapter 43

You've Reached the (First) Finish Line

After taking action on the advice outlined in the last 42 chapters, you've reached the finish line... or at least the first finish line: CLOSING!

Prior to going through the closing process, your lender should have already explained what will take place. Unlike a traditional residential closing, the bulk of the work is completed a few days before the scheduled close date. Three days beforehand, you – the sponsor – will sign the loan and title documents to approve the loan and transfer of title.

The day before closing, you will receive the closing document from the lender, which you will sign and overnight back to the lender. You will also wire the funds required to close into escrow with your lender, who will then review the documents to make sure all the T's are crossed and I's are dotted, before transferring the money to the title company, who will issue a new deed in your LLC's name. At that point in time, the property is officially yours!

Once you've received the word that the closing is completed, you will send your property management company to take over the property. Actually, scratch that! You should already have your property management team waiting in the parking lot. That way, you won't waste a single second.

You've got to get this business plan executed, right? No need to wait.

The old property management company should have been already notified of the transition, so your managers shouldn't receive any resistance. The property managers in the industry usually all know each other, but on the off chance that the old managers aren't in the know, it might not be a friendly interaction. Or they may be disgruntled about losing the business. Nonetheless, your experienced property managers should be able to handle any resistance to ensure a smooth transition.

As the asset manager of the property, you will have a few additional pre-close duties, and then you will have various duties to perform on an ongoing basis.

CHAPTER 44

ANTICIPATING THE FINISH

Your first official duty as the asset manager of the newly acquired apartment community is to notify your investors of the close. A few days before the scheduled closing date, you want to prepare an email that says, "Congrats! We Closed." You will send this once you've received word from your lender about a successful close. That is, after all, cause for celebration.

The purpose of this email is to not just notify your investors that you've closed on the property but to also set their expectations for the process going forward.

A few days before closing, create the email. Mention that you have taken over ownership and that your property management company has taken over the operations. You won't send it until the close has happened, but it's great to be prepared.

Also, set communication expectations. How often will you provide your investors with updates: weekly, monthly, quarterly, or annually? My company sends property updates each month, recapping the previous month's operations, plus we send the financials (profit and loss statement along with a current rent roll) each quarter. The frequency that you select and the information you send is based on your preferences and those of your investors.

You also want to include information about the distributions and taxes. My company creates a separate guide, an Investor Guide, and includes a link to download it in the email.

The Investor Guide proactively addresses common investor questions about the deal process. This document informs investors about ongoing communications and updates on the deal, tax information, distribution frequency, and any other piece of relevant information.

Examples of what to include in your Investor Guide are:

- **Communication information**
  - How often will you provide updates?
  - What form will they receive the updates in? Will it be an email, conference call, mailed newsletter, or what?
  - What will these updates include?
  - Will you be sending detailed financial statements or other operational reports?
  - When should they expect to receive their first update?
- **Tax information**
  - What type of tax documentation do you provide? Generally, you will send your investors a K-1 tax document, which outlines their annual distributions and depreciation.
  - When will you send out the tax documentation?
- **Distribution information**
  - How often will you send distributions? Monthly, quarterly, annually?
  - When will they receive their first distribution?
  - What will be the amount of their first distribution?
  - What is the distribution amount after the first distribution?
  - Will every distribution be the same, or will you distribute more at the end of the year?
  - How will they receive their distribution? Direct deposit or check in the mail?

A few days prior to closing, create your email and investment guide so you can send it to your investors immediately after closing.

BEST EVER APARTMENT SYNDICATION BOOK

A few days prior to closing, create your email and investment guide so you can send it to your investors immediately after closing.

PART 1: THE EXPERIENCE

KNOWLEDGE — Chapters 1 - 4
1. What is apartment syndication?
2. How to Get Started
3. What to focus on

GOALS — Chapters 5 - 6
1. How do you make money?
2. Set 12-month goal and long-term vision
3. Ultimate Success Formula

BRAND BUILDING — Chapters 7 - 12
1. Why you need a brand
2. Select a target audience
3. How to build a brand

MARKET EVALUATION — Chapters 13 - 16
1. 3 Immutable Laws of Real Estate
2. Evaluate 7 markets
3. Pick 1-2 Target Markets

PART 2: THE MONEY

BUILD TEAM — Chapters 17 - 19
1. Find core real estate team members
2. Hire a mentor or consultant

FIND CAPITAL — Chapters 20 - 24
1. Why will they invest?
2. Build passive investor database
3. Create partnership structure

PART 3: THE DEAL

FIND DEALS — Chapters 25 - 28
1. Set investment criteria
2. On-market vs. off-market deals
3. How to find your first deal

UNDERWRITING — Chapters 29 - 31
1. Information needed to underwrite a deal
2. The 6-step underwriting process

SUBMIT OFFER — Chapter 32
1. How to submit an offer on a deal
2. Best-and-final offer
3. Purchase sales agreement

PART 4: THE EXECUTION

DUE DILIGENCE — Chapters 33 - 37
1. 10 due diligence reports
2. Secure financing from lender

SECURE CAPITAL — Chapters 38 - 42
1. Create investment summary
2. New investment offering call
3. Secure investor commitments

CLOSE — Chapters 43 - 44
1. Closing process
2. Notify passive investors

EXECUTE BUSINESS PLAN — Chapters 45 - 46 *(YOU ARE HERE)*
1. 10 asset management duties
2. How to sell the apartment

CHAPTER 45

THE ROAD AHEAD

You've closed on the apartment community and notified your investors. Now, what are the next steps? Well, you will have certain duties and responsibilities to ensure that the apartment community is successfully taken over and managed by your team.

TOP 10 ASSET MANAGEMENT DUTIES

As you may have guessed, these duties can vary from syndicator to syndicator, but generally you will be responsible for the following:

1. Implementing the business plan

As the asset manager, your main responsibility is to ensure that the business plan is successfully implemented. This starts by determining an expense budget and projected rental premiums, and by confirming these assumptions with your property management company. You also must confirm these assumptions by data based on the results of the due diligence reports. These reports were completed **before** closing on the deal, so there's nothing you have to create at this point.

After you close on the deal, it is your responsibility to oversee the budget. Gain access to your property management company's online reporting system. At the end of each month, review the monthly financial statements. You want to look at how the projected, budgeted expenses and rent premiums compare with the actual figures (also called "actuals"). If there are discrepancies, work with your property manager to figure out the cause(s) and formulate a plan to get back on track.

2. Weekly performance reviews

To help in tracking the progress of the business plan, you will want to schedule a weekly call with your point person at the property management company to go over and track the property's key performance indicators (KPIs).

Our KPIs are broken into three categories: money, occupancy, and management, or M.O.M. (You have to take care of your property like you would take care of your MOM.)

We created a performance review spreadsheet that we send to our management company every week. They have to fill it out and return to us.

- **Money**

Gross Potential Income	$XXX,XXX
Gross Occupied Income	$XXX,XXX
Collected This Week	$XXX,XXX
MTD Collected	$XXX,XXX
MTD Delinquent	$XXX,XXX

- **Occupancy**

Units Pre-Leased	X
Notices Given This Week	X
Total # of Notices on Books	X
# of Set-Outs Scheduled	X
Applications Denied	X
# of Renewals	X
# on Waiting List	X

- **Management**

Current Occupancy %	X%
Total Occupied Units This Week	X
Total Occupied Units Prior Week	X
Total Move-Ins Prior Week	X
Projected Total Occupied Units	X
Projected Occupancy %	X%
Exposure	X%
# of Evictions Filed	X
# of Skips	X
# of Transfers	X
# of Set-Outs Scheduled	X
# of Units Vacant	X
Vacant Rent-Ready	X
Vacant NOT Rent-Ready	X

3. **Investor distributions**

On either a monthly, quarterly, or annual basis, you will need to send out the correct distributions to your investors. Before closing on the deal, make sure you know who will be sending these notices out. Ideally, your property manager handles the distributions with your oversight.

4. **Investor communications**

You will also be responsible for ongoing communication with your investors. Each month, I provide my investors with an email that recaps the activities of the previous month. On a quarterly basis, I also include the financials (trailing 12-month income plus expense report and a current rent roll) in my recap email. Annually, I provide my investors with their K-1. Talk to your CPA about when they will provide you with the K-1s so you can tell your investors when they will be receiving them.

To get the information required to create your update emails, use the most recent performance review spreadsheet. Obtain any additional information from your property management company.

- **Monthly Email Checklist**
    - Payment information to them (see "Important Milestones" below for more details).
    - Occupancy and pre-leased occupancy.
    - Renovation update: How many units have been renovated in total since buying property?
        - Provide pictures of renovated units.
    - Are rents on renovated units reaching the premiums we projected? Give specifics. (For example, we projected an increase of $75 a unit on renovated units. We are getting $100.)
    - Improvements/projects. (For instance, we got all the carports built and will begin leasing at $25/space, with website optimized by doing XYZ.)
        - Provide pictures when applicable.
    - Misc. – Holiday parties or local news about job growth.
- **Email Timing:** You have already set expectations with your investors for how often you will send them update emails. To make sure you always send these on time, start drafting the monthly recap emails at least two full weeks prior to the date on which you committed to send them. If you send them earlier, hey, even better.
- **Important Milestones:** Depending on your investor payout frequency – if it is tax season or if a quarter is ending, for example – the content of your monthly emails will vary slightly. Below is a list of certain milestones throughout the year and the additional information you'll want in your emails:

- At the end of each quarter
  - In addition to an update from the previous month (See "Monthly Email Checklist Template" above), you will send investors the rent roll and profit and loss statement for the trailing 12 months.
- If payout is monthly, in the email a month prior to the investor's first payout...
  - Let them know they will receive payment by the end of the month.
  - Provide an example of payout amount based on a $100,000 investment (e.g., $100,000 * 8% preferred return / 12 = $666.67 per month).
- If payout is quarterly, in the email a month prior to the investor's first payout...
  - Let them know they will receive payment by the end of the month.
  - Provide an example of payout amount based on a $100,000 investment (e.g., $100,000 * 8% preferred return / 4 = $2,000).
- If the payout is distributed annually, in the email a month prior to the investor's first payout...
  - Let them know they will receive payment by the end of the month.
  - Provide an example of payout amount based on a $100,000 investment (e.g., $100,000 * 8% preferred return = $8,000).
- Tax documentation
  - Once you have a conversation with your CPA, you will know when you will receive the K-1s.
  - Starting with your first recap email of the year, let your investors know when to expect to receive their K-1.

- **Other Best Practices**
  - I use the service MailChimp to send out my emails, but you can use any automated system, including Active Campaign, Constant Contact, Aweber, or any number of services. Research a few and choose the one that's right for you.
  - When sending images, rent rolls, or profit and loss statements, I upload those files to Dropbox and insert a link into the emails so there aren't massive pictures or data tables in the email. (Really large files slow a system up or can't be sent through regular email.)

5. Managing renovations

If you purchased the asset using a loan program where the renovation costs are included in the financing, you will have constant communication with the lender during the renovation period. You won't get a lump sum of money upfront for renovations and CapEx projects. Instead, you will receive draws from the bank. That means you need to interact with the lender about the construction draws as you implement your capital expenditure projects.

If your renovations are not included in the financing and you're covering the costs by raising equity from your investors, you'll have control of the capital expenditures budget and won't have to go back and forth with the lender.

6. Maintaining economic occupancy

Once you take over the property, you will begin to implement your value-add business plan. Since you are performing renovations, you've already accounted for a higher vacancy rate during the first 12 to 24 months. However, it is your responsibility to make sure you maintain occupancy so that you can hit your return projections.

Your property management company should be implementing their best practices for maintaining occupancy, too, like advertising and marketing to local businesses and competitors, adjusting rental rates as occupancy dips, and doing weekly market surveys to determine the market rents. That said, you are the asset manager. As such, it is your responsibility to advise the management company on the speed at which renovations are made. You don't want to handicap your property management company by forcing renovations. So don't be too aggressive with the pace at which you do your renovations. Stick to the pre-approved renovation plan, budget, and rent premiums you specified during the due diligence process.

Generally, you will start by renovating vacant units (ones that are vacant at closing or due to turnover). Other strategies include offering newly renovated units to residents who are living in unrenovated units so that you can renovate their unit once they move, or you can increase unrenovated rents to promote turnover. However, if you have a large influx of vacant, unrenovated units, don't feel obliged to renovate all of them. It's okay if for every five or six units that become vacant, you only renovate half and lease the remaining units back to the market unrenovated, because you'll get to them the next time people move out. Overall, you want to renovate at a pace that will not adversely affect occupancy rates and use a property management company that can deliver on the plan that they agreed to.

7. Plan trips to the property

Plan to visit the apartment community at least once a month. However, don't announce all your trips. If the management company is aware of your visit, they will have time to prepare, which means you may not get a true representation of how the property is typically managed. If you visit unannounced, you'll see how the property is actually operated on a day-to-day basis. This is not being sneaky; it's called good business practice.

8. Frequently analyze the competition
You want to set up a process for doing rent surveys of your property's competition in the area. The goal of the rent survey is to compare your property's rental rates with those of surrounding apartments, as well as the overall market rates, to determine whether you can further increase your rates while remaining under the leading competitor. Hopefully, this is something your property management company will perform and then provide you with the results and advice on rate increases.

9. Frequently analyze the market
Once you've completed your value-add business plan, you will also want to pay close attention to the market in which your apartment property is located. What are the prices and cap rates? What would you get if you sold right now or if you were to refinance? Determine a low, medium, and high property value by requesting a broker's opinion of value (BOV) from your real estate broker.

Even if your business plan is to sell in five years, don't wait until then to look at the market. You may be able to provide your investors with a sizable return if you were to sell after just two or three-and-a-half years. But you'll never know if you aren't constantly analyzing the market conditions. It is always best to determine how much return you'd achieve if you sold at least a couple times a year. It's kind of fun, too.

10. Expect the unexpected
Finally, as unexpected issues arise (and you can guarantee they will), you are responsible for making proper decisions to resolve the problems. For example, if you receive a call from the

property manager notifying you that the boiler unexpectedly broke down, you'll have to decide whether you will use money from the operating budget to replace, refurbish, or repair it.

How to Maintain the Occupancy Rate

If for some reason you find yourself with a bad property management company and you need to make things happen by helping them increase your property's occupancy level, here is a list of 19 proven ways to market your rental listings:

1. Set up a landing page online and direct people to it.
2. Create a postcard campaign and send it out to people living in similar buildings to tempt them to move into yours. **Note:** This strategy could anger the local owners, so if you decide to do this, don't expect to be popular. Also, expect others to do it to your residents. In general, while I want you to be aware of this tactic, I personally wouldn't do it.
3. Contact the Human Resources departments at all major employers in the area to let them know about your wonderful apartments.
4. Create a tenant referral program (e.g., offer $XXX for all tenants that refer someone that signs a lease).
5. Set up an open house and invite members of the local community to attend.
6. Offer a special discount on rent for military, police, and first responders (e.g., 50% off 1st month's rent).
7. Design "For Lease" banners and put them up at the entry way to your property.
8. Create a corporate outreach program. Would your apartments make great corporate housing for executives and workers new to the area? What about spaces for a corporation's visitors?

9. Design and place fliers at local establishments (e.g., laundromats, hair salons, nail salons) where you know there is a lot of foot traffic.
10. Purchase ads and place them in local newspapers.
11. Post a listing to Craigslist, Zillow, Realtor.com, Apartments.com, Rentals.com, and other online rental listing services. Listing a rental on HotPads.com or Cozy.co will post your listing to multiple rental listing platforms.
12. Partner with a real estate agent (or if you already have your license, use yours) and advertise on the MLS.
13. Create a Facebook advertisement, which allows you to hyper-target your preferred tenant criteria.
14. Create a Facebook page for your rental business, post weekly content to generate a following, and post your rental listings.
15. Pay close attention to what is nearby and cater to that audience (e.g., colleges, military bases, large corporations).
16. Provide stellar, good old-fashioned customer service! Be responsive and timely with requests/questions. It doesn't matter if you are a marketing wizard and get hundreds of responses to your rental listing if you don't pick up the phone or respond to emails quickly, politely answer their questions, and get them one step closer to viewing the property and signing the lease.
17. Call all residents who have previously notified you that they plan on leaving at the end of their lease to figure out why they are leaving. See what you can do to convince them to stay. Maybe they want to move to a different unit or want a minor upgrade, like an accent wall. Also, explain to them the costs associated with moving out (e.g., new security deposit, hiring a moving company

or U-Haul, cleaning costs, new furniture). This conversation should take place at least 90 days prior to the end of their lease.
18. Send marketing packages or gift baskets to preferred employers surrounding your property. You'd be surprised by just how effective thank-you cards and handwritten notes can be. (It means you cared enough to spend the time to write something. This will be remembered and appreciated.)
19. Reach out to old leads you received (older than 90 days).

The last step of the syndication process is where you and your investors make the BIG money – and that's at the time of sale... your exit strategy!

CHAPTER 46

FINISH STRONG TO COLLECT YOUR JACKPOT

You've acquired your first deal, completed your value-add business plan, and have been distributing higher than projected returns to your extremely happy investors.

Excellent!

You think your investors are satisfied now? Well, sure they are, but think about how excited they'll be when they receive a massive distribution upon sale of the property! That means it is important to understand the when and how of selling your apartment community.

If you get to the end of your business plan and the market conditions are not such that you can sell the asset and meet your investors' return expectations, take a breath. More important, if it's time to return their capital, you have some conversations with the investors coming. Don't be afraid to hold onto the property longer. If it doesn't make good fiscal sense to sell, it's likely better to hold onto it for a bit longer. You'd be surprised by how understanding your investors can be, especially when they are earning good returns before the sale.

EIGHT-STEP PROCESS TO SELLING YOUR APARTMENT COMMUNITY

When the market conditions are right, here is the eight-step process to sell your apartment community:

1. Request a Broker's Opinion of Value

Based on your evaluations of the market, if you are confident that you can sell your apartment at the price you need in order to get the returns you want, the next step is to find a listing broker. It's easy to write down a value that makes you happy, so you'll want to get a relatively unbiased second opinion without having to shell out a few thousand dollars for a full appraisal.

You want to find a broker who is the best fit to sell the property. Loyalty is important in this business, which means it's good if you can use the same broker who represented you when you purchased the asset in the first place. But there might be reasons to go with someone else. If that is the case, reach out to two or three of the best brokers in the market and ask them for a Broker's Opinion of Value (BOV). Send them whatever information they request (T-12 and/or rent roll). Based on the value of the BOV, select a broker to list the property.

2. Send Your Lender a Notification of Disposition

When you decide to sell, you need to notify your lender. To do so, you will send them an official notification of disposition. This is typically done two months prior to listing the apartment for sale to the public. Work with your experienced attorney to draft the notification and send it to your lender.

Depending on the loan program you used to purchase the property, you may have a pre-payment penalty as well as yield maintenance and defeasance. I referred to that in Chapter 37. Keep that in mind when deciding to sell, because a large pre-payment penalty will drastically reduce your sales proceeds.

3. Be Mindful of the Sale

The value of the asset is dependent on the market cap rate (which is outside your control) and the net operating income (which is inside your control). To maximize the value, you want to maximize the net operating income, which means maximizing the income and minimizing the expenses.

Once you've made the decision to sell, don't start certain projects if the payback period extends beyond the sale date. For example, if you plan on selling in a few months, don't put in a brand-new playground for $30,000 unless you are certain that it will increase the property's value by more than $30,000. Makes sense, right?

Optimize the rent roll, because the higher the rent roll, the higher the property value, which means the more money you will make at sale. Some people do this by spending a little bit more money on marketing to increase occupancy and by pursuing collections a little more aggressively than they normally do.

Look at your profit and loss statement. See which income and expense line items can be improved in the months prior to listing the asset for sale.

4. Start a Bidding War
Over the next six weeks or so, your broker is going to create the OM and market the apartment to the public to whip up a whole lot of interest. Interested parties will visit the property and they'll take the same approach you did when you purchased the property – they will talk to the property manager, tour units, inspect the exteriors, analyze rent comps, run the numbers, and submit an offer.

The goal for your broker is to create a bidding war to push up the offer price and get you the highest offer price possible.

5. Screen Out Newbies with a Best and Final Call
Once you cease accepting offers, you will review the submissions, and have a best and final call with the top offer or offers to qualify the buyers. Remember that? Now that you are on the other end of the best and final call, you get to ask the same

list of questions you were asked when purchasing the property. (Refer back to Chapter 32 to refresh your memory on what questions you need to ask to qualify the buyer.)

You want to learn as much as you can about their track record, funding capabilities, and proposed business plan to gauge their ability to close. Ideally, you sell to a sponsor or investor with a proven track record. That means, at minimum, they've purchased a similar-sized property in the past. You don't want a newbie who has to back out of the deal during the due diligence phase because they cannot fund the deal, can't qualify for financing, did poor underwriting, or don't have a qualified team.

6. Negotiate a Purchase and Sale Agreement
Select the best offer and negotiate a purchase and sale agreement (PSA). Have your experienced attorney draft the PSA. Don't let the buyer draft the PSA, because you want to start the negotiation with terms closest to where you need them to be, and not the other way around. Send the potential buyer the PSA for their attorney to review. You'll likely go back and forth to negotiate the terms of the contract, with the end result hopefully being reflective of what you read in their letter of intent.

This negotiation process typically takes about a week. (Sometimes longer, but usually not less time.)

7. Fulfill Obligations during Due Diligence
When the negotiations have concluded, and both you and the buyer have signed the PSA, the due diligence period begins. The buyer will be required to adhere to the schedule agreed upon in the PSA (i.e., they have X number of days to perform their due diligence, X number of days close). You owe them whatever it is you agreed to in the PSA (e.g., they can come to

the property with 24 hours' notice, they can look at your bank statements, financials, leases, marketing materials). Make sure you understand fully what you are to provide to them and by which date. That will be listed in your PSA. Otherwise, you will be in default of the contract, and that could provide an out for the buyer should they want to exercise it later.

Best-case scenario is that nothing comes up during the due diligence period and you sell the property at the price and terms defined in the PSA. If challenges pop up, there may be additional negotiations back and forth with the seller on either the terms, purchase price, or both.

Once the due diligence is completed, the buyer will work with the lender and the title company to finalize things in preparation for closing.

8. Close and Distribute Sales Proceeds

A few days prior to the official closing date, you will sign hundreds of execution documents. Then, on the day of closing, you will be wired the sales proceeds.

Distribute the sales proceeds to your investors according to what you and your investors agreed to in the partnership. They will then go from satisfied to ecstatic and will be ready to start the process all over again.

Yes, that's right. It is not uncommon for happy investors to want to reinvest with you!

CONCLUSION

By reaching this concluding chapter, you've officially acquired the necessary knowledge to overcome the four main challenges faced by aspiring apartment syndicators: lack of experience, lack of money, lack of a deal, and inability to execute a business plan.

Congratulations!

But knowing what to do and how to do it is one thing. Actually doing it is an entirely different matter.

It is understood among active investors that only 1 out of 10 who become interested in real estate actually follow through. And since apartment syndications are one of the more complicated, time-intensive strategies, I bet the odds are closer to 1 out of 100.

So, what differentiates the few who do from the many who don't? **Consistent action.**

It really is that simple. The few does something every single day that brings them closer to completing their first deal while the many are always putting it off until tomorrow or making excuses as to why they cannot become a syndicator.

That's why I challenge you to dedicate **at least 1 hour a day for the next 30 days to acting on the advice provided in this book**. Don't waste those feelings of inspiration and motivation that you're currently experiencing from completing this book. Leverage them to build up momentum and create the right habits starting TODAY. Because I can guarantee that once you put down this book and get back to your day-to-day tasks, those feelings will slowly dissipate.

Go to Amazon and purchase my book recommendations. Get the free Deal-Finding Tracker and Simplified Cash Flow Calculator by emailing info@joefairless.com. Visit www.TheBestEverBlog.com for more content on apartment syndications. Become a member of the Best Ever Community on Facebook to join in on the conversation with over one thousand active real estate investors at www.BestEverCommunity.com. Go to www.BestEverAptProgram.com and apply for a planning session in order to learn exactly what you need to do to launch your apartment syndication business based on your background.

The time is now! Get out there, take action, and you will be well on your way to creating your own apartment syndication empire.

If this book exceeded your expectations and added value to your real estate business, please leave a review on Amazon. Plus, if you send my team a screenshot of the Amazon review, we will hook you up with some free apartment syndication goodies to get you started on your journey. Just email the screenshot to info@joefairless.com.

To your Best Ever-ness,
Joe

GLOSSARY OF TERMS

Note: All examples use the same 216-unit apartment community referenced throughout the book.

A

Accredited Investor: A person that can invest in apartment syndications by satisfying one of the requirements regarding income or net worth. The current requirements to qualify are an annual income of $200,000, or $300,000 for joint income, for the last two years with the expectation of earning the same or higher, or a net worth exceeding $1 million either individually or jointly with a spouse.

Acquisition Fee: The upfront fee paid by the new buying partnership to the general partner for finding, evaluating, financing, and closing the investment. Fees range from 1% to 5% of the purchase price, depending on the size of the deal.

Active Investing: The finding of, qualifying, and closing on an apartment building using one's own capital and overseeing the business plan through to its successful execution.

Amortization: The paying off of a mortgage loan over time by making fixed payments of principal and interest.

Apartment Syndication: A temporary professional financial services alliance formed for the purpose of handling a large apartment transaction that would be hard or impossible for the entities involved to handle individually, which allows companies to pool their resources and share risks and returns. In regards to apartments, a syndication is typically a partnership between general partners (i.e., the syndicator) and limited partners (i.e., the passive investors) to acquire, manage, and sell an apartment community while sharing in the profits.

Appraisal: A report created by a certified appraiser that specifies the market value of a property. For apartments, the value is based on cost, sales comparable, and income approach.

Appreciation: An increase in the value of an asset over time. The two main types of appreciation that are relevant to apartment syndications are natural appreciation and forced appreciation. Natural appreciation occurs when the market cap rate naturally decreases over time, which isn't always a given. Forced appreciation occurs when the net operating income is increased by either increasing the revenue or decreasing the expenses. Forced appreciation typically occurs by adding value to the apartment through renovations and/or operational improvements.

Asset Management Fee: An ongoing annual fee from the property operations paid to the general partner for property oversight. Generally, the fee is 2% of the collected income or $250 per unit per year.

B

Bad Debt: The amount of uncollected money owed by a tenant after move-out.

Breakeven Occupancy: The occupancy rate required to cover all of the expenses of a property. The breakeven occupancy rate is calculated by dividing the sum of the operating expense and debt service by the gross potential income. For example, a 216-unit apartment community with $1,166,489 in operating expenses, $581,090 in debt service, and $2,441,050 in gross potential income ($2,263,624 gross potential rent plus $177,426 other income) has a breakeven occupancy of 71.6%.

Bridge Loan: A mortgage loan used until a borrower secures permanent financing. Bridge loans are short term (six months to three years, with the option to purchase an additional six months to two years), generally have higher interest rates, and are almost exclusively interest only. Also referred to as interim financing, gap financing, or swing loans. The loan is ideal for repositioning an apartment community that doesn't qualify for permanent agency financing.

C

Capital Expenditures (CapEx): The funds used by a company to acquire, upgrade, and maintain a property. Also referred to as CapEx. An expense is considered CapEx when it improves the useful life of a property and is capitalized – spreading the cost of the expenditure over the useful life of the asset. CapEx include both interior and exterior renovations. Examples of exterior CapEx are repairing or replacing a parking lot, repairing or replacing a roof, repairing, replacing, or installing balconies or patios, installing carports, large landscaping projects, rebranding the community, new paint, new siding, repairing or replacing HVAC, and renovating the clubhouse. Examples of interior CapEx are new cabinetry, new countertops, new appliances, new flooring, installing fireplaces, opening up or enclosing a kitchen, new light fixtures, interior paint, plumbing projects, new blinds, and new hardware (e.g., door knobs, cabinet handles, outlet covers, or faucets). Examples of things that wouldn't be considered CapEx are the operating expenses, debt service, fees paid to the general partner, and distributions to the limited partners.

Capitalization Rate (Cap Rate): The rate of return based on the income that the property is expected to generate. Also referred to as the cap rate. The cap rate is calculated by dividing the net operating income by the current market value of a property. For example, a 216-unit property purchased for $12,200,000 with a net operating income of $960,029 has a cap rate of 7.87%.

Cash Flow: The revenue remaining after paying all expenses. Cash flow is calculated by subtracting the operating expense and debt service from the effective gross income. For example, here is the cash flow of the 216-unit apartment community:

Effective Gross Income	$2,123,235
Operating Expense	($1,166,489)
Debt Service	($581,090)
Asset Mgmt. Fee	($45,272)
Cash Flow	**$330,383**

Cash-on-Cash Return: The rate of return based on the cash flow and the equity investment. Also referred to as CoC return. CoC return is calculated by dividing the cash flow by the initial equity investment. For example, the 216-unit apartment community with a cash flow of $330,383 and an initial equity investment of $3,843,270 has a CoC return of 8.6%.

Closing Costs: The expenses, over and above the purchase price of the property, that buyers and sellers normally incur to complete a real estate transaction. These costs include origination fees, application fees, recording fees, attorney fees, underwriting fees, due diligence fees, and credit search fees.

Concessions: The credits given to offset rent, application fees, move-in fees, and any other cost incurred by the tenant, which are generally given at move-in to entice tenants into signing a lease.

Cost Approach: A method of calculating a property's value based on the cost to replace (or rebuild) the property from scratch. Also referred to as the replacement approach.

D

Debt Service: The annual mortgage amount paid to the lender, which includes principal and interest. Principal is the original sum lent to a borrower and the interest rate is the charge for the privilege of borrowing the principal amount. For example, for a 24-month $11,505,500 loan with a 5.28% interest rate amortized over 30 years secured on the 216-unit apartment community, the monthly debt service is $60,977. If the loan required interest-only payments, the monthly debt service would be $48,424.

Debt Service Coverage Ratio (DSCR): The ratio that is a measure of the cash flow available to pay the debt obligation. Also referred to as the DSCR. The DSCR is calculated by dividing the net operating income by the total debt service. A DSCR of 1.0 means that there is enough net operating income to cover 100% of the debt service. Ideally, the DSCR is 1.25 or higher. A property with a DSCR too close to 1.0 is vulnerable, and a minor decline in revenue or minor increase in expenses would result in the inability to service the debt. For example, the 216-unit apartment community with an annual debt service of

$581,090 and a net operating income of $956,746 has a DSCR of 1.65.

Depreciation: A decrease or loss in value due to wear, age, or other cause.

Distressed Property: A non-stabilized apartment community, which means the economic occupancy rate is below 85% and likely much lower due to poor operations, tenant problems, outdated interiors, exteriors, or amenities, mismanagement, and/or deferred maintenance.

Distributions: The limited partners' portion of the profits, which are sent on a monthly, quarterly, or annual basis, at refinance, and/or at sale.

Due Diligence: The process of confirming that a property is as represented by the seller and is not subject to environmental or other problems. For apartment syndications, the general partner will perform due diligence to confirm their underwriting assumptions and business plan.

E

Earnest Money: A payment by the buyers that is a portion of the purchase price to indicate to the seller their intention and ability to carry out the sales contract.

Economic Occupancy Rate: The rate of paying tenants based on the total possible revenue and the actual revenue collected. The economic occupancy is calculated by dividing the effective gross income by the gross potential income. For example, here is the economic occupancy rate for the 216-unit apartment community:

Gross Potential Rent	$2,263,624
Other Income	$177,426
Gross Potential Income	**$2,441,050**
Loss-to-Lease	($67,909)
Concessions	($36,306)
Vacancy	($158,454)
Bad Debt	($55,147)
Effective Gross Income	**$2,123,235**
Economic Occupancy	87%

Effective Gross Income (EGI): The true positive cash flow. Also referred to as EGI, total income, or total revenue. EGI is calculated by subtracting the revenue lost due to vacancy, loss-to-lease, concessions, employee units, model units, and bad debt from the gross potential income (gross potential rent plus other income). For example, here is the EGI for the 216-unit apartment community:

Gross Potential Rent	$2,263,624
Loss-to-Lease	($67,909)
Concessions	($36,306)
Vacancy	($158,454)
Bad Debt	($55,147)
Other Income	$177,426
Total Income	**$2,123,235**

Employee Unit: An apartment unit rented to an employee at a discount or for free.

Equity Investment: The upfront costs for purchasing a property. For apartment syndications, these costs include the down payment for the mortgage loan, closing costs, financing fees, operating account funding, and the fees paid to the general partnership for putting the deal together. Also referred to as the initial cash outlay or the down payment. For example, here is the equity investment for the 216-unit apartment community:

Down Payment	$2,806,000
Closing Costs	$143,003
Financing Fees	$214,700
Operating Account Funding	$435,567
Acquisition Fee	$244,000
Equity Investment	**$3,843,270**

Equity Multiple (EM): The rate of return based on the total net profit and the equity investment. Also referred to as EM. The EM is calculated by dividing the sum of the total net profit (cash flow plus sales proceeds) and the equity investment by the equity investment. For example, here is the EM to the limited partners on the 216-unit apartment community:

Equity Investment	$3,843,270
Year 1 Cash Flow	$329,359
Year 2 Cash Flow	$323,507
Year 3 Cash Flow	$481,209
Year 4 Cash Flow	$510,755
Year 5 Cash Flow	$385,342
Profit at Sale	$3,803,677
Return of Equity Investment	$2,198,439
Total Net Profit	$8,032,288
Equity Multiple	**2.09**

Exit Strategy: The general partner's plan of action for selling the apartment community at the conclusion of the business plan.

F

Financing Fees: The one-time, upfront fees charged by the lender for providing the debt service. Also referred to as finance charges. Typically, the financing fees are approximately 1.75% of the purchase price.

G

General Partner (GP): An owner of a partnership who has unlimited liability. A general partner is usually a managing partner and is active in the day-to-day operations of the business. In apartment syndications, the general partner is also referred to as the sponsor or syndicator and is responsible for managing the entire apartment project.

Gross Potential Income: The hypothetical amount of revenue if the apartment community were 100% leased year-round at market rental rates plus all other income. For example, the 216-unit apartment community with a gross potential rent of $2,263,624 and other income of $177,426 has a gross potential income of $2,441,050.

Gross Potential Rent (GPR): The hypothetical amount of revenue if the apartment community were 100% leased year-round at market rental rates. Also referred to as GPR. For example, the 216-unit apartment community with an average monthly rent per unit of $873.31 has a gross potential rent of $2,263,624.

Gross Rent Multiplier (GRM): The number of years it would take for a property to pay for itself based on the gross potential rent. Also referred to as the GRM. The GRM is calculated by dividing the purchase price by the annual gross potential rent. For example, the 216-unit apartment community purchased for $12,200,000 with a gross potential rent of $2,263,624 has a GRM of 5.4.

Guaranty Fee: A fee paid to a loan guarantor at closing for signing for and guaranteeing the loan. The standard guaranty fee is 0.5% to 5% of the principal balance of the loan paid at closing and/or 5% to 30% of the general partnership. The size of the fee depends on the business plan, the guarantor's relationship with the syndicator and the type of debt (recourse vs. nonrecourse).

H

Holding Period: The amount of time the general partner plans on owning the apartment from purchase to sale.

I

Income Approach: A method of calculating an apartment's value based on the capitalization rate and the net operating income (value = net operating income / capitalization rate).

Interest-Only Payment: The monthly payment for a mortgage loan where the lender requires the borrower to pay only the interest on the principal.

Interest Rate: The amount charged by a lender to a borrower for the use of their funds.

Internal Rate of Return (IRR): The rate needed to convert the sum of all future uneven cash flow (cash flow, sales proceeds, and principal paydown on the mortgage loan) to equal the equity investment. Also referred to as IRR.

A very simple example is let's say that you invest $50. The investment has cash flow of $5 in year 1, and $20 in year 2. At the end of year 2, the investment is liquidated and the $50 is returned. The total profit is $25 ($5 year 1 + $20 year 2). Simple division would say that the return is 50% ($25/50). But since time value of money (two years in this example) impacts return, the IRR is actually only 23.43%. If we had received the $25 cash flow and $50 investment returned all in year 1, then yes, the IRR would be 50%. But because we had to "spread" the cash flow over two years, the return percentage is negatively impacted.

The timing of when cash flow is received has a significant and direct impact on the calculated return. In other words, the sooner you receive the cash, the higher the IRR will be.

L

Lease: A formal legal contract between a landlord and a tenant for occupying an apartment unit for a specified time and at a specified price with specified terms.

Letter of Intent (LOI): A non-binding agreement created by a buyer with their proposed purchase terms. Also referred to as the LOI.

Limited Partner (LP): A partner whose liability is limited to the extent of their share of ownership. Also referred to as an LP. In apartment syndications, the LP is the passive investor who funds a portion of the equity investment.

Loan-to-Cost Ratio (LTC): The ratio of the value of the total project costs (loan amount + capital expenditure costs) divided by the apartment's appraised value.

Loan-to-Value Ratio (LTV): The ratio of the value of the loan amount divided by the apartment's appraised value.

London Interbank Offered Rate (LIBOR): A benchmark rate that some of the world's leading banks charge each other for short-term loans. Also referred to as LIBOR. The LIBOR serves as the first step to calculating interest rates on various loans, including commercial loans, throughout the world.

Loss-to-Lease (LtL): The revenue lost based on the market rent and the actual rent. Also referred to as LtL. The LtL is calculated by dividing the gross potential rent minus the actual rent collected by the gross potential rent. For example, the 216-unit property with a gross potential rent of $2,263,624 and actual collected rent of $2,195,715 has a LtL of $67,909 or 3%.

M

Market Rent: The rent amount a willing landlord might reasonably expect to receive and a willing tenant might reasonably expect to pay for tenancy, which is based on the rent charged at similar apartment communities in the area. The market rent is typically calculated by conducting a rent comparable analysis.

Metropolitan Statistical Area (MSA): A geographical region containing a substantial population nucleus, together with adjacent communities having a high degree of economic and social integration with that core. Also referred to as an MSA. MSAs are determined by the United States Office of Management and Budget (OMB).

Model Unit: A representative apartment unit used as a sales tool to show prospective tenants how the actual unit will appear once occupied.

Mortgage: A legal contract by which an apartment is pledged as security for repayment of a loan until the debt is repaid in full.

N

Net Operating Income (NOI): All the revenue from the property (i.e., effective gross income) minus the operating expenses. Also referred to as the NOI. For example, the 216-unit apartment with an effective gross income of $2,195,715 and operating expenses of $1,166,489 has a NOI of $956,746.

O

Operating Account Funding: A reserves fund, over and above the purchase price of an apartment, to cover things like unexpected dips in occupancy, lump sum insurance or tax payments, or higher than expected capital expenditures. The operating account funding is typically created by raising extra capital from the limited partners.

Operating Agreement: A document that outlines the responsibilities and ownership percentages for the general and limited partners in an apartment syndication.

Operating Expenses: The costs of running and maintaining the property and its grounds. For apartment syndications, the operating expenses are usually broken into the following categories: payroll, maintenance and repairs, contract services, make ready, advertising/marketing, administrative, utilities, management fees, taxes, insurance, and reserves. For example, here are the operating expenses for the 216-unit apartment community:

Payroll	($244,630)
Maintenance	($66,717)
Contract Services	($84,509)
Turn/Make Ready	($44,478)
Advertising	($33,359)

Admin	($33,359)
Utilities	($194,592)
Mgmt. Fees	($74,313)
Taxes	($286,494)
Reserves	($54,000)
Insurance	($50,038)
Total Expenses	($1,166,489)

P

Passive Investing: Placing one's capital into an apartment syndication that is managed in its entirety by a general partner.

Permanent Agency Loan: A long-term mortgage loan secured from Fannie Mae or Freddie Mac. Typical loan terms lengths are 3, 5, 7, 10, 12 or more years amortized over up to 30 years.

Physical Occupancy Rate: The proportion of occupied units. The physical occupancy rate is calculated by dividing the total number of occupied units by the total number of units at the property. For example, the 216-unit apartment community with 199 occupied units has a physical occupancy rate of 92.1%.

Preferred Return: The threshold return that limited partners are offered prior to the general partners receiving payment.

Prepayment Penalty: A clause in a mortgage contract stating that a penalty will be assessed if the mortgage is paid down or paid off within a certain period.

Price Per Unit: The cost per unit of purchasing a property. The price per unit is calculated by dividing the purchase price of the property by the total number of units.

Private Placement Memorandum (PPM): A document that outlines the terms of the investment and the primary risk factors involved with making the investment. Also referred to as the PPM. The PPM typically has four main sections: the introductions (a brief summary of the offering), basic disclosures (general partner information, asset description, and risk factors), the legal agreement, and the subscription agreement.

Pro Forma: The projected budget with itemized line items for the revenue and expenses for the next 12 months and/or 5 years. For example, here is the 5-year pro forma for the 216-unit apartment community:

Rental Income	Year 1	Year 2	Year 3	Year 4	Year 5
GPR	$2,009,748	$2,263,624	$2,364,536	$2,436,455	$2,510,562
LTL	($60,292)	($67,909)	($70,936)	($73,094)	($75,317)
Total GR	**$1,949,455**	**$2,195,715**	**$2,293,600**	**$2,363,362**	**$2,435,246**
Concessions	($32,234)	($36,306)	($37,925)	($39,078)	($40,267)
Vacancy	($160,780)	($158,454)	($165,517)	($170,552)	($175,739)
Employee Units	$0	$0	$0	$0	$0
Model	$0	$0	$0	$0	$0
Bad Debt	($48,962)	($55,147)	($57,605)	($59,357)	($61,163)
Other Income	$172,189	$177,426	$182,823	$188,384	$194,114
EGI	**$1,879,669**	**$2,123,235**	**$2,215,375**	**$2,282,758**	**$2,352,190**
Expenses					
Payroll	($239,790)	($244,630)	($249,568)	($254,605)	($259,744)
Maintenance	($65,397)	($66,717)	($68,064)	($69,438)	($70,839)
Contract Services	($82,837)	($84,509)	($86,214)	($87,955)	($89,730)
Turn/ Make Ready	($43,598)	($44,478)	($45,376)	($46,292)	($47,226)
Advertising	($32,699)	($33,359)	($34,032)	($34,719)	($35,420)
Admin	($32,699)	($33,359)	($34,032)	($34,719)	($35,420)
Utilities	($190,742)	($194,592)	($198,520)	($202,527)	($206,615)

Mgmt. Fees	($65,788)	($74,313)	($77,538)	($79,897)	($82,327)
Taxes	($280,825)	($286,494)	($292,276)	($298,176)	($304,194)
Reserves	($54,000)	($54,000)	($54,000)	($54,000)	($54,000)
Insurance	($49,048)	($50,038)	($51,048)	($52,078)	($53,130)
Total Expenses	**($1,137,424)**	**($1,166,489)**	**($1,190,668)**	**($1,214,405)**	**($1,238,644)**
NOI	**$960,029**	**$956,746**	**$1,046,485**	**$1,090,132**	**$1,200,660**
Debt Service	($581,090)	($581,090)	($443,522)	($443,522)	($731,729)
Asset Mgmt. Fee	($40,195)	($45,272)	($47,291)	($48,729)	($50,211)
Cash Flow	**$338,743**	**$330,383**	**$555,673**	**$597,881**	**$418,719**

Profit and Loss Statement (T-12): A document or spreadsheet containing detailed information about the revenue and expenses of a property over the last 12 months. Also referred to as a trailing 12-month profit and loss statement, P&L, or a T-12.

Property and Neighborhood Classes: A ranking system of A, B, C, or D assigned to a property and a neighborhood based on a variety of factors. For property classes, these factors include date of construction, condition of the property, and amenities offered. For neighborhood classes, these factors include demographics, median income and median home values, crime rates, and school district rankings. These classes tend to be subjective, but the following are good guidelines:

Property Classes

Class A	New construction, commands highest rent in area, high-end amenities
Class B	10-15 years old, well maintained, little deferred maintenance
Class C	Built within last 30 years, shows age, some deferred maintenance
Class D	Over 30 years old, no amenity package, low occupancy, needs work

Neighborhood Classes

Class A	Most affluent neighborhood, expensive homes nearby, maybe golf course
Class B	Middle-class part of town, safe neighborhood
Class C	Low-to-moderate-income neighborhood
Class D	High crime, very bad neighborhood

Property Management Fee: An ongoing monthly fee paid to the property management company for managing the day-to-day operations of the property.

R

Ratio Utility Billing System (RUBS): A method of calculating a tenant's utility usage based on occupancy, unit square footage, or a combination of both. Once calculated, the amount is billed back to the tenant.

Recourse: The right of the lender to go after personal assets above and beyond the collateral if the borrower defaults on the loan.

Refinance: The replacing of an existing debt obligation with another debt obligation with different terms.

Refinancing Fee: A fee paid to the general partner for the work required to refinance an apartment.

Rent Comparable Analysis (Rent Comps): The process of analyzing the rental rates of similar properties in the area to determine the market rents of the units at the subject property.

Rent Premium: The increase in rent demanded after performing renovations to the interior and/or exterior of an apartment community.

Rent Roll: A document or spreadsheet containing detailed information on each of the units at the apartment community, including the unit number, unit type, square footage, tenant name, market rent, actual rent, deposit amount, move-in date, lease-start and lease-end dates, and the tenant balance.

S

Sales Comparison Approach: A method of calculating an apartment's value based on similar apartments recently sold.

Sales Proceeds: The profit collected at the sale of the apartment community.

Sophisticated Investor: A person who is deemed to have sufficient investing experience and knowledge to weigh the risks and merits of an investment opportunity.

Subject Property: The apartment the general partner intends on purchasing.

Submarket: A geographic subdivision of a market.

Subscription Agreement: A document that is a promise by the LLC that owns the property to sell a specific number of shares to a limited partner at a specified price, and a promise by the limited partner to pay that price.

U

Underwriting: The process of financially evaluating an apartment community to determine the projected returns and an offer price.

V

Vacancy Loss: The amount of revenue lost due to unoccupied units.

Vacancy Rate: The proportion of unoccupied units. The vacancy rate is calculated by dividing the total number of unoccupied units by the total number of units. For example, the 216-unit apartment community with 17 vacant units has a vacancy rate of 7.9%

Value-Add Property: A stabilized apartment community with an economic occupancy above 85% and an opportunity to be improved by adding value, which means making improvements to the operations and the physical property through exterior and interior renovations in order to increase the income and/or decrease the expenses.

Y

Yield Maintenance: A penalty paid by the borrower on a loan if the principal is paid off early.

ABOUT THE AUTHORS

Joe Fairless

From being the youngest vice president of a New York City ad agency to creating a company that in six months controlled over $7,000,000 of property, Joe Fairless lives up to his Fearless Fairless nickname.

He's the host of the popular podcast **Best Real Estate Investing Advice Ever**, which is the world's longest-running daily real estate podcast. Past interview guests include Robert Kiyosaki, Barbara Corcoran, and Emmitt Smith.

He currently controls over $400,000,000 worth of apartments in Dallas and Houston and consults for investors who want to raise money and buy apartment buildings.

He is on the Alumni Advisory Board of the College of Media and Communication at Texas Teach University and the Board of Directors for Junior Achievement.

Say hi to him at www.JoeFairless.com.

Theo Hicks

Theo controls over $1 million worth of real estate in Cincinnati, Ohio. He is also a Project Manager on an apartment syndication team that controls over $400,000,000 worth of apartments in Houston and Dallas-Fort Worth.

Prior to entering the real estate industry, Theo received a B.S. in Chemical Engineering from the Ohio State University and has a corporate background in Technical Sales, Project Management, and Logistics.

Theo is also the Key Underwriter and Content Creator for the Joe Fairless Apartment Syndication Consulting Program, co-host of "Follow-Along Friday" on the Best Real Estate Investing Advice Ever Show, and co-author of two real estate books: *Best Real Estate Investing Advice Ever* Volumes I & II.

Made in the USA
Monee, IL
26 June 2021